A Modest Major General

Major General RWL McAlister CB OBE

(Late the 10th Princess Mary's Own Gurkha Rifles)

by

Rupert Litherland

Published by New Generation Publishing in 2020

Paperback ISBN: 978-1-80031-840-3
Hardback ISBN: 978-1-80031-839-7

www.newgeneration-publishing.com

New Generation Publishing

Dedication

This book is dedicated to all 10th Gurkhas who lost their lives during their service but in particular to those who were killed in action during the Borneo Conflict

21140867	LCpl Sirkumar Rai
21140667	Cpl Shamsherbahadur Rai
21148753	LCpl Gopalprasad Rai
21154033	Rfn Dilbahadur Limbu
21139229	Cpl Birbahadur Rai
21147751	LCpl Kindraman Rai
21154072	Rfn Hangsabahadur Limbu
21148749	LCpl Tejbahadur Rai
426891	Capt T/Major RM Haddow
21151056	Rfn Budiman Rai
21156589	Rfn Chakrabahadur Limbu
21151092	Rfn Kharkabahadur Limbu
21155762	Rfn Motilal Rai
21155808	Rfn Bijuliprasad Limbu
21149938	Rfn Mangalsing Limbu
21149977	Rfn Bhalman Rai
21154193	Rfn Krishnabahadur Rai
21156591	Rfn Parsadsing Limbu
21156684	Rfn Lachhuman Rai

Foreword

General Sir Garry Johnson KCB OBE MC

It is a pleasure to write this foreword for Rupert Litherland's perceptive biography on Ronnie McAlister, a fellow 10th Gurkha, with whom I served in Malaya in the late 1950s and Borneo in the early 1960s. I thought I knew 'Ronnie Mac', as he was known, but Rupert's research and insights have revealed a great deal I did not know about Major General Ronnie McAlister's life and achievements; both are of interest.

Although this biography is essentially a contribution to the Regimental History of the 10th Gurkhas, it will be of interest to those who served in the Brigade of Gurkhas, supporters of the Gurkhas, the wider Army and those who study military history, as it brings to light the extraordinary events on the Hong Kong border in 1967, which are not widely known about and in some circles misunderstood. The biography also highlights the importance of staff officers and trainers and their essential role in ensuring success in combat. This biography also shows that gallantry on operations and an extrovert personality are not pre-requisites for high rank. Ronnie McAlister was an outstanding staff officer and trainer and was consistently selected for appointments that needed the attributes required to carry out those important appointments well. He was quite simply better than his contemporaries when it came to staff work and training, and as a result those who commanded him used him in those roles, and, unintentionally perhaps, limited his front-line operational experience. However, as the book brings out well, the operational successes of the 1st 3rd Gurkhas at the end of the Burma campaign and the 10th Gurkhas in Malaya and Borneo, which were second to none, owed much to the staff work and training support Ronnie McAlister gave to those in the front line. Staff officers and trainers may not get many gallantry awards, but without excellence in the roles they carry out those at the sharp end are less likely to succeed.

On assuming command of 1st 10th Gurkhas (1/10GR), he was, however, pitched into the sharp end with limited front line operational experience. He rose to the challenge and the Battalion's tour in the Bau sector at the end of the Confrontation with Indonesia was a notable success. Then, when Chairman Mao's Cultural Revolution swept across China, creating chaos as uncontrolled Red Guards purged Chinese elites and raged against the 'imperialist white pigs', and the turmoil threatened to spill over into Hong Kong, he was called upon to handle the extraordinary conflict on the Hong Kong border in 1967. When he led 1/10GR, the designated Hong Kong Frontier battalion, to relieve the border village of Sha Tau Kok nobody knew how the Chinese would react. The Hong Kong Police had suffered casualties, including fatalities, and were under siege by snipers and machine gunners from China. He had the misfortune to be taken hostage by Red Guards during the troubles; but later dealt with serious rioting and provocation by them, aimed at getting the British to open fire and escalate the conflict on the border to one of war. His calm reassurance and steely determination was a shining example to the officers and men of 1/10GR, and to those in other units who served in a unique conflict. Throughout that summer he handled all that was thrown at the Battalion with astonishing calmness; had hotter heads been at the helm, the outcome might well have resulted in bloodshed and lasting bitterness between Hong Kong and China.

This biography is a good read. I wish it well.

General Sir Garry Johnson

Contents

List of Illustrations

List of Maps[1]

---

[1] . Maps produced by Lovell Johns Ltd, Whitney, Oxfordshire

Preface

General Ronnie was on good form at Kit and Caroline Maunsell's curry lunch on 14 June 2015. It was a gathering of regimental friends, some of whom had come from abroad to celebrate Gurkha 200, the 200th anniversary of the enlistment of Gurkhas into service with the British. It was a breezy, bright summer day. At 92 General Ronnie was still the same dapper, fit 'General Ronnie', full of life, interested and interesting. Hand cupped over his ear to hear what I was saying about a presentation I was to take part in at the Gurkha Museum, he chuckled as we discussed how I might pour cold water on the Gallipoli myth that only Allanson's 6th Gurkhas in the 29th Indian Infantry Brigade fought with distinction at the Battle of Sari Bair. How might that be achieved without taking anything away from the splendid achievements of 1/6GR in that ill-fated and badly conceived attempt at a break out? His hearing might have gone at bit, but the clarity of his thinking and memory had not and he recalled with complete accuracy the article he had written on the errors and inaccuracies in the historical records on the part played by 2/10GR and other units in that awful battle. He knew Allanson's record of what happened was in several respects quite simply wrong but he felt, rightly, that my thoughts of exposing where Allanson had been guilty of embroidery, and my desire to point out that 2/10GR attacked as ordered on 9 August and on every day of the battle, suffering dreadfully as a result, would not be helpful. He suggested it would be better to let the daily casualty figures speak for themselves, because even if 2/10GR's part in the battle had passed largely unrecognised officially, nobody on the British side came out of the sorry tale with any credit. In the race to the Sari Bair heights that dominated the area, the Turks won, and hands down. I marvelled at his grasp of regimental history. When he got home that evening he suggested he had a slight backache. Within a few days pancreatic cancer was diagnosed. He was told it was terminal and he did not have long to live.

He did not want anyone apart from his immediate family to know, but the word got out through his golf club and in a reply to an e-mail from Bill Dawson, a regimental colleague, he replied: 'I am fully at peace with my future and having lots of laughs with the family (down for the bank holiday) ..... So don't feel sorry for me .... I have had a great life. No church or memorial service for me – a quiet family affair. Tell everyone.' He died on 8 September 2015, surrounded by his family, two days after his illness forced him to bed. It was typical of the man to want no fuss, no memorial service, no celebration of his life and no sadness. Though he declared he was happy and had no regrets, his decision that there should be no memorial service or celebration of his life left a void. Many of his numerous colleagues and friends would have wished to mark his passing with a celebration of his life and achievements. At a regimental lunch a month after his death General Sir Garry Johnson, President of the 10th Gurkha Rifles Regimental Association, took the opportunity to say a few words about 'Ronnie Mac', reminding those who knew him, and informing those who did not, what a tremendous contribution he had made to the Regiment and what an exceptional soldier and person he had been. General Ronnie had every right to be content. He was one of life's contributors: a man who gave more than he took; a man, who, in the process of giving, was modest to a fault. He never blew his own trumpet, never sought the limelight, never wanted a fuss; but he never failed to carry out his responsibilities and do his duty.

This biography is an attempt to place on record a celebration of his life. Ronnie McAlister may well be remembered and associated with the extraordinary events on the Hong Kong border in the summer of 1967, when he commanded 1/10GR in situations that required a cool head, quick thinking and an assured touch. He had the misfortune to be taken hostage by Chinese Red Guards and to see his photograph as a captive splashed across the world's media. This undoubtedly hurt him, personally, and it was damaging in the minds of others who almost certainly did not appreciate the difficult and challenging situations that the Police-Military campaign on the Hong Kong border in 1967 presented. If I have covered that period in his life more comprehensively than might be expected in a biography I make no apology: it deserves to be recorded thoroughly and put in perspective, so that the key part played by 1/10GR under Ronnie's command is better understood. There was, however, much more to Ronnie McAlister than the extraordinary events in Hong Kong during the summer of 1967.

A biography is said to be either a hero worshipping exercise or an assassination. This one on a distinguished senior officer in my Regiment is unlikely to be the latter; I accept therefore that the enormous respect I had for him may be reflected in it. It is for you, the reader, to judge whether I have got the balance between the two extremes right. That coverage of parts of his life story is patchy and thin compared to other parts simply reflects that written information on a modest person, who did not indulge in self-promotion, is sadly lacking for periods of his life or I have failed to find it. Some readers will be able to add to Ronnie McAlister's story: I am sorry I did not reach you and learn more about him – such is the lot of a biographer. The omissions, errors, oversights and interpretations in this biography are mine.

Rupert Litherland
April 2020

Chapter 1

Family Background and Growing Up

Ronald William Lorne McAlister, known in the family as Lorne, was born on 26 May 1923 in Teddington, Middlesex, when his father, Ronald James Frier McAlister, was in Aldershot, serving as an officer in the Argyll and Sutherland Highlanders.[2] His elder brother Brian Frier was born on 8 April 1922 and David Neil, the youngest of the three boys, on 11 October 1928. Their mother, Nora Prosser, was English, but the family was proudly Scottish.

The McAlister clan is a sept, or junior branch, of the clan Donald or the McDonalds. The prefix 'Mac' means 'son of' and in the 13th century the sons of the Chief Alasdair were MacAlasdairs. Over the years various spellings of the name MacAlisdair came into being and were used. In some the 'lisd' became 'list', the 'dair' became 'tair' or 'ter', in some 'Mac' became 'Mc' and in others there were two 'ls' rather than one. By the 18th and 19th centuries McAlisters could be found in the south-west corner of Scotland on the Mull of Kintyre, on the isles of Bute and Arran, in Argyllshire and further east around Stirling. It was a strong recruiting area for the Argyll and Sutherland Highlanders. McAlister of Loup, the Chieftain, has a house on the Mull of Kintyre.

The crest of the McAlisters is a mailed fist holding a dagger, blade pointing upwards, and the motto 'Fortitier' (Bravely); however, for reasons that are not apparent, the family always wore the McDonald crest – a gauntleted hand holding, blade down, a crosslet handled dagger and the motto 'Per Mare per Terras' (By Land and Sea). This describes the McDonald chieftains' ancient title of 'Lord of the Isles', which gave them sovereignty over all the western isles around which a boat could be navigated, and authority over large tracts of the Argyllshire shore.

---

2 . Abbreviated to Argylls.

Writing in later life Lorne regretted that he did not know more about his McAlister forebears. What he did know was that his great-grandfather James McAlister was born in about 1827 and married Helen, born in 1825, in 1861. It is thought James McAlister was a doctor. His son William, Lorne's grandfather, born in Kilmarnock, Ayrshire in 1862 was a doctor. He married Williamina Frier of Currie, Midlothian, in St Andrew's church in Edinburgh on 30 July 1884. Their son, Lorne's father, R.J.F. McAlister, known as Ronnie, was born in Kilmarnock on 13 June 1897 when Williamina, or Minnie, was 36.[3] Sadly she died in 1907 when Ronnie was 10, and it is thought he was looked after and brought up by his two elder sisters, Susan and Mary, when he was not at boarding school. Lorne, as far as he could recall, never met his aunts. Ronnie was educated at Fettes in Edinburgh. He was a School prefect, Head of Carrington House and played in the 1st XV. A fellow Carrington House pupil was David Prosser and Ronnie stayed with the Prosser family in Helensburgh from time to time in the school holidays. It was there that he met the Prosser's eldest daughter Nora.

In 1916 almost straight from school, at the age of 18, with only the military training of the Fettes Officer Training Corps (OTC) and a cursory period as a cadet in the Edinburgh area, Ronnie Senior was commissioned into the Argyll and Sutherland Highlanders. He served in Belgium during the last few months of the Great War and received the 1914-18 War Medal and the Allied Victory Medal. At the end of the war he took a regular commission in the Argyll and Sutherland Highlanders and on 15 September 1920 he and Nora Prosser were married.

Lorne's early life involved following the drum with his mother and brothers, as his father's Army postings demanded. His father was stationed in Aldershot from 1921 to 1925 and then, until 1928, he served as the adjutant of the 9th Argylls based at Dumbarton Castle on the north side of the Clyde, west of Glasgow. He returned to regimental duty with his battalion at Shorncliffe Barracks, Folkstone in 1929, before returning to Scotland again in 1930 as adjutant at Edinburgh Castle. In 1932 the Argylls were sent to the Shanghai International Settlement where the British had stationed a battalion following

---

3   . 'R.W.L. McAlister – CV'. The family thought her name was Wilhelmina but her birth certificate indicates she was Williamina. This led to speculation that the family were expecting the baby to be a boy.

disturbances at the Hankow concession in 1927. Ronnie went with the Battalion on what was an unaccompanied tour of duty. Nora and the boys remained in their Army quarter in Edinburgh, a hiring on Ormidale Terrace, and it was from there, in 1932, that Brian and Lorne, at the ages of 9 and 8 respectively, started boarding at the Dreghorn Castle Preparatory School, Colinton, Edinburgh.

At the end of their Shanghai tour in 1933 the Argylls were sent to Rawalpindi, which was one of the biggest permanent garrisons in India. Nora went out by troopship to join Ronnie leaving Brain and Lorne behind. When not at boarding school, the boys were looked after by granny and grandpa Prosser in Glasgow. Neil, who was only four, went to live with auntie Honor, Nora's sister, who was married to uncle Frank Ingham Clark, because their son Alan was the same age as Neil. This was a difficult period. Nora had found her separation from Ronnie for more than a year difficult and the world depression had had a profound effect on both families. The Prossers' motor car business in Glasgow was hit hard and they had to sell the family home in Helensburgh, a house called 'Arduli', with a large garden, a chicken run at the back over a stream and a wooded dell, where the boys played out adventures. In the McAlister family, Ronnie suffered a pay cut when all public service salaries were cut by 10% and his shares became worthless. The Prosser family went to live in a private hotel at Lancaster Crescent on Great Western Road, Glasgow, run by two McDonald spinsters. It was at Lancaster Crescent, with granny and grandpa Prosser, uncles David and Pat and aunts Eily and Joy, that Brian and Lorne spent their holidays from 1932 to 1938. The few other permanent residents at Lancaster Crescent used the hotel's main drawing room while the Prossers enjoyed the privacy of their own private drawing room, which they called the West Room, after the day room at 'Arduli'. From Lancaster Crescent first David, then Eily, followed by Pat and finally Joy, got married and left the family 'home', and in 1938, with the family business recovering, granny and grandpa Prosser bought 'Whincroft' a lovely house in Helensburgh.

Keeping Brian and Lorne occupied during the holidays was a problem for granny Prosser. For three or four years in the Easter holidays they were sent for two weeks to a sheep and cattle farm at Call Ender, Stirlingshire, run by Mr and Mrs Barr, which they much enjoyed. On two or three occasions in the summer holidays they were invited to Glen Caladh Castle in the Kyles of Bute by uncle Frank's father. This was exciting for the boys as it involved taking a steamer from Helensburgh down the Clyde to Tighnabruich, from where they were met by launch, there being no road to Glen Caladh, and taken to the castle's private harbour. There was usually a house party while they were there and they enjoyed the air of opulence and good living. They enjoyed things they never knew *chez* Prosser, such as whole stiltons, cocktails before dinner – although they were too young to be offered those – and a help-yourself breakfast from a large sideboard with a dazzling array of eggs, bacon and mushrooms under large silver lids. They had a room and bathroom en suite. They roamed the vast grounds, where there were peacocks, and spent a lot of time at the boat yard and anchorage that was sheltered by a small island which was the family's private burial ground. All the various boats were run by 'Young Archie', the boatman, and his less active father, 'Old Archie', who had been family retainers for years and lived in one of the five staff cottages in the grounds. At the time 'Young Archie' was about 40. On one occasion they sailed in Pop Clark's large motor yacht 'White Heather' from Glen Caladh to the boat yard at Sandbank, about twenty sea miles away, where the yacht was to be overhauled.

In addition to time spent at Glen Caladh, the Potters, the parents of Douglas Potter one of their friends at Dreghorn Prep, always invited the boys to stay with them in the house they rented in the summer holidays, near Dumfries in Perthshire or on the Moray Firth. This continued even after the boys left Dreghorn and Douglas was at Merchiston School while Brian and Lorne were at Sedbergh. In the summer of 1939 while picnicing on the Moray Firth with the Potters, they witnessed the Fleet sail out from the dangerously constricted anchorage at Invergordon for Scapa Flow.

Otherwise, while in Glasgow during the holidays, the boys enjoyed swimming in the fine pool, the Western Baths; also outings to the cinema that sold reduced price tickets for the morning and afternoon shows, and the boating pool where a rowing boat could be hired for sixpence an hour; and they could get to these facilities easily by tram.

It was uncle David who drove Brian and Lorne across to Edinburgh for the start of term at Dreghorn and picked them up at the start of the holidays. The boys loved their uncle David. He was always immaculately dressed, calm and cheerful. He had won his wings in the RAF in 1918, at the age of 18, and served in the Great War. He had crashed an aircraft in training and had been given the broken wooden propeller which was mounted above the door of the West Room at Arduli. Although grandpa Prosser headed up the family business selling Worsley motor cars and went to the office every day until 1940, he was often asleep in his chair and it was actually uncle David who ran and managed the business. He told the boys he had to instruct the staff to knock loudly and pause before they entered grandpa's office. Uncle David lunched at the same restaurant in Glasgow every day and often, at granny Prosser's request, gave the boys lunch there, which was a treat and involved another tram ride to the Prosser showrooms. Uncle Reggie, who ran and managed the Prosser engineering works, also took the boys out to lunch regularly, but Lorne could only remember one occasion when uncle Pat took them out to lunch. It was memorable because he ordered chilli con carne, which was a new dish for Lorne. Later in life Lorne wondered whether his uncles David and Reggie felt put-upon by their demanding mother when asked to take the boys out to lunch, but concluded that if they did, they never showed it. Lorne recalled that granny Prosser was very kind, soft spoken, and quietly but unobtrusively strict, and that she brought them up with good manners. She was greatly respected in Helensburgh where she had many friends. She got on well with all the shopkeepers which helped with wartime rationing and ran Whincroft comfortably and efficiently. When the boys were in their teens and had a problem she would say, 'If I were you I would get up very early tomorrow and go straight to the telephone.' Grandpa Prosser stayed in the background. He was a Victorian gentleman who was keen on winter shooting and interested in the garden, and of the generation who believed children should be seen and not heard.

The boys did not see their brother Neil often. In 1935 Alan Ingham Clark died at the age of six from diphtheria and Neil had to be moved to stay with uncle David and Bunty who were recently married. When their son Harry was born Neil was moved again and went to stay with uncle Reggie and his wife Jane, a wealthy widow, who had a son, Colin Fergusson, who was the same age as Neil. They lived in a lovely house at Gartocharn, Loch Lomondside.

In 1935 the boys' mother, whom they had not seen for three years, returned from India to tell them she was divorcing their father and was going to marry Terrence Collins, known as 'Bunjy', an officer in the Indian Police. She took the boys on a very nice holiday at Totland Bay on the Isle of Wight. Lorne thought she did it as a sweetener for leaving their father, yet the divorce had little impact on the boys. From the age of nine Lorne had spent three years living with his brother and grandparents among his uncles and aunts.

Ronnie's parents – Colonel Ronald James Frier McAlister OBE and Nora McAlister (nee Prosser)[4]

That life was the boys' home and it did not change with the divorce. He was aware his grandparents disapproved of his mother's behaviour and that she was out of favour because they thought divorce was disgraceful. Much to his mother's fury her lovely old dining room chairs, in store while she was in India, were removed and given to uncle David and Bunty on their marriage. In 1937, his mother and Bunjy visited Lorne and Brian at Sedbergh when they were back on leave from India. They were based on the Isle of Man for tax reasons and Lorne doubts that Bunjy ever went to Helensburgh to meet granny and grandpa Prosser. Later in life Lorne understood that his mother met Bunjy on the ship out to India in 1933 and married him out there. He was told by her that in her marriage to Ronnie 'the Regiment came first, golf came second and I came third'. He thought that marriage to a junior officer who had no great promotion prospects and was of a similar age may have been

4   . The McAlister Family Collection.

dull and unexciting for his mother. The only thing she said to Lorne about her first husband that was in any way endearing was, 'Your father always had impeccable manners'. Bunjy, who was older, moved in altogether different circles. He had good friends in Government, in the judiciary and the Indian Civil Service. He had joined the Indian Police in 1913 at a time when entry was more demanding than for Sandhurst and the army. He had served with the 2/2nd Gurkhas in France in 1916 and then transferred to the 2/3rd Gurkhas and served with them in Palestine in 1918. He tried to stay with Gurkhas as a regular officer after the Great War but was recalled to the Indian Police. Soon after his marriage to Nora he was promoted to Deputy Inspector General of Police at Nagpur in India's Central Provinces, and was later promoted to Inspector General in the Central Provinces. Sadly the marriage was not to last long, as Bunjy died in harness in 1947, and the war separated them for five of the 12 years they were married. Nora returned to England in May 1940 and then could not get back to India until the Suez Canal reopened in 1945.

The Headmaster at Dreghorn, Mr Osborn, was an Old Sedberghian and sent a large number of boys to Sedgewick House at Sedbergh. He secured a bursary for Brian at Sedbergh that was for the sons of army officers. Given the family's financial circumstances, this was eagerly taken up, so Brian, aged 14, went to Sedbergh starting in the summer term of 1936. At the end of that same term Dreghorn Prep was forced to close as it occupied War Department land that was required for new barracks, as the belated rearmament programme to counter the rise of Nazi Germany took shape. Sedbergh agreed to take Lorne, aged 13, in the Christmas term of 1936 but he had to live out as a day boy for his first term. He lived with the family of a teacher, Mr Cortazzi, who later taught him history in the sixth form. The Cortazzis had a son, Hugh, who was the same age as Lorne and they walked to school together for his first term.[5] There was a large Scottish contingent at Sedbergh from Cargilfield and Dreghorn in Edinburgh, Warriston and St Mary's Melrose and the boys considered it quite a cachet to be at Sedbergh rather than at Fettes, Loretto, Glenalmond or

---

5   . Lorne recalled that Hugh Cortazzi never shone at school: he was rather overweight and no sportsman. He joined the Foreign Office after the war. He was knighted (KCMG) and was the British Ambassador in Japan.

Merchiston, but their parents did not share that view. Their mother had put them down for Wellington, where Neil subsequently went, and their father was a Fettesian.

Lorne and Brian with their mother at Sedbergh probably taken in 1937[6]

Lorne was at Sedbergh in Sedgewick House from the Christmas term in 1936 until the Spring term of 1941. He was sound academically, a good sportsman and an able pupil. He was particularly good at fives. The April 1940 report in 'Rouge et Noir', the Sedgewick House chronicle, on Senior Fives stated that L.McAlister was much improved, 'he makes up for his lack of strength by nimbleness of foot', and, 'L. McAlister was competently efficient and stood up very well to the hard hitting (and rather dangerous) Hammond'. The April 1941 report states: 'L. McAlister captained the side and it is to him we owe so much of our success. His infectious enthusiasm and his real skill in teaching others the secrets of his own craft were immense assets, and we are duly grateful.' It is interesting to note that at the age of 18 he was already a noted instructor. He had to leave Sedbergh early because the money ran out. His AU REVOIR entry from Sedbergh records:

> RWL McAlister. Came September 1936. 1939 – House XV (Cup). House Colours. 1940 – Senior Fives. House XI. House XV (Cup). 2nd XV Colours. House Prefect. 1941 – School Secretary of Fives and Captain. School

6 . The McAlister Family Collection.

Prefect. Left March 1941. McAlister is trying for a Paymastership in the Navy.

Sedgewick House XV – Cup Winners 1940[7]
RWL McAlister Standing Fourth from the left in the backrow

The AU REVOIR entry does not record that he also captained the squash side, made several appearances in the 1st XV at scrum half and scored 105 not out in the 3rd XI in the summer of 1940. He was also in the Sedbergh Officer Training Corps (OTC) from 1937 to 1941 and passed his 'Certificate A'. He wrote that he regretted not being able to further his cricket career in the summer of 1941, and it would be reasonable to assume, had the money not run out, that his record at Sedbergh might have included his appearance in the 1st XI.

On leaving Sedbergh he taught at Limehouse Preparatory School in Carlisle during the summer and Christmas terms of 1941. He took over the job from his brother Brian who taught there during the Christmas 1940 and Easter 1941 terms, and it was essentially a time-filler before he was called up in May 1941. Brian elected to enlist in the Coldstream Guards as an ordinary soldier. Lorne joined the Army as a potential officer at Aldershot in November 1941. The mention in his 'AU REVOIR' from Sedbergh that he was seeking a paymastership in the Navy is something of a mystery, not least because whoever had editorial responsibility should have known that the Navy has pursers and not paymasters.

---

7   . The McAlister Family Collection.

At the start of the war Ronnie Senior was serving on operations in Palestine. By the time his two older sons enlisted he was in North Africa. He was on the staff of the Middle East Staff College in Haifa but re-joined the 1st Argylls for the desert battles of 1941. In May 1942 he was commanding the 1st Argylls at Ruweisat Ridge in the First Battle of Alamein, for which he was Mentioned in Despatches.

Lorne's early life and upbringing was somewhat peripatetic; as an Army child he lived in several places when he was very young and then, just as his formative years started, his parents went abroad and subsequently separated; he rarely saw them and he lived with and was brought up by his grandparents. Grandma and grandpa Posser were almost certainly quite Victorian and strict. He and his brother were farmed out to family and friends in the holidays and financial pressures and the first two years of the war meant life was by no means easy; it might even have been challenging if not Spartan. Sedbergh was a fine school but pre-WW2 boarding schools were not for the faint-hearted or the non-conformist. The strict ethical code of his grandparents, the importance they placed on manners and grandma Prosser's no-nonsense running of the household were examples that moulded him. That and the regime of a good boarding school combined to create a well-educated young man, who had a natural confidence in his own ability, a mature understanding of life and a quiet assuredness that allowed him to recognise that although he did not have an impressive stature he did not have to impose himself to achieve things. He had a sharp, independent mind; he was proudly Scottish and ready to cope with the world beyond home and school.

Chapter 2

Enlistment and Preparation

On the day of his enlistment in November 1941, the recruiting officer asked him what name he was known by and when he replied 'Lorne' the recruiting officer said he had never heard of it and asked him to offer an alternative. Understandably, as his full name was Ronald William Lorne McAlister, Lorne suggested 'Ronald'. The recruiting officer accepted that as a name he recognised; so, on joining the Army, Lorne became Ronnie and he was known as Ronnie throughout his army career. He enlisted in The Royal Scots on 19 November 1941. His enlistment papers record that he was 5 feet 8½ inches tall and weighed 10 stone. His education standard was listed as 'B' and his profession as 'Teacher'.[8]

Ronnie joined about 20 other public school boys who, after dormitory life, took barrack room life in their stride. The only unfamiliar thing was beds without sheets and the lack of heating other than the occasional coal fire at a time when coal was severely rationed. For three weeks three Scots Guards sergeants 'square bashed' them in an attempt to turn them into soldiers quickly. On 11 February 1942 he was appointed an officer cadet bound for the Officer Cadet Training Unit (OCTU) in Bangalore and a commission in the Indian Army. This swift route to a commission had not been an option when Brian was called up: he had to earn his recommendation for a commission. Ronnie and his fellow officer cadets were then taken by train at night to an undisclosed destination. It turned out to be a troopship anchored off Greenock on the Clyde opposite Helensburgh, an area Ronnie recognised and knew only too well. They sailed from there on the night of 15 February 1942 on the P&O liner, the SS *Stratheden*. As befitted their status as cadets – the lowest of the low – they were accommodated on troop deck G, below

---

8   . It is debatable whether teaching could reasonably be called his profession. The two terms he taught at Limehouse Prep were essentially a time-filler until he was called up.

the waterline and there they lived, ate and slept for six weeks. They slept in hammocks, a new experience for them all, which were set up at night and rolled up during the day. Part of their daily routine was to don their life jackets and go on deck. On the first morning an awesome sight met their eyes. They were part of a convoy of about 50 passenger and merchant ships, accompanied by a powerful naval escort of a battleship, aircraft carrier, two or three cruisers and several destroyers that were in full view and quite close. Aircraft were continuously taking off and landing on the aircraft carrier and the destroyers constantly roamed up and down the convoy, often at speed. On that first day they reckoned they were somewhere north of Ireland and had been joined in the night by other ships, probably from Liverpool and other ports on the west coast of England. They later learned that the convoy zig-zagged for some days heading out into the western Atlantic before turning south to Freetown, by which time that part of the convoy that was headed for India was accompanied by a meagre escort of a few destroyers. They did not go ashore at Freetown but did get ashore at Durban. They finally reached Bombay in early April 1942.

From Bombay they went to Bangalore by train to begin a new and seemingly wonderous life for 18 year olds: two cadets to a bedroom, with a bearer who attended to their every need, from *chota hazri*, a 'small breakfast' of tea and biscuits on waking, through organising their *dhobi* (laundry) and laying out their smartly starched uniforms and polishing their boots, to giving them tea at the end of the day's parades. Breakfast was at about 0900 hours after two hours of parades in the cool of the day. This meal, lunch and dinner were all taken in the cadets' mess, where they were waited on by smart bearers in white uniforms with green cummmberbunds and turbans. All movement during the day to and from lessons on drill, tactics and Urdu was on bicycles in formed squads two lines abreast. Bicycle drill was based on cavalry drill, so shared the basic orders: 'Prepare to mount' and 'Mount', to be followed later by 'Prepare to dismount' and 'Dismount'. For those who passed the course their commissioning parade and commissioning date was 3 October 1942.

Although they were Emergency Commissioned Officers (ECO) and held that commission in British Army regiments, in Ronnie's case the Argyll and Sutherland Highlanders, the cadets were asked to make three choices of regiment in the Indian

Army. Ronnie's first choice was the 3rd Gurkhas. He had been told by his mother to opt for the 3rd Gurkhas and then any other Gurkha Regiment. He got his first choice not knowing that Bunjy Collins had written to the Commandant of the 3rd Gurkha Rifles Centre at Dehra Dun, who he had served with in 2/3GR in Palestine 24 years earlier, asking him to find Ronnie a place in the 3rd Gurkhas. With hindsight Ronnie realised how lucky he had been, as other capable chaps on his course with no connections went to units like the Royal Indian Army Service Corps (RIASC), which was considered inferior and known unkindly as 'The Rice Corps'.

After being commissioned on 3 October 1942, Ronnie travelled north to Nagpur where he was met at the station by his step-father Bunjy, who he recognised easily from his uniform. He stayed with Bunjy for a few days and it was the first time he had really met him at close quarters. Ronnie was impressed by Bunjy's household staff and the obvious devotion they showed to him. He thought it was a wonderful example of how a proper gentleman should run a household. He was thrilled to be called *chota sahib*, or 'little sir', by the head of the household staff and chief bearer, Yenkenna. Bunjy showed Ronnie all his old 2/3GR photographs and generally made him aware of what splendid soldiers he was about to join.

Ronnie recalled that the 3rd Gurkha Centre at Dehra Dun exceeded all his recently-learned expectations. Years later he wrote an article titled 'First Impressions':

First impressions are important and I was, perhaps, aged 19, too easily impressed, and indeed impressed by little things. But my earliest experiences of the 3GR Depot at Dehra Dun will always remain with me; they endeared me to Gurkhas at once and forever.

I arrived at Dehra Dun at about 7am on 7th October 1942 by the night train from Delhi. After breakfast in the mess I walked down the road, as bidden, to report to the Adjutant. On my way, I noticed a number of soldiers saluting, it seemed at some considerable distance far across the parade ground and eventually realised with a mixture of amazement and pleasure that they were saluting me.

Two days later it was Dashera and the Kalarati Nautch. I was generously entertained by the GOs with rum, to which I was in no way hardened and, around midnight, felt I must go back to my tent under my own steam or risk being carried.

Vaguely aware that I was being followed, I staggered off towards the mess area and somewhere on the edge of the top most parade ground I fell into one of those weapon training slit trenches. I was undamaged, as drunks usually are, but at once two young Gurkha soldiers, luckily I now realise, detailed off to see me home by a kind and perceptive GO, hauled me out and mumbling thanks in Bangalore Urdu, I went on my unsteady way, followed by the soldiers who saw me to my tent.

A few days later, 'Grumpy' Hornsby detailed me to supervise a working party building a new Assault Course. Over a ten day period the Pioneer Havildar in charge contrived to make me feel that I was directing, requisitioning and gathering the necessary tools from the QM store each day and designing a wall and ditch, the immediate focus of the work. I was flattered but not deceived. In truth, he did it all.

In early November 1942, I marched out of the Depot with 100 Gurkhas to a jungle camp north of Raiwala, about 15 miles away. At one halt, we ate our haversack ration of cold *chapati* and vegetables and Jemedar Pabe Pun generously shared with me some very tasty chutney made for him by his wife. I remember asking him how far he could march in a day. His answer 'as far as you order me to go' made an indelible impression. By now I was hooked forever.

Everyone will have some definition of a good soldier. But the one I like best comes from Lieutenant Harry Lumsden who raised the Guides. Asked what sort of man he wished to enlist, he did not ask for brawn or brains, sharpness of eye, stamina, strength, not even courage. He said 'The sort of man I want must be alert and ready; he must do his duty, be the matter great or small; he must not be taken aback in an emergency; and he must be a congenial comrade.' The Gurkha soldier surely fills all these criteria.

I would like to feel that most of our readers would agree, above all, that as a genial comrade to go to war with, the Gurkha soldier is the finest in the world.[9]

---

9   . 3GR Association Journal No.49, April 1995, p.29.

2nd Lieutenant RWL McAlister 3GR – October 1942[10]

At the 3GR Centre he lived in a large tent with a thatched roof for protection from the heat. He had his own bearer who as he went on parade at 0730 hours asked him what he wanted for breakfast. He usually asked for fried eggs, bacon and sausages and his bearer would be at the Mess at 0900 hours and promptly produce his breakfast. His bearer stood behind him while he ate – ready to pass him toast and marmalade. It was a lifestyle likely to turn the head of any young officer of Spartan upbringing and not long away from the austerity of war-torn England.

Ronnie was at the 3GR Gurkha Centre for three months during which he did some very minor jobs and a mortar course at the Small Arms School at Saugor. To his astonishment he was then sent to be an instructor in jungle warfare at a newly established camp at Raiwala not far from Dehra Dun that was under the command of Major Angus Rose. Major Rose was an Argyll and a friend of his father and he had been specially

---

10 . The McAlister Family Collection.

withdrawn from the jungle in Malaya in order to pass on his battle experience to the as yet 'green' Indian Army. When Ronnie protested that he did not know anything about jungle warfare, Major Rose's response was: 'That is why you have been chosen – you will teach exactly what I tell you to.' Ronnie enjoyed the six months he spent at Raiwala and observing what seemed like an endless stream of soldiers formed in companies of 100 men. He saw men from various Indian Army regiments and liked them all, but none it seemed to him were as good as the Gurkhas.

Back at the 3GR Centre in July 1943 he was immediately put to work running jungle training for 3GR recruits. It did not last long, as out of the blue he was posted to a training establishment at Poona. His protests were of no avail and the efforts of the Commandant, Colonel Barltrop, Bunjy's friend from 2/3GR, failed to stop the posting. Ronnie had to go as the school at Poona had absolute priority in getting the officers they wanted. He wondered why him, and he was in for a surprise. One day in September 1943, on the station platform at Poona, he found uncle Frank Ingham Clark, by then a Lieutenant Colonel in the Argylls, waiting to greet him. In the staff car on their journey to the school, the Eastern Warfare Centre (EWC), that his uncle was running, Ronnie learned that his uncle had heard from Major Angus Rose, a fellow Argyll, that Ronnie had been a jungle instructor. So there were family and regimental connections, but Angus Rose probably recommended Ronnie because he was a good instructor. Although very young he had shown he was good at passing on his skills, as Captain of Fives at school; he had taught for two terms at a prep school and instructed at the jungle school for six months. He was undoubtedly competent and because the Eastern Warfare School (EWC) needed a jungle instructor his uncle asked for him. The EWC was a highly secret training school at Kharakvasla beside a big lake south of Poona. It was part of the Special Operations Executive (SOE), subsequently known in India as Force 136, and was set up to train guerrilla parties from Burma, Malaya, Laos and Vietnam, including French officers, to go back to into those countries to harry the Japanese from behind the lines. On the journey to the school Ronnie was promised that he would only be required to instruct there for a year.

The training included canoeing on the lake for landings in enemy held territory from submarines, living and operating in the jungle and the use of explosives to disrupt the enemy's railway lines and communications. On one occasion Ronnie's enthusiasm for realism almost got him into trouble. He ran an exercise to practice French officers in derailing a train, and he chose a mock derailing of the night express on the main Madras to Bombay line. After a site recce and the posting of 'stops' on the flanks of the chosen site, a mock charge was laid. The night express duly arrived and set off the low powered detonator with a muffled bang. There was no danger to the train, as intended, but the driver heard the bang and the train screeched to a halt. The driver and others tumbled out to inspect the damage while the exercise saboteurs beat a hasty retreat in the darkness. No damage was found and the train continued on its way, but the driver reported the incident. His report shot up the chain of command to police and government officials, who at first thought it was a real attempt at sabotage that had gone wrong. By chance, uncle Frank was dining with senior Poona policemen and other government officials that evening when the news came in. The meal ceased immediately. However, after a quick telephone call to the school and an explanation of the exercise, Lieutenant Colonel Ingham Clark was able to reassure all present that there was no threat. Ronnie heard no more about it, but could not help feeling that any other commanding officer would have given him a severe reprimand.

It would have been while he was at the EWC that Ronnie heard that his brother Brian had been killed in action. Brian, a Lieutenant in the 2nd Gurkhas, was killed at Litan in the Sangshak battle near Imphal in 21st March 1944 while serving with 153 Gurkha Parachute Battalion. It is unlikely that Ronnie knew the circumstances of Brian's death at the time, namely that he would have been part of the frantic and heroic self-sacrifice made by 50 Indian Parachute Brigade at Sangshak, when the eastern approach to Imphal lay open and virtually undefended following a withdrawal mix-up. The two battalions of 50 Indian Parachute Brigade, without direction from 4 Corps, with little or no information about the enemy, and without ammunition and stores of the most basic kind – not even barbed wire – was thrown into a defensive position to hold a gap. The brigade held off General Miyazaki's 58 Regiment from the 20th to the 26th of March 1944. 50 Indian Parachute Brigade was almost wiped out. 152 Gurkha Parachute Battalion went into the battle 700 strong and after seven days could only muster two British officers and

90 men.[11] 153 Gurkha Parachute Battalion's casualties were similar; however, Japanese casualties were high and Miyazaki's advance was delayed for a week, which bought Slim and Scones valuable time to reorganise and reinforce the defences around Imphal. The stubborn – even fanatical – resistance by 50 Indian Parachute Brigade at this time took the Japanese by surprise. It was an early indication that their plans to drive into India were going awry.[12]

It is probable that Brian's death had a profound effect on Ronnie. Brian had been the only member of his immediate family who had been a constant companion during the long periods that they were separated from their parents. Although they lived with loving and understanding members of their wider family, the bond between Ronnie and Brian must have been especially strong. As brothers they had had to stick together and support each other. Over the years and especially during their formative school years it is likely that they shared adventures that cemented a special bond between them. That that bond was shattered was part of the price, sacrifice and reality of war, and it would have brought home to Ronnie that he too might have to pay the ultimate price for what had to be done.

Lieutenant Brian McAlister 2GR killed in action Burma 21 March 1944 aged 22[13]

He returned to the 3GR Centre at Dehra Dun in September 1944 and the following month attended the regular commission board which he passed. He was granted a regular commission in the Argyll and Sutherland Highlanders. At the time it was policy

11   . McAlister, RWL, 'Battle Casualty Statistics – Do they tell a story?', Bugle & Kukri journal,1998, p.18.
12   . Lyman, Slim, Master of War, Burma and the Birth of Modern Warfare, pp.193–194.
13   . The McAlister Family Collection.

for all regular officers to get active service experience so the centre could not keep him and much to his delight he was posted to the 1st Battalion of the 3rd Gurkhas (1/3GR).

Chapter 3

Burma

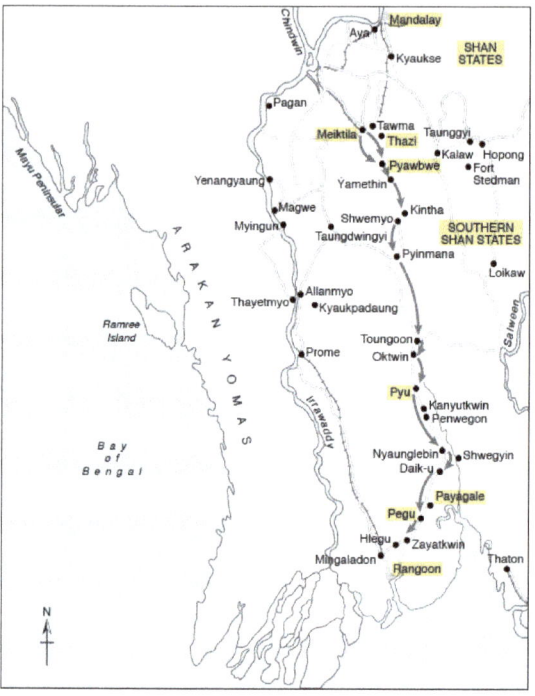

Burma 1945
1/3GR's advance as part of 99 Brigade in 17 Indian Division

Ronnie joined 1/3GR at Ranchi in eastern India. The Battalion had fought as part of the famous 17th 'Black Cat' Indian Division in Burma from 1942 until September 1944. It had been withdrawn after the ferocious fighting around Imphal for a hard-earned and well-deserved rest: years of fighting and dysentery and malaria had taken their toll and the Battalion was exhausted. It had rested, retrained and been re-equipped and reinforced and was about to return to Burma on operational service when

Ronnie joined them in mid-December 1944. By then he had been serving for almost three years.

On 14 January 1945 the Battalion moved by train and then river steamer on the Brahmaputra river to the rear logistic base at Dimapur near the India - Burma border. From there it went forward by lorry to Wanjing near Imphal, where it trained for deployment as an airportable battalion. At Wanjing, on 28 January, Ronnie was appointed adjutant. He was immediately involved in helping the Commanding Officer, Lieutenant Colonel WJM Spaight, work out details of how to fit the Battalion's men, weapons and a limited amount of equipment into USAAF Dakota DC3 aircraft, not knowing when or where they might be used in an airportable role. It was not long before they learned both.

As a young and green battalion adjutant Ronnie would have known little of Slim's grand strategy for XIVth Army to drive the Japanese out of Burma, but he played an active role in 1/3GR's activities and battles, as part of 99th Brigade in Major General 'Punch' Cowan's 17th Indian Division. Slim's masterstroke was to persuade the Japanese that XIVth Army's main objective was an attack by the British 2nd Division and the Indian 20th, 19th and 7th Divisions on Mandalay, while in the greatest secrecy he ordered the 48th and 63rd Brigades of 17th Indian Division, supported by the 255th Tank Brigade, to make a bold thrust through Japanese lines to capture the main Japanese logistic base at Meiktila well to the south. This was the strategic ploy that broke the back of the Japanese resistance in Burma.

The force attacking Meiktila captured an airfield at Thabukon 15 miles north of Meiktila on 26 February, and once that was secure 1/3GR were flown in, along with the rest of 99th Brigade (1st Sikh Light Infantry and 6/15th Punjab Regiment) to join the rest of 17th Indian Division. 1/3GR's task was to defend the Thabukon airfield aggressively and secure the Division's rear as it fought to capture Meiktila. From the time 1/3GR arrived on 26 February through to the end of March, Meiktila was under siege as the main Japanese force turned south to try to recapture the town and clear their line of retreat to Rangoon. On 3 March Meiktila was captured by 48th and 63rd Brigades. On the same day B Company of 1/3GR supported by tanks sallied out to the north of Thabukon and killed 32 Japanese in a three-day operation. 1/3GR then moved south to the main Meiktila airfield, helped to clear the surrounding villages and secure the airfield on 4 and 5 March. Cut off from the north and supplied by aircraft landing at the airfield and by airdrops, the Division did not adopt a static defensive posture but sallied forth conducting offensive all-arms operations to all points of the compass.

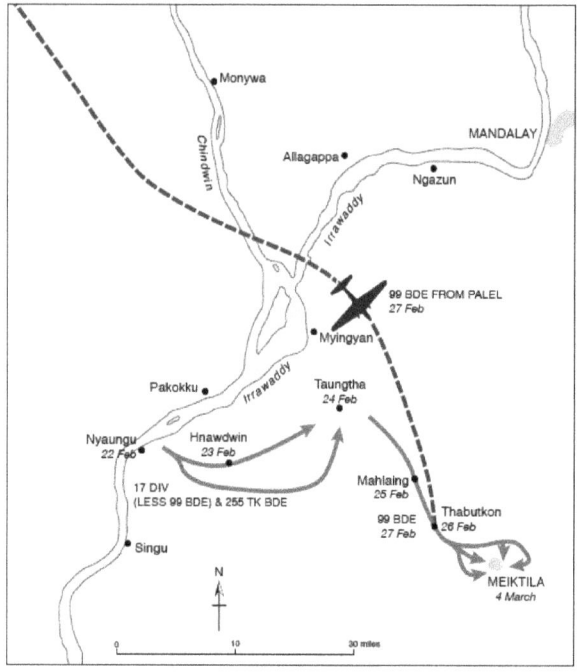

1/3GR Fly-in to Thabutkon 27 February 1945

Carrying four days' rations, by 9 March the Battalion had marched to a position west of Thazi, which was still in enemy hands, and on 10 March it was ambushing the roads into Meiktila from the north, down which the Japanese were approaching. For a brief period in the middle of March Japanese shelling and attacks prevented aircraft from landing on the airfields and the Division had to be supplied entirely by airdrops. To counter this pressure, on 17 March, 99th Brigade launched an attack to the north, supported by tanks and artillery. The infantry were put under command of the tank units, but it quickly became apparent that this arrangement was unsatisfactory, because the only way the infantry could communicate with the tank crews was via a telephone on the back of each tank – a tricky business when under fire. This, and the arrangement was not repeated subsequently. 1/3GR led the attack, but when they asked for permission to clear a village on their left flank, Divisional HQ over-ruled Brigade HQ and the 1st Sikh Light Infantry passed through 1/3GR and made a frontal attack without tank support. They, and to a lesser extent 1/3GR, were shot up from the flank, and suffered significant casualties when the Japanese held their fire until the unsupported Sikhs were almost on top of them. What Ronnie would not have known was that this and other operations on the same day were aimed at relieving pressure on Meiktila which allowed Slim to commit his only reserve, 5th Indian Division, by flying it into Meiktila to ensure the town was held and the Japanese onslaught to recapture it defeated. Extensive aggressive patrolling continued over the next few days, greatly enhanced by the arrival of 5 Indian Division. On 22 March 1/3GR carried out a battalion attack to the south-east of the airstrip, against a battalion-strength Japanese unit dug in in foxholes and bunkers in villages. In bitter fighting that lasted all day 1/3GR suffered 42 killed and wounded, but killed 169 Japanese. A Company 1/3GR cleared a Japanese position on the butts of the Meiktila rifle range on 24 March. On the same day Ronnie had a narrow escape. D Company was advancing north towards high ground that had been occupied in strength by the Japanese when wireless communication was lost. The commanding officer told Ronnie to go forward and find out what was going on. He took a jeep and, unable to find his own orderly, took the Jemadar Adjutant's orderly as his escort. When he returned to Battalion HQ he found it had been hit by a salvo of Japanese shells. Two direct hits on the HQ killed nine people, including the Jemadar Adjutant and Ronnie's orderly, and, among others, wounded the Intelligence Officer, Subedar Narbahadur Chand, and the Signal officer, Captain Heft. In the fast-moving situation Battalion HQ had not dug in, a precaution that should always be taken no matter how short the halt. That evening in its overnight position Battalion HQ was shelled again, but being better prepared the occupants were able to take cover in their slit trenches. Throughout these battles Ronnie, as Adjutant, manned the Battalion forward wireless link and received reports from the forward companies, also by runner, and the rear link to brigade. He kept the commanding officer informed of what was happening and passed orders to the companies, the Quartermaster and Motor Transport Officer, as required. To be at the centre of the Battalion's activities as it advanced and defeated the Japanese using superior weapons, tanks and aircraft was exhilarating for a young officer, and he was learning fast.

By 30 March the siege of Meiktila had been lifted and with the 5th Indian Division holding the town, the 17th Indian Division was ordered to advance south down the main road to Pyawbwe. On 2 April 1/3GR attacked Okpo with the help of close bombing and strafing by RAF Hurricanes and on 7–8 April the Battalion attacked an isolated Japanese position at Yindaw, killing 22 enemy. Every day there was some action as the Battalion cleared village after village. However, Pyawbwe was strongly defended and the tanks were held up by anti-tank guns on a hill on the main road, so 1/3GR was ordered to turn from the left flank and take the hill. In a nine-hour battle lasting into the evening, 1/3GR captured two enemy anti-tank guns and killed 250 Japanese, while their own casualties were nine killed and 42 wounded. The two anti-tank guns captured in this battle now stand outside the 1/3GR Quarter Guard. 17 Indian Division and the armour rested at Pyawbwe for a few days while 5 Indian Division took over the lead.

By this stage of the war in Burma, Japanese resistance was crumbling, so Slim called for a swift armoured thrust down the road, the aim of which was to get to Rangoon before the monsoon rains arrived. An armoured brigade consisting of Probyn's Horse, the Deccan Horse and the 16th Light Cavalry, with their supporting infantry, the Bombay Grenadiers and 4th/7th Rajputs, were to be augmented by another infantry battalion mounted in lorries. The Commanding Officer of 1/3GR, Lieutenant Colonel Robert O'Lone, who had relieved Lieutenant Colonel Spaight on the 25 March, went to see General 'Punch' Cowan and asked that 1/3GR should be that battalion, on the grounds that it had been with the Division ever since the first battles in 1942 and it deserved to be at the front for the final battles. Cowan agreed. The force took over the lead from 5 Indian Division in mid-April and had the exhilarating experience of brushing aside enemy resistance until it met the Japanese rearguard at Pyagale, which 1/3GR cleared in a brisk action, losing Bill Scurr, a newly joined young officer. The Japanese were short of anti-tank guns and resorted to suicide squads. This involved individuals hidden in holes in the road, each with a live aircraft bomb and a brick to strike the nose cap if a tank went over his position. At Pyagale Ronnie was at Battalion HQ waiting for the attack to go in when, not 100 yards away, there was a mighty roar and a Probyn's Horse tank rose high off the ground and toppled over, a victim of this tactic. 1/3GR cleared the village but some Japanese could not escape and hid in foxholes within 1/3GR's night perimeter. Suddenly, in the dark, there was shooting, then silence. C Company's Subedar came to Battalion HQ to report that one Japanese had made a run for it but was chased by a Gurkha who killed him with his kukri. A bunker full of Japanese lying low in the midst of C Company's position was also discovered and Ronnie went over to witness their elimination. A Company was sent to ambush a road leading towards the Sittang River and safety for the retreating enemy. At about midnight a Japanese staff car, clearly unaware how far south our forces had advanced, approached the ambush from the east. A Company opened fire killing all the occupants, which included two Japanese officers and a red-tabbed full Colonel in the Indian National Army, but not before they had returned fire and mortally wounded the company commander, Richardson. The next day Ronnie, as part of his responsibilities as Adjutant, went to find out how Richardson was, and found him lying on a stretcher in one of the casualty clearing stations, clearly dying.

On 30 April 1/3GR took part in the attack on Pegu, an important road centre 10 miles north of Rangoon. In stiff fighting the Battalion killed 47 Japanese forcing them to abandon large quantities of weapons and equipment, however once again Japanese appeared in the dark within the area the Battalion had just captured and tried to shoot their way out to safety in the darkness. In the ensuing skirmish another British officer, Joe Low, was mortally wounded. It was a sad end to a successful final battle and 15 exciting days of fighting, during which 1/3GR performed splendidly. Throughout the period from 26 February to 30 April 1945 1/3GR was engaged in almost continuous fighting. It was Ronnie's baptism of fire, but the only Japanese he saw were dead and he never fired his rifle.

In early May 1945, following the recapture of Rangoon, Ronnie was granted a spell of leave. He sailed from Rangoon to Calcutta and went from there by train to Pachmari, the summer 'hill station' for Nagpur, where he joined Nora and Bunjy for a week. It was the first time he had seen his mother since saying farewell to her at Whincroft in January 1942, when he sailed off to war. He attended a dinner at Government House at which the others wore black tie or mess kit. Doubtless he felt distinguished, and probably cooler, dressed in his open-necked jungle green. He was back in Burma by the end of May.

Temporary Major RWL McAlister – Pachmari, India – May 1945[14]

1/3GR was ordered north and travelled along Burma's north-south road for the fourth time in the war. It was a road of either continuous dust or a muddy quagmire; on this occasion it was the latter. The Battalion conducted operations in the southern Shan States area, advancing eastwards and for the most part against minor opposition, up into the hills at Kalaw and Taunggyi. These operations ended after the dropping of the atomic bombs on Japan and orders to 'cease fire' were given on 14 August 1945 when the Japanese accepted the surrender terms that had been offered to them on the 1 August 1945. No Japanese came forward to surrender in 1/3GR's area but the Battalion was soon involved in guarding Japanese prisoners gathered in other areas and within a short period of time they had to assist in the difficult task of helping the local police deal with dacoits,[15] who were well armed with looted weapons. This

---

14   . The McAlister Family Collection.
15   . Dacoits were gangs of armed bandits.

required 1/3GR to go back onto a 'war footing' and assisting the civil authorities involved some serious low-level fighting. It is not clear what Ronnie's role was during part of this period. His record of service suggests he relinquished the appointment of Adjutant on 20 October 1945 and as a Temporary Major was given command of a company. The next two entries show he embarked at Rangoon for India on 31 January 1946 and disembarked at Calcutta on 6 February. Confusingly the entry after that suggests he relinquished the appointment of Adjutant on 28 January 1947 to be a company commander again. I suspect he was reappointed Adjutant when 1/3GR returned to India in early 1946.

The London Gazette dated 19 September 1946 published that Ronnie had been awarded a Mention in Despatches. There appears to be no citation for the award and it is not clear precisely what it was awarded for. At the time of the announcement 1/3GR was back in India but it would have taken time for the recommendation for the award to get through the honours and awards system. In his undated notes, titled 'R.W.L. McAlister – CV', Ronnie recorded much of what happened and his part in 1/3GR's activities up to his short leave in May 1945. His record for the period May 1945 to January 1946 is at best sketchy; he made the simple entry: 'Kalaw–Taunggyi (Despatches)' in a series of notes that are not fleshed out. This might suggest that the award was in recognition of a specific incident in that area at that time. However, this seems unlikely, as some record of a specific incident ought to have become known. It is more likely that the award was for distinguished service as Adjutant during the last 8 months of the war and from August to October 1945, and then as a company commander from October 1945 to January 1946 in the challenging circumstances in Burma immediately after the war ended.

By the end of the war Ronnie was entitled to wear four medal ribbons: the 1939–45 Star; the Burma Star; the Defence Medal and the War Medal. The oakleaf indicating he had been Mentioned in Despatches was worn on his War Medal ribbon. By contrast, his father (Ronnie Senior) was entitled to wear 11 medal ribbons. He had been appointed an Officer of the Order of the British Empire (OBE) for his work in command of the 1st Argylls, so this, as an honour, was the first of his medal ribbons. It was followed by the WW1 British War Medal and the Allied Victory Medal, which he had earned as a 20-year-old. These were followed by the 1918 General Service Medal with the clasp 'Palestine 1936–39' for his service there on operations in 1939, and then there were his WW2 medals: the 1939–45 Star, the Africa Star, the Italy Star, the France and Germany Star and the War Medal, on the ribbon of which he too wore an oakleaf, to represent the two Mentions in Despatches he had been awarded. The first was for services on the Ruweisat Ridge that was part of the El Alamein Line and the second was for services in command of the 1st Argylls in Sicily and Italy. Then, after his British medal ribbons, he wore ribbons representing the Order of Leopold and the Belgian Crois de Guerre, which he was awarded as a Colonel in Normandy, when he was a special adviser to a Belgian brigade commander. Ronnie Senior's medal ribbons tell a remarkable story: he served throughout the war and in three of its major theatres of operations. It may well have been his father's record and medals that kindled in Ronnie a keen interest in military medals.

1/3GR left Burma and returned to the 3GR Regimental Centre at Dehra Dun in February 1946, arriving in India during a period of considerable unrest. In June 1946 the Battalion was deployed to Chittagong in Bengal to deal with serious rioting and civil disobedience. On this period, in his undated document 'R.W.L. McAlister – CV', Ronnie simply wrote 'Returned to India 1946, Dehra Dun, then Chittagong and Calcutta riots'. He remained in his appointment as Adjutant until 28 January 1947 when he was appointed B Company Commander. In the period up to 15 August 1947, when India and Pakistan gained independence, and afterwards, the Battalion was involved in the difficulties associated with partition. Serious communal fighting broke out in Calcutta in September 1947 and 1/3GR was sent to deal with it. Lieutenant Colonel Rose, the CO, recalled:

After our uneventful life in Chittagong the drama of the September riots in Calcutta seemed to open on a world suddenly gone mad; all the necessary theatrical effects were there, corpses lying unburied in the shops and street, abandoned trams, houses in flames and sporadic firing. The Battalion first took over an area in the City near the Medical University where we lived in requisitioned houses. The Officer's Mess was located in the Museum devoted to anatomical specimens and the memory of those rows of grisly bottles combined with the pervading odour from the adjacent and overflowing mortuary, will, I have no doubt, linger long in the memories of all of us.

The men behaved magnificently in the very difficult conditions which prevailed and we soon established close liaison with the police and civil authorities. After a couple of weeks we returned, for a short spell, to our lines, only to be moved into another area, this time near Sealdah Railway Station.

The worst rioting occurred in this period, necessitating several full scale company attacks upon 'Terrorist' strong-points, usually located in the upper stories of buildings. The railway station, which was strongly cordoned by the police, became a sanctuary for refugees.

As the cold weather approached the situation was slowly brought under control and we found ourselves back in our own lines.

The 3GR Regimental History does not reveal what part B Company played in the Chittagong riots and civil disobedience, or in the dreadful, senseless violence in Calcutta; probably those involved, including Ronnie, felt that the awfulness of what happened was best left unrecorded. In August 1947 1/3GR received the news that it was not one of the four regiments selected for transfer to the British Army, so it then prepared for service in the Army of independent India, and the handover of the Battalion to its new Indian Army officers. Instructions were received that all the regimental funds and property, mess silver, trophies and other effects of the British Officers' Mess were to be handed over. On 29 November 1947 Lieutenant Colonel HV Rose handed over to Lieutenant Colonel PO Dunn, the first Indian Officer to command 1/3GR. Ronnie had by then transferred to the British Army. His record of service indicates he was posted to 2/10GR on 15 November 1947. Quite when he was actually released from 1/3GR is not clear, but he was not with the Battalion, or in the Indian Army, on 15 August 1947; had he been, he would have qualified for the Indian Independence Medal. In a period of uncertainty he was no longer in the British Indian Army. He may have had a spell on local leave in limbo, while the British Army decided what to do with him. Ronnie served in 3GR for five years and with 1/3GR for three years. He briefly commanded a company in Burma shortly after the war ended in 1945, and again for about six months in

India in 1947; however for most of his time with 1/3GR he was Adjutant. This suggests that the commanding officers at that time recognised and appreciated his competence as a staff officer.

Chapter 4

Into the British Army

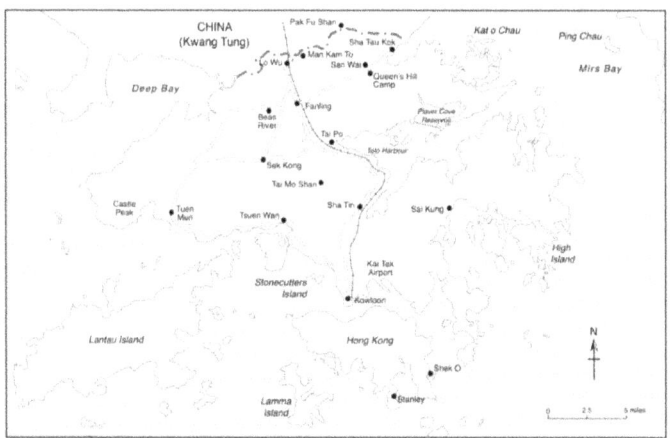

Hong Kong ca 1948

On 15 August 1947 India and Pakistan gained their independence from Britain. The run-up to Independence was a period of considerable uncertainty for everyone, Gurkha and British alike, in the Gurkha Brigade. Mountbatten had assumed that the whole of the British Indian Army would transfer to the new Indian Army. However, it was pointed out that the soldiers in the Gurkha Brigade of the British Indian Army were Nepalese and not Indian citizens and their enlistment and employment outside Nepal would require the agreement of the Nepalese Government. A treaty known as the Tripartite Agreement between the Governments of Britain, India and Nepal was drawn up. As part of that agreement four regiments[16] of the Gurkha Brigade were selected for transfer to the British Army and the other six regiments[17] were to be part of the new Indian Army. It was a difficult time for both the Gurkhas and their British

---

16 . 2GR, 6GR, 7GR and 10GR.
17 . 1GR, 3GR, 4GR, 5GR, 8GR and 9GR.

officers. In the regiments selected to be transferred to the British Army, the Gurkhas were given the choice of remaining in the Indian Army or transferring to the British Army. The 'opt' as it was known strained relationships, as British officers were not allowed to advise their men. It was a difficult time not least because of the paucity of information.

> ... this was a time of great bitterness in the Indian Army in general, and in Gurkha regiments in particular. Men and officers alike were treated badly by a government and War Office only half-heartedly committed to them. Montgomery's lack of enthusiasm for the 'private army', as he called it, which he had helped to have transferred to British service, was well known, and his attitude was reflected in War Office policy: Gurkhas were not to have their own permanent cadre of officers, but were to be commanded by officers on secondment from British regiments.[18]

> British Gurkha officers were in the same position as other Indian Army officers in that they were required to decide by 15 July 1947 whether to take redundancy terms and leave the army altogether, or transfer to British service, or to continue serving in one of the new Dominion armies for a limited period, thereby rendering themselves ineligible for future service in the British Army. There was no option for staying on with a British Gurkha regiment because at that stage there were no British Gurkha regiments. Even when agreement was reached for the transfer of four regiments, subject to ratification by the Nepalese government, the War Office continued to shilly-shally until finally, on 28 November 1947, the Director of Personnel Administration, Major General J.E.C. McCandlish, wrote to all British Gurkha regular officers, giving them the opportunity of opting for continued service with Gurkhas ..... whatever their previous election.[19]

As a regular officer in the Argyll and Sutherland Highlanders, Ronnie was in British service, albeit in a Gurkha regiment, so he would not have received the 28 November 1947 letter. However, it was clear by then that the Gurkha regiments

---

18 . Gould, Imperial Warriors, p.299.
19 . Gould, Imperial Warriors, p.300.

selected for transfer to the British Army had to be officered, and in line with War Office policy he was transferred as a seconded officer. Many of those on the list of regular British officers selected to transfer to those Gurkha regiments earmarked for the British Army[20] either elected not to transfer, or had a modest war record, so there was a shortfall particularly in the younger age groups. By the time this was happening, Slim relieved Montgomery, and the plan to officer British Gurkha regiments with seconded officers from British regiments was overturned. The Brigade of Gurkhas was now to have its own permanent cadre officers. There was a concerted effort to recruit officers to fill the gaps in the age and rank-structure and it is probable that Ronnie was talent-spotted at the time. He had done well in 1/3GR and was asked to join the permanent cadre. Although 10GR and the three other selected Gurkha Regiments did not officially transfer to the British Army until 1 January 1948, Ronnie was posted to the 10th Gurkhas and joined 2/10GR at the 10th Gurkha concentration area at Lahore in Pakistan on 15 November 1947. He was appointed Officer Commanding B Company and immediately became embroiled in the difficulties surrounding Partition and the 'opt'. Again his entry in 'R.W.L. McAlister – CV' is remarkably brief, stating merely 'Partition problems in the Punjab as OC B Company.' However, on the 'opt' he later wrote more fully:

I joined 2/10GR from 1/3GR in mid-November and was apprehensive about the opt. My senior Subedar, Jitbahadur, and my Company Havildar Major (Deshman Rai, BEM, MM a fine soldier of some influence) both wished, I quickly learnt, to stay in the Indian Army, and I visualised many waverers following their lead. But both made it clear they would not try to influence others and this left the door open to Subedar Manbahadur Rai, OC 6 Platoon and an ex 4/10GR Gurkha Officer (GO). He unashamedly advised those with prospects of a good career to stay; doubters, weaklings or those at their ceiling to leave the Army or join an Indian Gurkha battalion. He calmly told me one morning the opt was over. 'These are staying', he said (handing me a list with about 40 names, all good men he assured me) 'and the rest are going.' He then confided, 'We shan't miss

20 .Gurkha Museum, War Office letter 100/INDIA/3754/AG1 (Offrs P), 28 November 1947.

them.' He was a splendid officer, and I could not have been more appreciative or grateful at this my initiation into the Battalion. For me that was all the dreaded 'Opt' amounted to.[21]

This was not quite the case. Later events were to expose concerns about the way British Gurkhas were treated and how strongly the Gurkhas felt about it.

The Battalion moved from Lahore to Ranchi on 17 January 1948 and from there, on 28 February 1948 it travelled by train to Bombay and embarked on SS *Strathnaver* on 3 March 1948, bound for Hong Kong via Singapore. The Battalion disembarked on 17 March 1948 and moved to a hutted camp at San Wai on the Fanling – Sha Tau Kok road a mile, as the crow flies, from the Hong Kong border with China. Ronnie's first spell in Hong Kong lasted only two months, as he was due long leave. He sailed from Hong Kong on 28 May 1948 and disembarked at Liverpool on 26 June. While he was on leave he was granted a regular commission in the Brigade of Gurkhas on 21 August 1948.[22]

On completion of his leave he sailed from Liverpool on 1 October 1948 and disembarked in Hong Kong on 30 October. He assumed the appointment of Adjutant 2/10GR on 4 November. In peace time it was a very different role to the one he had undertaken in 1/3GR during the war, in the turbulent period in Burma just after the war and in India in 1946. He was immediately thrown into the work involved in moving the Battalion from its rural location at San Wai to Whitfield Barracks on Nathan road in the heart of downtown Kowloon. One company was based 12 miles away at Erskine Camp on the Sai Kung Peninsular. The accommodation in Whitfield Barracks and Erskine Camp was a marked improvement on San Wai but the distance from the training areas, predominantly in the New Territories, was a disadvantage. At the time, in China, the communists were gaining sweeping victories in the civil war. This led to fears that aggressive guerrilla forces might threaten the Hong Kong border and the garrison was reinforced in April 1949 by two British infantry brigades and medium and field artillery units, all of which required accommodation. In May 1949, just as the Battalion had settled into its new

21   . McAlister, Bugle & Kukri, Vol.2, p.268.
22   . APC, RWL McAlister, British Army Record of Service.

accommodation in Whitfield Barracks, it was moved back to the New Territories, to the Jockey Club Stables at Beas River near the Fanling Golf Club. Four men in bunk beds occupied each horse box – the accommodation had been designed for horses and the previous occupants had been horses. This was difficult for the Gurkhas to stomach and understandably they felt they were being badly treated.

When the decision to move the Battalion was made, the Commanding Officer, Lieutenant Colonel Jim Vickers DSO and Bar, immediately protested. He was only too aware that one of the most telling aspects of the anti-British propaganda at the time of the 'Opt' was an assertion that British Gurkha units would be used where both the climate and the accommodation were bad, and that the British Government's aim was to save money by paying the Gurkha soldier far less and by providing him with a lower standard of living conditions than his British counterpart. On his arrival to command the Battalion in July 1948 Lieutenant Colonel Vickers had a deep suspicion that the assertion might well be true, and he knew that Major Bagdhan Rai, the senior Gurkha Commissioned Officer (GCO), held the same view, as did all the other Gurkha officers. They all knew accommodation had to be found for the reinforcing units and Lieutenant Colonel Vickers was assured that the real reason for the move was operational. The General Officer Commanding (GOC) wanted troops who knew the ground near the border. Vickers accepted this in good faith and was able, with some difficulty, to persuade the senior Gurkha officers. The situation then got worse. Barely six weeks after the Battalion's move to the Jockey Club Stables the Commanding Officer received a warning order to move out into a tented camp so that a newly arrived British battalion could move into the accommodation the Battalion had spent a month cleaning out and improving. The news soon reached Bagdhan, who went to see Jim Vickers. Bagdhan was white with rage and found the Commanding Officer in a similar condition. Bagdhan made it clear that if the order was not rescinded he and the other senior Gurkha officers wished to resign their commissions. Ronnie, as Adjutant, almost certainly shared their outrage. Vickers demanded an interview with the GOC, which was granted only after he had been threatened with being put on a boat back home and to which he retorted that if that was the case he would not be alone.

In what was clearly an evolving response to what was happening in China, the reality was that it was again an operational decision. On its arrival in Hong Kong the Battalion had been in the Kowloon Brigade. When Hong Kong was reinforced, in April 1949, the Kowloon Brigade was re-designated as 26th Gurkha Brigade, comprising 1st Cameronians, 2/6GR and 2/10GR. Just after the Battalion had moved into the Jockey Club Stables, it was given the task of defending the eastern sector of the frontier from Fanling to Sha Tau Kok. (See Map page 31). The Jockey Club Stables camp was in the western sector and the Battalion was in the wrong place. Vickers forcefully expressed the feelings of the Gurkhas and the sensitive nature of the situation, and this gained an agreement that he could select his own site for the Battalion's camp, get priority for the completion of the works services, and an assurance that the 2/10GR would not be moved again during its tour in Hong Kong. Armed with these concessions he managed, again with difficulty, to persuade Bagdhan and the other senior Gurkha officers to accept the situation. He and Bagdhan then selected a hilly area just south of the Fanling–Sha Tau Kok road, opposite San Wai camp. It was near the Birds Hill, Cloudy Hill and Robin's Nest features that the Battalion was tasked to defend. The new site became known as Queen's Hill camp. In a superhuman effort the Battalion created a pleasant tented camp where each company had its own hill area.

Almost as soon as they had completed the task a Force 9 typhoon named 'Maggie' hit the colony on 9 September 1949. The tents had to be struck and tied down and the men, in the open and exposed to the elements, took such cover as they could find behind their respective hills. It was an unpleasant experience and one soldier was killed when he was decapitated by a flying sheet of 'wriggly tin'.[23] In an effort to provide some comfort to the men Ronnie felt that a rum issue would be appropriate and might help raise morale. An extraordinary rum issue could only be authorised by the Commanding Officer or Regimental Medical Officer in exceptional circumstances. The circumstances were indeed exceptional and the doctor agreed. However, it was immediately apparent that issuing the rum would be difficult, as the men were safer sheltering from the high winds and rain in the lee of their respective hills. The rum

---

23 . Army slang for corrugated iron.

was stored in the ammunition compound, where there were numerous fire buckets filled with sand to extinguish any fire. Reckoning that the sand was superfluous, because there was running water everywhere and rain was lashing down, Ronnie ordered the sand buckets to be emptied, cleaned and filled with rum, straight from the rum barrels. A small fatigue party from each company was called for and the rum filled-buckets were carried Chinese coolie style, with a bucket at each end of a pole, to the respective company areas. The rum did much to fortify the men and was much appreciated. About a week later after the typhoon had abated and life had returned to normal, the rum NCO presented the extraordinary rum issue figures for verification and signature. The amount issued had to be confirmed, signed off and counter-signed by the Commanding Officer. After signing, Vickers eyed his adjutant rather severely, and said words along the lines of, 'It was a very good idea Ronnie, but issuing the equivalent of three months' worth of rum on a single night was a bit excessive, don't you think?'

It would have been a challenging time for an adjutant. Unfamiliar British Army peacetime administrative and accounting procedures had to be learnt, applied and taught to others. Most of this work was carried out by the Battalion's clerks, who were commanded by the adjutant. The clerks were recruited and enlisted as clerks and served throughout their careers as such. Most came from the Darjeeling area in India and many had attended missionary and church schools. They were a specialist platoon, better educated than the average Gurkha and essential at a time when paperwork and written English was not a forte in Gurkha battalions. Ronnie was the principal staff officer in Battalion HQ and responsible for the clerks and their tasks of producing and issuing written orders, correspondence and record keeping. These were considerable challenges, similar to those faced during the creation of a new battalion. 2/10GR had been brought up to strength during 1948 and it was expected to be operational by 1 January 1949, shortly after Ronnie was appointed adjutant. Although it officially became operational on that date the reality was that more training and time were needed to mould officers and men from various different units into cohesive and effective fighting groups, at section, platoon and company level. Trying to achieve this was not helped by three unit moves in less than a year. It is hardly surprising that in commenting on Ronnie's performance in his annual confidential report, Vickers wrote, 'The volume of office work has kept him tied too much to his office and this has not enabled him to give sufficient time or attention to the normal peacetime duties of the Adjutant.' This may have been accurate but given the circumstances it seems harsh. They were, however, remarks that were not repeated in his next report.

The Battalion enjoyed a more settled period from September 1949 to March 1950, during which it trained hard and concentrated on putting right its collective ability and all-round effectiveness from section to battalion level. It was not all hard work, as 2/10GR ran two football sides in the Hong Kong Army Football League. The 1st XI did moderately well, considering that most of their opponents were British units, by holding a position in the middle of the league. As recorded in *The Kukri* the 2nd XI was not quite so successful:

> … the 2nd XI maintains its positon without any fluctuation (unfortunately at the bottom of the league). In the 2nd XI Lieutenant Colonel Vickers is a frequent member of the team at centre forward and in fact scored one of the few goals the team has scored during the season. McAlister tries very hard at centre half to plug up some of the holes in the defence whilst Twelvetrees reclines in goal with a goal average of 65 against and 16 for.[24]

On 6 March 1950, and it did not come as a complete surprise to everyone, it was announced that 26th Gurkha Brigade was to prepare to move to Malaya to help deal with the Communist Terrorist threat known as the Malayan Emergency.

---

24 . The Kukri, No.1, May 1949, p.85.

Chapter 5

Malaya

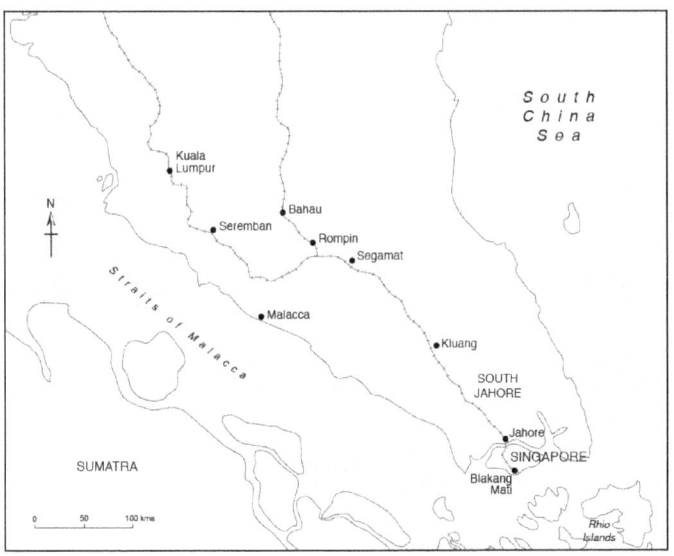

South Malaya ca 1955

The Battalion embarked on SS *Orbita* on 16 April 1950 and arrived in Singapore on 22 April. It moved straight across the causeway to Johore Bahru in Malaya, where it joined the 1st Battalion of the Regiment in Majedee Barracks. The 1st Battalion was on a break after 17 months on operations, and it was able to help the 2nd Battalion in its hasty preparations for anti-terrorist operations. The help was significant, as the Battalion began operations against the terrorists on 24 May 1950. By the middle of June it had been in action and killed four terrorists for the loss of Lance Corporal Sahardhoj Limbu. By December it had killed 18 terrorists, for the loss of one Gurkha officer and one Gurkha other rank killed and one Gurkha officer and four Gurkha other ranks wounded, when it was unexpectedly called upon to deal with serious rioting in Singapore.

2/10GR was ordered to gather as many troops as could be released from jungle operations and move at once to Singapore. The call went out after dark on 12 December 1950 and before first light on 13 December Ronnie, as Tactical Adjutant (Operations Officer) in Battalion HQ, was moving with a composite force of six cobbled together platoons across the Causeway into Singapore and heading for the Beach Road Police Station. Serious racial rioting had broken out over the tragic case of a young Dutch girl called Bertha, also known as Maria, Hertogh. Her Dutch father and Malay mother were taken into custody in Java by the Japanese in 1943 and Maria was looked after by Malay Muslim foster parents and moved to north Malaya. In 1948 when her parents discovered where she was and claimed her back. Baptised a Catholic Maria was 13 years old at the time of the riots. Towards the end of protracted custody battles that aroused strong religious feelings, Maria was rushed through a Muslim marriage to a Malay. The Supreme Court in Singapore ruled the marriage invalid and granted custody of the child to her parents. Anti-European and Eurasian sentiments and Malay Police ineptitude led to widespread rioting during which nine people were killed and 173 injured, 26 of them seriously, and there was considerable damage to property. The situation was out of control and the Army was called in to act in aid of the civil powers. The hastily gathered *ad hoc* force from 2/10GR arrived at the Beach Road Police station early in the morning. This was close to a Mosque that was thought to be a riot headquarters and the Battalion was immediately asked to deal with an angry and hostile mob. Major 'Bunny' Burnett, OC Headquarter Company, was the only company commander available, and was asked to deal with the situation. Over 60 years later Ronnie recalled:

The CO told Bunny to gather some men. The only ones available were Bunny's own men from the Pipes & Drums and with these, led by a Police inspector, he dashed off in two 3-tonners. The time was about 0800 hours. This body of men, as you can imagine, was a much less effective force than one which, an hour later, we might have been able to deploy. But Bunny's presence was reassuring. It seemed to me to be just half an hour later that one of the 3-tonners came back to us at Beech [*sic*] Road with a heap (it looked like six or seven) of dead and wounded in it – a gruesome sight! We had no RMO with us yet, I seem to recall, and I told the driver to go at once to the nearest hospital. A policeman guide must have been produced for our driver surely did not know where to go.[25]

Seven rioters were killed and a number wounded when Major Burnett's troops opened fire. The rioting stopped abruptly and, as Ronnie wrote, 'the effect of this one stern but limited action in Arab Street played a major role in bringing law and order back to Singapore. Before the rest of the Battalion arrived in Singapore, the rioting was effectively over and after two days of enforcing a curfew and patrolling quiet streets, we returned gratefully to the jungle.'[26] The exact details of what happened when Major Burnett's troops opened fire may never be known. The official inquiry into the Maria Hertogh riots, the Leach Report,[27] concluded, 'We are satisfied that fire was never opened unless it was absolutely necessary, and, where possible warning was given beforehand. Indeed, this might be regarded as an excellent example of the use of the Military in aid of the Civil Power in that a minimum of force was used to restore law and order without delay.'[28]

Operations continued at a demanding pace and it was not until September 1951 after 16 months of testing jungle warfare that the Battalion was taken off operations for re-training. By then it had killed or captured 31 terrorists, but by Malayan Emergency standards it had suffered high casualties, having had two KGOs and six GORs killed and one BO, one KGO and 12 GORs wounded. It was a mark of the quality and fighting ability of the hard core terrorists in the Johore area, and in particular of 5 and 9 Platoons of the Malayan Races Liberation Army (MRLA), who were regular adversaries.

Throughout this operational period Ronnie remained Adjutant, coping with the usual demanding administrative responsibilities of that appointment, and, when Battalion HQ was in the field, also the operational responsibilities of running Tactical HQ, as the Operations Officer. His task was not made

25 . RWL McAlister, E-Mail 4 February 2010.
26 . McAlister, Bugle & Kukri, Vol.2, p.289.
27 . TNA, CO 537/7247 and 537/7248, Report of the Singapore Riots Inquiry Commission, (Government Printers, Singapore 1951). Known as the Leach Report, May 1951.
28 . Leach Report, p.71.

any easier by changes in personalities. In September 1950 the Commanding Officer, Lieutenant Colonel Jim Vickers, was taken to hospital very seriously ill. He did not return to the Battalion. Major Terry became the officiating CO until Lieutenant Colonel John Waldron from the Gloucestershire Regiment assumed command in August 1951. Providing the continuity in Battalion HQ almost certainly created more work, and Ronnie unselfishly rose to the challenges. His 1951 annual report records, '[He is] a tireless worker, who tends to do more than his fair share of work and should learn to decentralise more.' He was graded B – 'Up to the Standard of his rank and service' – but in his remarks as the first Superior Reporting Officer, the Brigadier records that Ronnie has carried out 'a far from easy task with success', and upgrades the grading to 'A' – 'Above the standard of his rank and service'. However, the same Brigadier does not upgrade Ronnie's 1952 report in the same manner. This may be because after three years as Adjutant Ronnie had handed over the appointment in November 1951 and was commanding a company on operations for the last three months of the reporting period. It is note-worthy that for the operational awards period July 1951 to December 1951, a period that falls in his 1952 report period, Ronnie was awarded a second Mention in Despatches (MID). There is no citation for the award so again it is not clear what he received it for. After two months of re-training the Battalion returned to operational duties in November 1951, so Ronnie spent four months on operations commanding a company before proceeding on long leave on 9 March 1952. For two months of the operational awards period relevant to his MID he was commanding a company, though there is nothing in the regimental records to suggest there was a specific incident on operations for which the award might have been made. In the absence of any other evidence it would be reasonable to assume that his MID was awarded for 16 months distinguished service on operations as Adjutant.

Ronnie disembarked in the United Kingdom and began his long leave on 12 April 1952. His leave address was the Prosser family home at Whincroft. In October 1952 he reported to the School of Infantry at Warminster and attended the Company Commanders Course before being appointed as an instructor on the Platoon Commanders Course at the same school. The latter was a specialist course for recently commissioned infantry officers, with the remit of teaching them how to command a rifle platoon of about 30 men, which would usually be the first command in their career. The ten-week course aimed to teach them how to command a platoon in battle, with all the skills and knowledge which that requires, including basic tactics, fieldcraft, weapon handling, the use of supporting arms, fitness, first aid and hygiene, along with the management and administration of the platoon. The course was the essential first building block in the leadership and command of men and it had to be good. Ronnie received his first report a mere three months into the appointment. He was now away from the Brigade of Gurkhas and competing with his peers, drawn from a cross-section of infantry regiments. He quickly made his mark. The Chief Instructor who initiated his report described him as 'an excellent instructor', adding that 'He takes considerable trouble in the preparation of his work, is thorough and has the ability to put his instruction across in an interesting manner.' By the time of his second report in the post Ronnie's ability as a staff officer had not passed unnoticed, and in addition to his instructing responsibilities he was employed as a staff officer to the Chief Instructor, a certain Lieutenant Colonel HJ Mogg, who went on to be the Deputy Supreme Allied Commander in Europe, as General Sir John Mogg. By the time Mogg was the Chief Instructor at the School of Infantry he had already been a member of the Directing Staff at the Staff College at Camberley and he recognised talent when he saw it. Throughout his time at Warminster Ronnie was graded 'A' – 'Above the standard of his rank and service'. He got strong recommendations for Staff College and in addition to his 'flair for instructing' it was noted that 'with more experience he will undoubtedly become a high grade 'all rounder''.

In April 1955, after a little over two years as an instructor at Warminster, Ronnie returned to regimental duty with 2/10GR. Curiously, the Regimental Journal *Bugle & Kukri* records in its 'Arrivals' column the return of 'Major Lorne McAlister'.[29] It would appear this was the only time in his military career that he was referred as Lorne, the name of his youth and the one his family knew him by. The Battalion was still involved in the

---

29 . 'Arrivals', Bugle & Kukri journal, Vol.2 No.6, Dec 1955, p.227. In his Army service, this is the only reference found that suggests his Christian name was Lorne rather than Ronnie.

struggle to defeat the Communist Terrorists (CTs) in the Malayan Emergency and it was still based at Majedee Barracks in South Johore. On arrival Ronnie assumed the appointment of OC Support Company.

At this stage of the Emergency the intensity of the earlier battles against large and well-armed terrorist groups had decreased; there was increasing civil control with an emphasis on protecting and controlling the civil population and denying the terrorists access to their sources of food, information and funds. Most of the Battalion was tied up in static duties to guard the 'protected villages', enforce curfews and search through and control the flow of produce in and out of the villages, as information on the enemy was gathered by the police special branch in particular. Such troops as could be spared from these static duties continued to conduct operations in the jungle against an increasingly elusive and rarely encountered enemy, but a long period with no contacts was broken almost as soon as Ronnie returned. What followed was typical of the time. On 7 April, A Company killed a terrorist in some jungle cultivations (Sakai Ladangs) south of Bahau. Then, on 11 April, a small ambush party composed of men from B and D Companies killed two terrorists near Rompin. On 12 April a small patrol from Support Company was fired on and had one man wounded. The enemy was not seen and the one effective shot was the only one fired. On 23 April a patrol from A Company caught a fleeting glimpse of a CT party of six who moved into the jungle before they could be engaged. On 11 June B Company killed a terrorist north of Rompin near some jungle cultivations and on 22 June Support Company killed another in jungle cultivations east of Bahau. Over a period of three months the Battalion had seven contacts and killed five CTs in an area the size of Wales. The author of the 2nd Battalion entry for the 10th Gurkha contribution to the Brigade magazine, *The Kukri,* wrote: 'In April, May and June, A, B, D and Support Companies killed five bandits between them, whilst their company commanders successfully reduced their handicaps on the Bahau Estate Golf course.'[30] There may have been some truth in this, however light-hearted the remark was intended to be; but the enemy activity and 2/10GR's kills in the area prompted the Brigadier to mount a large-scale operation in the Battalion area under his

30   . The Kukri, No.8, April 1956, p.61.

personal control. Ronnie commanded the composite company that carried out the sweeps through a cordoned area, seeking to flush out the enemy towards the surrounding troops. The operation was called off when no enemy were found.

In September the Battalion was taken off operations for re-training. The Sultan of Johore was celebrating his Diamond Jubilee and on 17 September 2/10GR provided the Pipes & Drums and a detachment from Support Company as part of an all-Services and Police contingent for a ceremonial parade for the Sultan. The parade's marching pace was set at 110 paces per minute and was a challenge for Gurkhas whose normal parade marching pace was 140 paces per minute. Ronnie was Second in Command of the parade and it exceeded all expectations in its precision. Those who took part were able to watch their performance, when a newsreel covering the parade was shown at the local cinema a few days later.

Re-training was unexpectedly cancelled on 4 October and the Battalion went back on operations. It was tasked with going after a CT gang of 15 and in a period of five days killed three, wounded four and enticed three to surrender. Those who surrendered led Support Company to a small food dump on 12 October. Two days later Support Company engaged three CTs, killing one and wounding two. Further drives through the area led to the capture of a female CT by Support Company on 21 October, and although she did not talk under interrogation it was possible to deduce from the medical supplies she had on her that she was looking after a wounded person. Her wounded comrade, another female CT, surrendered to the Police 36 hours later. This was the last contact with the enemy during Ronnie's eight-month tenure in command of Support Company. He had been selected to attend the Army Staff College at Camberley and left the Battalion on 7 December to take up his place on the prestigious and career-enhancing course.

Before he left he had time to play in the annual Brigade of Gurkhas golf tournament, held on 15 and 16 November. He became the Brigade of Gurkhas 1955 Open Champion, playing off a handicap of 12, winning with a gross score 169 over 18 holes.

Chapter 6

Onto the Staff

The Staff College at Camberley was housed in a stylish Grade II listed building, designed by James Pennethorne and built in 1862 in the grounds of the Royal Military Academy at Sandhurst. Its setting was ideal for learning, away from the challenges of soldering, operations and the management of men. The course provided an opportunity to study the profession of arms and to network while working alongside and mixing socially with contemporaries in the numerous branches of the Army and, to a lesser extent, in the other services and some foreign nations. The year-long course aimed to teach the best senior captains and junior majors, aged about 30 to 34, the operational and administrative duties required of staff officers at brigade and divisional level, and some of the leadership skills needed to command. Entry was by examination, recommendation they selection. The staff-promotion exam consisted of written papers on international and current affairs, war studies and military law and administration with two levels of pass; a promotion pass being lower than a staff pass. A promotion pass was required for promotion to substantive major and a career beyond 16 years, and a staff pass was required to be eligible for selection to attend a staff course.[31] An exam pass at staff level was only the first hurdle; it did not guarantee attendance and some officers who passed at staff level were either not recommended for staff training or they missed the selection cut in a competitive age group. Teaching on the course was done in syndicates that were assessed by a member of the Directing Staff (DS), usually a lieutenant colonel, who had done well on the same course earlier in his career. The competitive atmosphere in what was effectively the Army's university was enhanced because both the students and the directing staff knew they were being assessed

---

31 . Staff training was not restricted to the course at Camberley. A small number of officers attended the RN or RAF staff courses or comparable courses overseas.

by the system. Those who did well at their respective levels were undoubtedly earmarked as having potential for higher rank.

Ronnie did well at the Staff College and achieved a B Grading, which would have placed him in the upper quartile of the course. His report suggested he used the course well and developed throughout it. He was assessed as being extremely sound tactically and could be relied upon to produce sound, concise, logical solutions in writing and verbally. Described as a pleasant, rather quiet personality with much common-sense and self-confidence the report suggested he would make a reliable, above-average staff officer. In answer to the question: 'Is he likely to be suitable for the Directing Staff after further experience?' his Divisional Colonel wrote 'No'. At the 'Black Bag Meeting'[32] held in October 1956 he was nominated for his first job as a trained staff officer. It was the important appointment of Brigade Major 99th Gurkha Infantry Brigade. His nomination was accepted. It meant returning to Malaya and taking on enhanced operational responsibilities on the staff in the Brigade HQ. He left England on 1 February 1957, travelling back to Singapore by sea via the Cape and Durban because the Suez Canal was still closed following the Suez crisis. Len Lauderdale, who had just been commissioned into the 2nd Gurkhas, travelled out to Singapore on the same ship. He recalled how thoughtful and considerate Ronnie was and how he helped Len start learning Gurkhali by teaching him on the voyage.[33] Ronnie disembarked in Singapore on 5 March 1957, and went straight to Brigade HQ to start taking over his new appointment, which he assumed on 25 March.

99th Gurkha Infantry Brigade was one of four brigades[34] in 17th Gurkha Infantry Division, all heavily involved in the Malayan Emergency. The Division was commanded by a major general who in addition to being the General Officer Commanding (GOC) 17th Division was also the Major General Brigade of Gurkhas (MGBG). The brigade majors were the principal staff officers in the brigade HQs, reporting to and working directly for the brigadiers, who in turn reported to the major general. In a key appointment and under the spotlight, Ronnie received his first report in the appointment after only

---

32 . The Black Bag Meeting allocated appointments to students, depending on how they had performed on the course.

33 . Telephone conversation Lauderdale–Litherland 6 January 2017.

34 . The others were 26th, 48th and 63th Brigades.

four months because there was a change of brigade commanders. Brigadier Townsend, on relinquishing the appointment, reported that Ronnie had got quickly into his stride and had made a good start. Townsend was replaced by Brigadier Walter Walker. Walker was a dynamic and determined Gurkha officer who knew that 99th Brigade had been tasked to fight the battle against the most formidable remaining communist terrorists in South Johore. At the time command of 99th Brigade was deemed to be the most demanding and important of any in the Army. If the battle could be won decisively, it should administer the *coup de grace* to the terrorists in Malaya. Walker wanted to deliver that blow personally.[35] Although the decision that 99th Brigade was to fight the battle was taken before Walker arrived in mid-1957, he immediately set about challenging the way operations had been conducted to date. He selected the code-name 'Tiger' for the operation, insisting that he expected the brigade to show 'the cunning, stamina and the offensive spirit of a tiger'. He believed the operation could only be successful if the Army and Police shared responsibility and was appalled at the paucity of informants in the area and the lack of usable information held by special branch on the enemy. He recognised the battle could not be launched based on the little information available, so delayed it, and immediately set about changing the mentality of those involved. Commanding officers were ordered to prepare their own assessments and theories about where the enemy were in the 1,800 square miles of jungle in which they operated, and how they might be found, trapped and killed. Study days followed. Training was harder and soldiers were taught to think and act like terrorists – no noise, no smoking, no give-away smells like soap and toothpaste – and taught the skills required for protracted ambushes and patient patrolling. The application of pressure on the enemy, in particular his sources of food, and the slow and deliberate piecing together of snippets of information from all sources took time, and it also required time to out-think and defeat an experienced and jungle-wise opponent. At the heart of the work involved in this re-thinking and training was the Brigadier's principal staff officer – Ronnie. Initially he supported the Brigade re-training programme and in the first confidential report that Walker wrote on Ronnie he described his staff work and dedication in glowing terms, but

---

35 . Pocock, The Fighting General, p.101.

identified that Ronnie had had limited experience as a company commander. In fact he had commanded a company on several occasions: firstly, in 1/3GR after the war in Burma for three months, October 1945 to January 1946; secondly, in India for seven months from March to October 1947; thirdly for three months on joining 10GR in Pakistan from November 1947 to March 1948, as it prepared to transfer to the British Army and move to Hong Kong, but one month of those three months was spent at sea; fourthly, on relinquishing the appointment as adjutant in 1952 he had another three-month stint as a company commander when the Battalion was on re-training, and lastly he had an eight-month spell as OC Support Company in 1955 before going to Staff College. Walker was right, Ronnie's five periods in command of a company had been *ad hoc* and his career profile lacked a protracted spell of command at company level. Walker recommended that he should command a company for at least a year on completion of his time as Brigade Major.

By the end of 1958 South Johore was finally declared 'White';[36] the last major campaign of the Malayan Emergency, Operation 'Tiger', had defeated the insurgents. In a series of flexible, overlapping military and police operations throughout 1958 the terrorists' losses had been 22 killed, one captured, 16 surrendered, 12 deserted or executed by their comrades and 39 surrendered by negotiation. Their ruthless commander Ah Ann, who executed five of his own men, was still at large, but then Special Branch provided the icing on the cake when Ah Ann, his wife and a District Committee member were killed, after a terrorist messenger was persuaded by the attraction of a large reward to betray them. Two other terrorists surrendered but one made good his escape – the sole survivor of the 96 terrorists that were in the area at the beginning of the year. For his exceptional work as Brigade Major during the highly successful operation 'Tiger' Ronnie was appointed a Member of the Order of the British Empire (MBE). The citation for his award says this:

For the last two years Major McAlister has borne the full brunt of the heavy and diverse responsibilities that befall a Brigade Major of an active Brigade engaged against the Communist terrorists in MALAYA.

---

36 . A term meaning 'clear of terrorists'.

During the last six months in particular, when the Brigade has been in control of Operation TIGER, a Federal priority operation aimed at the elimination of the Communist Terrorist organisation in SOUTH JAHORE – an aim which has now been achieved – he has proved himself to be a staff officer of exceptional professional ability, and one possessed of tact and complete integrity.

Not only has he won the respect and confidence of the many Army units both within and in support of the Brigade, but, and probably of more importance in this type of operation, he has been instrumental in cementing the most harmonious relationships with the Civil Administration, the Police, Special Branch, Home Guard, the Planters, and the Royal Air Force. The result has been that at all stages the War Executive Committee of Operation Tiger has spoken with one voice and secured the maximum co-operation from all classes and creeds.

In the operations which have recently concluded, there has been a requirement for an experienced General Staff Officer to be constantly available, day and night, to control the activities of the Security Forces. Major McALISTER readily accepted this task as his personal responsibility. For a protracted period, it has entailed working long hours at night collating last-light reports of unit activities and implementing subsequent command decisions regarding future operations. Frequently, he was again engaged shortly after dawn, receiving and processing first-light air reconnaissance reports and taking the appropriate staff action. In foregoing his leisure and relaxation he has never lost his balance under pressure, his sense of humour or his tact. Certainly the troops who he has served have never been in want.

As the principal staff officer of the Brigade, Major McALISTER has not only set a fine example of untiring devotion to duty, but has also – through his display of professional efficiency, his readiness to shoulder other peoples' burdens and his high sense of loyalty – done a tremendous amount to enhance the reputation of the British Officer in MALAYA, at a crucial time when the

country is in the process of establishing a new relationship with the British Crown after attaining independent status.

Certainly his personal contribution to the successful outcome of Operation TIGER has been in keeping with the highest traditions of the Service. [37]

Almost as soon as South Johore was declared 'white' and jungle operations curtailed, 99th Brigade became responsible for internal security throughout Singapore. At a time when passions among the Chinese population were high and being stirred up by a young politician called Lee Kuan Yew[38] it was thought that there was a high chance that anti-British rioting would break out. The change away from the application of whatever lethal force was necessary to kill terrorists and towards using minimum force to discourage civil unrest was a severe challenge, and without guidelines the units of 99th Brigade performed badly on exercises to test their internal security skills. Re-training and a change of mind-set were required and the principal drawback was that there was no manual on urban internal security operations. Walker determined that 99th Brigade would write one. In a month the Brigade had produced a new military manual titled *Internal Security in a City*, which passed into official use throughout the Army.[39] Much of the staff work that went into its production fell on Ronnie's desk.

Grading Ronnie 'outstanding' as a staff officer in his final report as Brigade Major, Brigadier Walter Walker wrote: 'I have met no officer who can express himself with such clarity and brevity, both verbally and in writing, whatever the subject. He is gifted with a better brain than most and at the same time has abundant common sense. He has an ability to reduce the most complicated problems to simple proportions and he does so with remarkable speed. Hard work under pressure for a sustained period holds no fear for him.' Ronnie received a very strong recommendation to attend the Joint Services Staff College, at a time when such a recommendation was a clear indication that the career of the officer in question should be managed with care. The final sentence of the report: 'He is an officer who will

37   . TNA, WO 373/135/103.
38   . Lee Kuan Yew (1923–2015) President of Singapore 1965–1990.
39   . Pocock, The Fighting General, p.109.

go far both as a commander and a staff officer' reinforces the point.

Despite Walker's recommendation in an earlier report, that Ronnie should command a rifle company for at least a year, Ronnie was appointed the Battalion Training Officer on his return to regimental duty with 2/10GR in early July 1959. Shortly after he returned the Battalion moved from Madjedee Barracks in Johore, Malaya, to Norwegian Farm Camp in the New Territories of Hong Kong. He was undoubtedly a fine trainer and probably the officer best suited, given his experience as an instructor at the School of Infantry, for the difficult task of retraining the Battalion and changing its mind-set from operations against small groups of elusive terrorists in the jungle to the greater demands of limited warfare against conventionally-armed opponents. He carried out this important appointment well and the perceived weakness in his career profile, as identified by Walter Walker, was not corrected. Somewhat surprisingly, after six months as Training Officer, he was then given command of a company for three months before being sent on long leave in March 1960.

He elected to travel home under his own arrangements and went overland by jeep from Calcutta to Glasgow, with Major Stuart Watson of the 13th/18th Hussars. The journey took them six weeks. They were invited to make observations on the circumstances and conditions at certain places along their route and to call on various diplomats to report on places their journey took them through. On some occasions they felt that discretion was the better part of valour and stuck to the accepted main routes through sensitive and risky areas.

On completion of his long leave, during which he did a two-week airportability course, he returned to 2/10GR in Norwegian Farm Camp in October 1960. There he commanded a company for 10 months, which was recorded in his annual report as being 'a little under a year', which might indicate that the recommendation made by Walter Walker had been picked up and acted on, even if he did not command the company for a full year. With hindsight, and without knowing the details and what impact his employment might have had on others, it is easy to be critical and question why on earth his long leave was not brought forward by three months: this might have eased the disruption and the bitty nature of his tenure in appointments over the two years in question, and given him the opportunity to command a company over a continuous period of a year as had been recommended.

He was selected to attend the Joint Services Staff College (JSSC) and returned to England for a short spell of leave before attending the 25th JSSC Course from 9 October 1961 to 13 April 1962.

The Joint Services Staff College was located at Latimer House in Buckinghamshire. The course focussed on managing tri-service operations, and the officers attending it were typically of lieutenant colonel or the equivalent rank[40] and needed to have the potential to rise at least two grades in rank. Ronnie's selection as a major, well before he was selected for battalion command, was an indication of the potential those who were reporting on him and managing his career felt he had. Three courses, each of nine months, were held every two years for 60 students; 17 from each service and nine others from the civil service or the police was the typical mix of students. Those officers passing the course received the post-nominal letters '*jssc*'.

Ronnie was graded above average on the course and his report states that he was 'a particularly good chairman in syndicate', 'thoroughly conscientious' and that his 'very good written work' was 'prepared with great care'. The reporting officer also noted that he was going on to 'an exacting appointment in the Chiefs of Staff Secretariat' and added 'I am certain he will do well.' However, he was not recommended to return as an instructor. The Commandant at Latimer, at that time a Naval officer, commented on Ronnie's performance with admirable brevity: he wrote simply: 'A very sound officer.'

Ronnie held the appointment of Assistant Secretary in the Chiefs of Staff Secretariat from April 1962 to May 1964. He was responsible for producing the minutes of the meetings of the Chiefs of Staff Committee.[41] Apart from being exceptionally hard work and long hours it must have been a fascinating appointment, as he listened to and recorded the deliberations and decisions of the highest military committee and observed its

---

40 . Commander in the Royal Navy and Wing Commander in the Royal Air Force.
41 . The Chief of the Defence Staff (CDS), Vice-Chief of the Defence Staff (VCDS), the three Service Chiefs: the First Sea Lord, Chief of the General Staff and Chief of the Air Staff.

interface with the Government. During his time in the secretariat the Chiefs of Staff would have had to deal with the military operations that took place during the Brunei Revolt[42] and the first year of the Indonesian Confrontation (Borneo);[43] Britain's special forces' involvement in Vietnam[44] and various United Nations operations, including the difficult operation in Katanga in the Congo, which involved British troops. It was a period when many African nations were gaining their independence from Britain and when the last national service conscripts into the armed forces completed their service in May 1963. The Profumo affair and the defection of the British spy Kim Philby rocked the political establishment in Britain and caused considerable embarrassment. America, Britain and Russia all conducted nuclear weapons tests and the space race had started in earnest. The world held its breath during the Cuban Missile Crisis in October 1962. The first Limited Nuclear Test Ban Treaty was signed on 5 August 1963.

On the social scene the Beatles rose to fame with the Rolling Stones were not far behind, in an era when post-war austerity had become a thing of the past and the social fabric of Britain was changing in the face of greater liberalisation and shared wealth. Standards were different; Ronnie went to work in a pin-striped suit and bowler hat, as was the practice in MOD at the time, and he wore hand-made shoes. All that was changing, and Ronnie's bachelor life was about to undergo a seismic change too. In August 1963 he met Sally Marshall, the daughter of Dr and Mrs Marshall of Thanet, Kent. Sally was working as a nurse at St George's Hospital, then near Hyde Park Corner. Her flatmates, who were trainees at St Mary Abbott's Hospital, met Ronnie and his flatmates before she did. They told her there was a 'rather quiet one'. Before he met Sally he was told by her flatmates that she was 'sailing to the Channel Islands with naval friends'. When they did meet, in a pub near Cadogan Mansions close to Sloane Square, and Ronnie told her he was a Gurkha officer, Sally asked what a Gurkha was. Ronnie owned a yacht and took her sailing which she did not enjoy. She was not a sailor and her trip to the Channel Islands had been on an ocean going boat – a poor start, but Sally challenged him to a game of

---

42   . 8–23 December 1962.
43   . 24 December 1962–11 August 1966.
44   . 24 December 1962–29 May 1964.

squash. He narrowly won the game but she won his heart. Ronnie proposed three weeks after they met. Not long after they were engaged 'Men from the Ministry' called on Sally to interview her and ask her about her background. Given the classified nature of Ronnie's job, and one can only surmise the sensitivity surrounding the recent Profumo scandal, Sally needed to be vetted. Ronnie faced an altogether different trial. He joined the Marshalls – a young, lively, joking family known as The Clock House clan, because their home included a clock tower. It had been part of Lord Northcliffe's estate Elmwood at Broadstairs in Kent. Sally thought Ronnie had never been teased until he met The Clock House clan. He loved it and thereafter Broadstairs was home. In 1971 Sally's grandmother, who thought women should be independent financially, bought The Chalet for Sally. It was on the Elmwood estate and had originally been Lord Northcliffe's office building; it was also a stone's throw from The Clock House with its large garden, tennis court and swimming pool for the girls to enjoy. The Chalet was to be the only home Sally and Ronnie ever had or needed.

Ronnie and Sally were married on 25 January 1964 in St. Peter-the-Apostle Church in Thanet. The very old Norman church was about a mile from the Marshalls' home and the reception was held in a marquee on the lawn of The Clock House.

Major and Mrs Ronnie McAlister – 25 January 1964[45]

---

45 . The McAlister Family Collection.

Shortly after he completed his appointment in MOD in May 1964, Sally and Ronnie travelled out to the Far East when Ronnie was posted back to 2/10GR, now based on Blakang Mati island[46] off Singapore, and appointed the Battalion Second-in-Command.

His return to regimental duty must have been a wonderful change of pace. From the pressures of a very demanding appointment in the Ministry of Defence during which the United Kingdom had its coldest winter since 1946, the sunshine of Blakang Mati, married life and the warmth of the regimental fold must have been as much as he could have wished for. He had done well in the Chiefs of Staff Secretariat, his reports commenting that: 'He has acquired a mastery of a wide range of subjects, and his quick intelligence contributes materially to the high quality of his work, particularly in periods when there is a high pressure of work', also that he has 'a ready sense of humour, which remains unaffected by very long working hours'. His report towards the end of his time in the appointment records: 'Major McAlister has set himself a very high standard of staff work in his present appointment which he has consistently maintained in the period of nearly two years he has served under me. He has the valuable quality of calmness in moments of stress, is very intelligent, and produces finished work accurately and swiftly. He has an ease of manner which has served him well in his regular dealings with officers of all Services, up to the highest rank.' The Vice Chief of the Defence Staff wrote: 'I have seen a good deal of his work and have been very impressed by his ability to record most efficiently the proceedings of the Chiefs of Staff Committee.' He was very strongly recommended for promotion on the staff and in command. Back in the Battalion there was little he could say about the work he had recently undertaken, because most of it was highly classified. His modest and quiet demeanour suited the situation perfectly.

Within two months of returning to the Battalion he deployed with 2/10GR on its third tour in Borneo during the Confrontation against Indonesia. The Confrontation, or 'Undeclared War' as it was also called, had by then been waged for 21 months. The threat from Indonesia had begun when the Indonesian Government issued statements supporting the Brunei rebels during their revolt

---

46   . Blakang Mati is now known as Sentosa and is no longer an island.

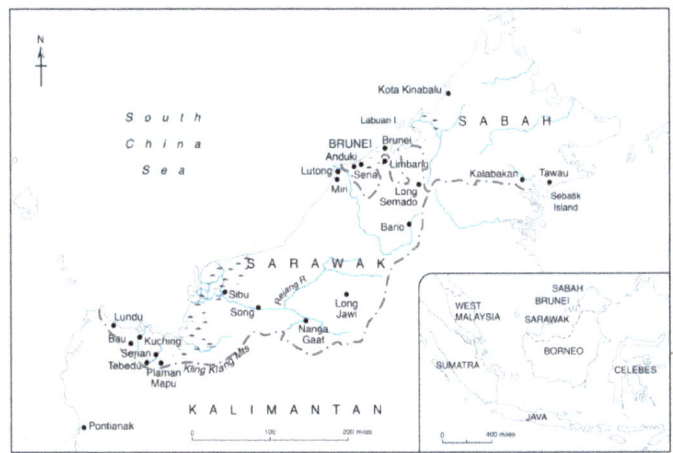

North Borneo (East Malaysia) - Sarawak, Brunei and Sabah

in December 1962, and made clear its opposition to the plan for the Federation of Malaysia to include Malaya, Singapore, Sarawak, Sabah and Brunei. The Brunei revolt was dealt with in 21 days by the rapid deployment of British troops from Singapore and the United Kingdom as part of Britain's responsibility for the defence of Brunei. During a period of mopping up after the Brunei revolt the Indonesian President, Sukarno, stepped up his propaganda against the proposed Federation and suggested that two divisions of 'volunteers' were ready to liberate North Borneo (Sarawak, Sabah and Brunei) from colonialism.

Just when the Brunei situation appeared to have been resolved, and Major General Walter Walker, who was both Commander British Forces Borneo and Major General Brigade of Gurkhas, had been instructed to return to Malaya, Sukarno's 'volunteers' attacked the border Police Station at Tebedu, 40 miles south of Kuching in Sarawak. It was subsequently learnt that the raid was carried out by regular Indonesian soldiers, and Indonesian claims that the attacks were by 'volunteers' against colonialism hid more sinister intentions. The Federation of Malaysia was formed on 16 September 1963 and although Singapore and Brunei subsequently withdrew, Indonesia continued to express its opposition and showed it was prepared to express its displeasure through the use of force. It mounted armed incursions from Indonesia into North Borneo (Sarawak,

Brunei and Sabah), which bordered Indonesia (Kalimantan) to the south.[47] It was to counter this aggression that British and then Commonwealth Forces were deployed.

Initially there were two enemy threats, the first being from cadres of the Clandestine Communist Organisation (CCO) among the local Chinese populations, which were at an elementary stage of development and not armed. These were affiliated to and supported by the *Parti Komunis Indonesia* (PKI). The second was from Indonesian-supported militants or Indonesian regular soldiers. Military confrontation started shortly after the *Partai Ra'ayat*, or People's Party, won all the seats in Brunei's only democratic election in September 1962. It had a military wing known as the *Tentera Nasional Kalimantan Utara* or the TNKU. In 1962 several of its officers had been trained in clandestine warfare in Indonesian Kalimantan and in Jakarta, and the force was thought to muster some 4,000 men, armed with a few modern weapons and about a thousand shotguns, enough they thought to stage a *coup d'état* in Brunei. It failed in Brunei, but throughout 1963 Sukarno used gangs of TNKU reinforced by regular Indonesian 'volunteers' from the *Tentara Nasional Indonesia* or TNI, the Indonesian Army, to carry out attacks and raids into North Borneo in an attempt to overthrow the newly-formed Federation of Malaysia. To simplify the nomenclature the TNKU gangs became known as Indonesia Border Terrorists or IBT.[48]

By August 1964 the fighting had escalated. Initial talks between Malaysia and Indonesia to resolve their differences had broken down and Sukarno decreed it was time for Indonesia to increase hostilities. He launched marine and parachute attacks on West Malaysia (mainland Malaya) and further attacks across the border in Borneo. Indonesian raids and attacks were carried out by units of a hundred men or more, the raids were planned better, the attackers were better armed and the units had a higher proportion of Indonesian regular soldiers. On the Malaysian side of the border, border posts became company-sized forts that were well defended bases, surrounded by wire obstacles, *panji* pits and mines with medium machine guns, mortars and artillery. Up to two thirds of the company groups in these bases would be

47 . Background to Borneo campaign taken from McAlister, Bugle & Kukri Vol.2, pp.160–164; Pocock, The Fighting General, pp.160–173, and van der Bijl, Confrontation: The War with Indonesia 1962-1966, pp.23–28.
48 . McAlister, Bugle & Kukri, Vol.2, pp.161–163.

out on patrol seeking to identify enemy incursions and along the length of the entire border, along which helicopter landing zones were cut at 1,000-metre intervals to allow troop-lifting helicopters to deploy personnel quickly to deal with Indonesian raids. The most significant change, however, was that permission had been given for friendly forces to undertake offensive action across the Indonesian border, albeit under very strict control. No longer were the Indonesians the only side able to violate the ill-defined international frontier.

2/10 GR took over from 1/6GR and was based in the Lundu area in the First Division west of Kuching. On arrival Ronnie asked to see the Standing Orders. That night the other officers in Battalion Headquarters observed that the light in his *atap* accommodation remained on well into the night. In the morning updated and substantially amended Standing Orders were in the duty clerk's in-tray for typing. The Battalion's 97 mile front along the border with Indonesia was covered by C Company in the north, A Company in the central sector and B Company in the south. D Company was held in reserve and for 'special operations'. At the time this was the phrase used for 'cross-border' operations that were subsequently conducted under the codeword 'Claret'. Great secrecy surrounded these 'special operations' and only the Commanding Officer and one selected company per battalion were to be fully aware of 'special operations' planning and execution. This caused some resentment, as Ronnie recorded:

> Even as Battalion 2IC I was not allowed to know about Mike St. Martin's[49] tasks. I felt quite out of it. How much more so must the other British officers and the QGOs in A, B and C Companies have felt. Morale was almost certainly undermined by this over-secretive attitude. It was not until the end of 1964 or early 1965 that the authorities, realising the effect that their strict orders were having at unit level, relaxed the security rules. Once all companies, and not just one, became liable for cross border operations and were allowed to discuss the problem amongst ourselves, morale improved almost at a stroke.[50]

---

49 . Major Mike St. Martin MC was OC D Company.
50 . McAlister, Bugle & Kukri Vol.2, p.398.

'The Golden Rules' – guidelines for cross border operations, drawn up by the Director of Borneo Operations (DOBOPS), Major General Walter Walker, were as follows:

1. Every operation to be authorised by DOBOPS – as authorised by the Commander-in-Chief, Far East.

2. Only trained and tested troops to be used. No soldiers were to cross the border during their first tour of duty in Borneo.

3. Depth of penetration must be limited and attacks must only be made to thwart offensive action by the enemy and must never be made in retribution or solely to inflict casualties. Civilian lives must not be risked.

4. No operation which required close air support – except in an extreme emergency – must be undertaken.

5. Every operation must be planned with the aid of a sand-table and thoroughly rehearsed for at least two weeks.

6. Every operation must be planned and executed with maximum security. Every man must be sworn to secrecy, full cover plans must be made and the operation given code names and never discussed in detail on telephone or radio. Identity discs must be left behind before departure and no traces – such as cartridge cases, paper, ration packs, etc – must be left in Kalimantan.

7. On no account must any soldier taking part be captured by the enemy – alive or dead.[51]

The rule that civilian lives were not to be risked was strictly adhered to and sometimes a fear of breaking this rule meant that the enemy, if they could not be positively identified by their clothing, or when mixing with civilians, were not engaged by our security forces.

Later, when the strict 'need to know' secrecy had been eased, the Adjutant, Captain Garry Johnson, and the Intelligence Officer, Captain Kit Maunsell, were thankful that Ronnie took out of their hands the operational order for the Claret operation that they had been tasked to write for the approval of the

51   . Pocock, The Fighting General, p.197.

Director of Operations. Ronnie quickly produced an immaculate operational order.

The Battalion's third tour in Borneo ended in early March and it was complete back on Blakang Mati by 18 March 1965 after a successful tour. It did not, however, mean that the Battalion could stand down. In late 1964 the Indonesians had established camps on the Indonesian Rhios Islands a few miles off Blakang Mati; and as the guard island for Singapore it and ships in the area became targets. While the Battalion was in Borneo a Liberian freighter was attacked and then a French ship was attacked with grenades hurled from a sampan. In April 1965, shortly after its return from its operational tour, a bomb planted near the stop-butts of the rifle range on Blakang Mati exploded during the night and two other unexploded bombs were found later. Malaysian Navy and Police boats patrolled the Straits and had regular night contacts with the terrorists, as could be seen from some of the officers' married quarters overlooking the Straits. On one occasion the families watched the Malaysian patrol boat *Sri Pahang* and some Police launches fight a small naval battle with a flotilla of sampans by the light of flares and the glow from the local Shell refinery on Pulau Bukom. Two sampans were destroyed, survivors picked up and the following morning a captured sampan with a bomb on board was blow up just out to sea. Although the excitement prompted some wives to suggest that they too should now qualify for the recently instituted 1962 General Service Medal,[52] it was a disturbing development. It was decided that a platoon should be left on Blakang Mati to guard the families when the Battalion deployed to Borneo on any future operational tour. When it did so, sentries were posted during the hours of darkness and Sally recalled that it was reassuring to hear them loading their rifles on taking post, and unloading after an uneventful night.

On 15 May 1965 Ronnie and Sally became parents when Angela Frances McAlister was born in the British Military Hospital in Singapore.

In July 1965, although he had only been out in the Far East for a little over a year, Ronnie and Sally returned to England on leave. Ronnie had been selected to command 1/10GR. On promotion to Lieutenant Colonel he was to take over from a

52   . Instituted under Ministry of Defence Order No.61 dated 6 Oct 1964.

former Second Tenth colleague, the redoubtable Lieutenant Colonel EJS 'Bunny' Burnett, DSO, OBE, MC.

Chapter 7

Command

Almost without exception, every officer aspires to command a battalion in his Regiment. It is the highest appointment he can hold within the Army's strongest family entity – the Regiment. Officers join a regiment as young men; they serve with it during their formative years, are nurtured by it, learn and grow up in it and rise through its ranks. Their brother officers are friends and colleagues and they are all involved in the collective and demanding responsibility of looking after their soldiers, while preparing them for circumstances when the orders they receive might result in them having to give their lives on the battlefield. If the following chapters on Ronnie's time in command of 1/10GR seem disproportionately long, and unbalance this biography, it is because his time in command was a high point and full of incidents that had a significant impact on his subsequent career.

Ronnie, Sally and Angela flew to Hong Kong in late October 1965 in time for Ronnie to take over from 'Bunny' Burnett on 5 November and assume command of 1/10GR, then based in Cassino Lines in the New Territories. 'Bunny' Burnett had had an exceptionally successful tour in command. 1/10GR had spent 24 months of his 30-month tenure in command on operations and had enhanced its distinguished fighting reputation. Much of what it had achieved could be attributed to 'Bunny' Burnett's determination, tactical skill and charismatic leadership. 'Bunny' had been decorated three times during his tour in command; being awarded a Mention in Despatches, the Distinguished Service Order (DSO) and being appointed an Officer of the Order of the British Empire (OBE). Out-going, jovial and popular he was going to be a difficult man to follow. Although both 'Bunny' and Ronnie had been brother officers in Second Tenth since November 1947 they had rarely served together and did not really know each other. In researching for a biography on 'Bunny' Burnett I asked General Ronnie whether he and 'Bunny' were friends. His measured and direct answer was, 'No.

We were different'. It was General Ronnie's polite way of telling me that while they were brother officers, they were not kindred spirits; and his comment was entirely accurate. Despite being in the same battalion for most of their careers their military experience, career paths and characters could hardly have been more different. The proverbial 'chalk and cheese' simile is apt. Both wore dark-rimmed glasses but there the similarities ended. Bunny was large-framed and impressive; he had difficulty controlling his weight and was not particularly smart personally. He enjoyed parties, he smoked and he enjoyed a drink and had a loud infectious laugh. In contrast Ronnie was slightly built, dapper, smart and reserved. He did not smoke and had moderate drinking habits. 'Bunny' was staff trained by appointments rather than staff courses and he had spent most of his service in Gurkha appointments. He did not expect to have to tell his officers how to do their jobs – he expected them to know and believed most jobs were best learned by doing them. Ronnie's career was very different. He was staff trained and had attended both the Army Staff College and the Joint Services Staff College. He had been an instructor at the School of Infantry and done well in two demanding staff appointments; an operational one as the Brigade Major of 99 Gurkha Infantry Brigade in Malaya and the other at the highest echelons of the Ministry of Defence, in the Chiefs of Staff Secretariat. He was also an excellent trainer. On the handover between the out-going and the in-coming commanding officer Ronnie wrote, 'There was no handover, we hardly spoke, no notes, no advice, no help, no welcome, no warmth – he just went.'[53] It is unlikely that Ronnie dwelt on the matter long; he was his own man and there was a great deal to be done as the Battalion prepared for its fourth tour in Borneo and its fifth spell on operations in three and a half years. 1/10GR was to take over from 2/10GR in January 1966 in the Bau Sector of Sarawak.

By the beginning of 1966 the situation in Borneo had changed. 'Claret' operations had become the norm and were an integral part of the strategy to deter the Indonesians from launching attacks into Malaysia. To keep the Indonesians off-balance and to make it difficult for them to launch attacks from secure bases close to the international border, 'Claret' operations, usually at company level, were undertaken to force

53   . RWL McAlister, E-Mail dated 4 Feb 2010.

The Officers of 1/10GR with General 'Tottie' Anderson, Colonel of
the Regiment, January 1966[54]

Standing L to R: Capt Hatrick (RMO), Maj Scott (Pmr), 2nd Lt
Worthington, Lt Cook, Capt Hughes, Capt Corden-Lloyd, Lt Watt,
Lt Walker, 2nd Lt Dawson, Capt Kay (Edn Offr)

Sitting L to R: Maj (QM) Miller, Maj Thomson, Maj Robertson, Lt
Col McAlister, General Anderson, Maj Phillips, Maj Maddison,
Maj Pike, Capt Chandrabahadur Rai

the Indonesians back from the border, to limit their offensive
options and to make their commanders think defensively. This
involved assaults on their bases and ambushing their supply
lines. The limited depth of penetration across the border laid
down in the 'Golden Rules' had been relaxed and operations, in
particular reconnaissance missions, were permitted to penetrate
up to 10,000 yards into Indonesia. It was thought the ideal would
be to try and force the Indonesians to abandon all their bases
within 10,000 yards of the international border, but operations to
a depth of 5,000 yards were more practical because another
major change was an improvement in the Indonesians' fighting
capabilities. More Indonesian regular troops had been deployed,
they were better armed and trained, more aggressive and
generally better supplied. Their bases were more strongly
defended, with improved use of mutual support between bases,
light artillery, mortars and anti-aircraft guns. When undertaking
a 'Claret' operation our forces were more likely to be counter-
attacked and harassed by artillery and mortar fire when returning
from an operation. No cross-border helicopter evacuation was
permitted and the 'Golden Rule' that no soldier was to be

---

54 . 1/10GR Photograph Album, Gurkha Museum.

captured dead or alive meant the hazardous extraction of casualties had to be planned for in detail. All this was well-known. What was less well-known, at battalion level, was that there was considerable political unrest in Indonesia. The economy was in trouble, President Sukarno was ill, and there were serious points of friction between factions of the Indonesian Armed Services. Some of the unrest was undoubtedly orchestrated by the CIA, who had some senior Indonesian officers in their pay, as it sought to avert the spread of communism that was sweeping South-East Asia. By October 1965 law and order had broken down and factional fighting occurred between the Indonesian Army and the armed communist cadres of the PKI (*Parti Komunis Indonesia*). The Indonesian Army smashed the PKI but to do so units had to be withdrawn from North Kalimantan and the Indonesian–Malaysian border area. Some of this percolated down to battalion level but what was not known on the front line was that in November 1965, in highly secret talks, Brigadier General Achmad Sukendro, from the Indonesian Army's Special Operations Group, met Dato Ghazali Shafie, Permanent Secretary of the Malaysian Ministry of External Affairs, and told him that British operations in North Kalimantan were hurting. A US Intelligence assessment at the time suggested:

> Although there was a massive Indonesian build-up along the Borneo border and in Sumatra beginning last December [1964] and largely completed by May [1965] military activity against Malaysia has declined in the last six months. In Borneo, effective British cross-border operations have disrupted Indonesian planning and placed the approximately 17,000 Indonesians in the area on the defensive.

Although the turmoil inside Indonesia was significant and helped divert Indonesian political attention away from the border in Borneo, and the first seeds of the Indonesians wishing to end hostilities had been sown, none of this was known to the officers and men of 1/10GR, nor was it particularly relevant. It was not time for Commonwealth Forces to ease the pressure on their opponents and 1/10GR had no intention of doing that.

The First Battalion took over from the Second Battalion on 25 January 1966. A Company, commanded by Major Colin Maddison, was based at Gumbang in the south of the Bau

Sector; B Company, commanded by Major Bruce Niven, was at Stass in the centre and D Company, commanded by Major Chris Pike, at Bokah in the north. C Company, commanded by Captain Chris Hughes, was the Brigade and Battalion reserve based at Bau, together with Battalion Headquarters and Headquarter Company, commanded by Major Chris Thomson. Cross-border operations had been restricted in January for political reasons and no cross-border patrols were permitted in the first 14 days of a tour, which were to be used instead for border reconnaissance and acclimatisation, so the Battalion did not become fully operational until 8 February 1966. This meant the Indonesians had not been under pressure for over a month and the first task was to check whether they had crept forward. Only two companies were allowed to be over the border at one time, so the first deployments were recces in strength by A and B companies of their parts of the front.

The Bau Sector, Sarawak, North Borneo

In B Company's area a fighting patrol was sent out to the Kaik–Kindau track to cover the flank of a recce party looking at Kaik, and had a fire-fight with an unknown number of enemy using the track, and was also mortared from the enemy base at Kindau. Niven pressed ahead with his recce and established that the enemy base at Kaik was still unoccupied. More importantly he established that the enemy base at Kuala Babang, which was thought to be occupied, was also deserted. A Company crossed the Koemba river north of Siding, watched the river for boat traffic and searched the area up to a depth of 4,000 yards, but found no signs of enemy activity.

While A and B companies were across the border the tracks of an Indonesian force of about 50 were found on 15 February 1966 just north of the right forward base of the 1st Battalion of the Argyll and Sutherland Highlanders at Tebedu (See Map p.57). The tracks were leading towards 2/7GR's area. 2/7GR threw a cordon around the area, and C Company 1/10GR, as the Brigade Reserve, was deployed to the north of the original sighting. A fighting patrol from 7 Platoon, C Company 1/10GR contacted a mixed force of Indonesian Shock Troops (RPKAD) and Chinese infiltrators at 1200 hours on 16 February and in a sharp fire fight inflicted casualties on the numerically superior enemy, who disengaged on the arrival of Captain Hughes with the rest of C Company. A rifleman wounded in the fire fight was evacuated by helicopter; then following up fast without packs, C Company made contact again at 1300 hours and killed one enemy. At 1715 hours contact was again made, however the enemy had taken up a position on a hill with good fields of fire overlooking a bare knoll where Hughes, his Company HQ and 8 Platoon had taken up positions. The enemy had also laid anti-personnel mines on the likely approaches to their position. A fierce firefight ensued. Heavy automatic fire swept the bare knoll and an attempt to outflank the enemy failed in the face of accurate fire, one rifleman was killed and two wounded in the firefight and two were wounded in a minefield, and as night fell the enemy broke off the action. C Company spent a wretched rain-soaked night with their dead and wounded with them and without their packs, but their morale and aggressive spirit was undaunted. After evacuating the wounded and the dead rifleman, the pursuit continued and on 20 February 1966 a small patrol comprising of Hughes and his Company HQ contacted two enemy and killed them both. A Company when back from its cross-border recce on 20 February was sent in to act as a long-stop, but the action had by then became a protracted chase carried out by 2/7GR and 1A&SH, so both A and C companies were returned to 1/10GR on 25 February. For his leadership, determination to close with the enemy and aggressive spirit Hughes was awarded the Military Cross.

Once the Battalion was back in balance it was D Company's turn to cross the border on a reconnaissance. The company was lifted by helicopter from Bokah to LZ 1693 at 0830 hours on 27 February 1966 and was complete there by 1200 hours. From there it moved up to LZ 1673, rested and crossed the border at 1400 hours. Pike took the company south-west towards Poeri to check river movement on the Sungei Koemba. The river had been used to supply Siluas until 2/2GR mounted several successful river ambushes in the area in 1965. Political constraints and changes in units meant the area had not been visited for some time and it was thought river traffic might have resumed, which proved to be the case. At 1630 hours on 28 February a recce patrol moving forward saw 16 enemy patrolling along an old logging track; they had their weapons slung and did not seem very alert. At first it was thought they were a patrol from Poeri north of the river but when Poeri was found to be unoccupied it was deduced it was a routine bank-clearing patrol from south of the Koemba river. By 1 March Pike had established a firm base 1,000 yards from the junction of the Koemba and Separan rivers and learned from recce patrols that the river was being used, the enemy were patrolling the area and a new enemy base was under construction on the south bank of the Koemba. By 1200 hours on 4 March all three platoons of D Company were in, or moving into, ambush positions on the river. At 1300 hours a landing craft type vessel with 35 enemy on board moved downstream into 11 Platoon's ambush position. The Platoon engaged the vessel at a range of 10 to 15 yards and killed all but two of the enemy on board, and those two were severely wounded. The boat canted over to port, its engine stopped and it slewed into the bank 30 yards downstream. There was complete silence; no screams or groans. However, almost immediately heavy small arms and machine gun fire was directed at the ambush area and six 81mm mortar rounds fell near 11 Platoon's position. Pike ordered 11 Platoon to withdraw but told 10 and 12 Platoons[55] to remain in position to cover 11 Platoon's withdrawal and to inflict further casualties. Nearly four hours later two boats carrying nine enemy entered 12 Platoon's ambush area and were despatched. Again the ambush area was subjected to mortar and small arms fire and 12 Platoon withdrew to the firm base to counter any follow-up or counter attack by the enemy, but there was none. Pike then sent 12 Platoon back into its ambush position where it remained until 2100 hours. In the early hours next morning continuous engine movement up and down the river could be heard, and believing the enemy were landing on the north bank in search of D Company, Pike decided it was time for discretion. In the darkness the Company crept through 300 yards of swamp and was out into primary forest and heading for the border by first light.

In the Regimental History Ronnie wrote this of D Company's action:

> For sheer impudent daring, cold courage and determination to extract maximum results from what was a planned reconnaissance, this operation of Pike's was in my view unique. And yet with the daring, went immaculate planning and briefing and, in tactical execution, a faultless attention to detail. Pike had the company on balance from start to finish. The result, not less than 37 killed, was the highest number of casualties inflicted on the Indonesians in one action in the whole of Confrontation. The way in which Pike held onto his ambush position for so many hours after the initial success, stamped him as a leader of extraordinary ability. When past precedent, orders from above, and every human instinct in one's soldiers, counselled immediate withdrawal, it takes exceptional courage to say 'Stay where you are: there's more work to be done.'[56]

In his CO's Comments on Pike's post-operation report Ronnie wrote:

1. This factual account, reading like a precisely planned surgical operation conceals the tremendous effort put in

---

55 . 11 Platoon was commanded by Lt(QGO) Indrajit Limbu MC, 10 Platoon by WO2 Jamanbahadur Rai and 12 Platoon by Lt Bill Dawson.
56 . McAlister, Bugle & Kukri, Vol.2, p.227–228.

by the Company over entirely new territory. The tactics used (three man patrols and movement in extended line) are not new but indicate high morale, supreme confidence and acceptance of the need for great physical effort to achieve results.

2. The reconnaissance of the ambush position was thorough and unhurried. However, four major risks were then taken;

   a. The ambush position was laid within two hundred yards of two enemy positions, heard and located if not seen, on the south bank of the river.

   b. No flank protection was provided for 11 Platoon on the left: an enemy attack on the flank at any stage could have been embarrassing.

   c. Permission was given for 11 Platoon to open its ambush before the rest of the company was in position. To this extent the company was 'off balance' when the first ambush was sprung.

   d. After the first ambush, the other two platoons were maintained in ambush long after their task of covering 11 Platoon's withdrawal might have been deemed to be accomplished.

3. Both ambushes were sprung correctly and devastatingly.

4. Of course, luck played a part. But Major Pike is, to my mind, to be commended for his cool assessment and acceptance of all the risks he knew he was taking. In particular, the three and a half hour wait in ambush positions by the company less 11 Platoon after the first massacre must have seemed like hours to those concerned. But Major Pike had a complete grip on the situation and, even under enemy MF (Mortar Fire), exuded confidence and determination which brooked no argument and silenced any doubters. As a result another 9 enemy were killed.

5. The decision to stay the night in the ambush area was also bold but not rash.

6. As regards the casualties inflicted, it is likely that 35 enemy died in the main ambush or in the next 12 hours. However, on 7 March trans-border traders came in with a story of an ambush of a large boat, of a type normally carrying 30 troops, and said that only two wounded had survived. I believe therefore that we should accept the conservative figure of 28 killed in the launch, plus 9 in the second ambush making a total of 37 killed.

7. Certainly in respect of leadership, boldness of concept and cold, calculating courage in execution, this operation has some lessons to teach.[57]

D Company Officers on the return to Bokah Camp after the 5 March 1966 River Ambush

2nd Lt Nick Worthington (Coy Officer 10 Pl), Capt (QGO) Bhimbahadur Sunwar (Coy 2IC), Lt (QGO) Indrajit Limbu (11 Pl Comd), Maj Chris Pike (Coy Comd). Lt Bill Dawson (12 Pl Comd) and Capt James Templer (FOO)[58]

57 . Gurkha Museum, Pike, CJ, Post-Borneo Operational File.
58 . Photograph taken by Lt Col RWL McAlister, courtesy of Lt Col WJ Dawson OBE.

On Monday 14th March 1966 Colonel Ronnie's Special Order of the Day published at Cambrai Camp, Bau for the Battalion to read omits the lessons learned:

SPECIAL ORDER OF THE DAY

BY

LIEUTENANT COLONEL RWL McALISTER, MBE

COMMANDING

1st BATTALION THE 10th PRINCESS MARY's OWN GURKHA RIFLES

(The Brigade of Gurkhas)

1. On Saturday 5th March 1966 in the border area near BOKAH, D Coy carried out a most successful ambush in which 37 Indonesians were killed without loss to our own men.

2. In reconnoitring the ambush area OC D Coy and all Platoon and section Commanders showed a high degree of skill and perseverance.

3. The ambush was sprung by No 11 Platoon commanded by Lieut (QGO) Indrajit Limbu, MC killing 28 of the enemy. In the face of heavy enemy mortar and automatic fire 11 Platoon was withdrawn. With great coolness Major Pike decided to maintain 10 and 12 Platoons in ambush, both to cover 11 Platoon's withdrawal and in the hope of inflicting further casualties on the enemy.

4. Four hours later 9 enemy entered 12 Platoon's ambush and were killed. Even now, near last light, when withdrawal would have been fully justified, Major Pike determined to hold in the ambush area to inflict further casualties next morning. However during the night the enemy started to patrol forward and it was clear the company should regroup. This was effected only after a difficult march, partly in darkness.

5. The number of enemy killed is the highest ever inflicted in one action in the Borneo campaign.

6. The Commanding Officer wishes to congratulate Major CJ Pike and all ranks of D Company on their coolness, courage and professional skill.

(RWL McALISTER, MBE)
Lieutenant Colonel
Officer Commanding[59]

Following these successes the Battalion's morale was high and the situation on which to base further operations was clearer, as Colonel Ronnie recalled:

The situation as it then appeared to me was:

a. On our left, the Siding area was 'dead', but we must still check the Koemba river further west towards Siluas and the south slopes of Brunei ridge (where in August/September 1965 the Second Battalion had had two very successful actions against enemy occupied posts).

b. In the centre Kindau was occupied, but Kaik, for certain, and probably Kuala Babang also, was abandoned. Kindau was thus isolated and could be harried from the north or east.

c. On the right, the Koemba river, north of Siluas, was still being used for troop and stores movement, but political sensitivity now precluded further ambushing.

C Company checked the south slopes of the Brunei ridge and Koemba river to its south and found the old enemy camps on the river were still abandoned and there were no sign of boat traffic or enemy activity forward from Siluas. A Company searched the Jagoi ridge and found they had to familiarise themselves with the much-used enemy tracks leading to Risau 1, Risau 2, Babang, Boon Kui's House and the hilltop post above Babang where Lance Corporal Rambahadur Limbu had won his Victoria Cross, when C Company 2/10GR attacked the position on 21 November 1965. Recce patrols and artillery sound ranging devices confirmed that all the positions were occupied but the enemy were on the defensive. It was a complex area and it was clear that further detailed reconnaissance was required. B Company confirmed Kuala Babang and Maskertas had been abandoned and found a jungle-covered rock west of Kindau that

---

59 . The Special Order of the Day was classified merely as RESTRICTED. This suggests the action took place near BOKAH rather than well over the border inside Indonesia, as in fact was the case.

74

was an ideal observation post. Later nicknamed 'Upper Macham' it overlooked the Kindau area even if it was too far away for observers to get the details of the enemy camp there. Based on the information found by these recces it was decided that a closer look at Kindau was required, and the task was given to Headquarter Company.

Thomson with the Recce and Pioneer Platoons carrying 10 days rations set out on 12 March 1966. As far as available records showed Kindau had never been visited or recced before, and the approach was through difficult and uncharted jungle, but Kindau was eventually located by bold patrols led personally by Thomson and his platoon commanders. So inaccurate and uninformative were the maps and air photographs that Thomson was prompted to send a morse code wireless message that read, 'I don't know where I am nor where the enemy is, but I can assure you we are both in the same place.'

This prompted Colonel Ronnie to write:

> Never could a First Battalion Commanding Officer have been blessed with better company commanders than I. I had five British officers whose eager courage, skill, resource, physical strength and initiative left me with a problem only of reining them in; never having to demand more. What so impressed too, at this time, was that while the fieldcraft and patrolling skill of the junior NCOs was as high as one has always come to expect in a good Gurkha battalion, this skill was repeated upwards through the sergeants, Gurkha officers and the British officers too. This was unusual.

The Battalion then received bad news. On about 15 March 1966 it was told that it was to be moved from the Bau sector to the Serian sector in mid-April, and take over from 1st Argyll and Sutherland Highlanders (1A&SH). This was to make way for the 3rd Battalion Royal Australian Regiment (3RAR). Militarily, to change a unit's operational area in mid-tour was a nonsense: the full value of early patrolling in the uniquely demanding conditions across the border could only be realised towards the end of a unit's operational tour. The decision just as the Battalion's local knowledge was paying off caused much resentment. Political factors prevailed: Australian money had been used to build and improve the Bau base and the Australian

Government insisted that on its return to operations 3RAR had to occupy the Bau Sector.

On this development Colonel Ronnie wrote:

> In the one month left to us, I decided to apply co-ordinated pressure on Kindau: we would attack it, harass it, probe for and ambush its L of C.[60] If we could force the enemy to abandon this post, I felt this would be a significant achievement.

This might suggest that Ronnie was determined to mount a significant operation before the Battalion had to move, and to make sure it would be a good one.

Thomson and the Recce and Pioneer Platoons were still across the border, based 800 yards from Kindau, improving their knowledge of the approaches to it and the layout of the enemy garrison there. The plan for the attack on Kindau developed into a battalion-size operation and the roles given to the companies were as follows:

HQ Company and C Company. Assault the southern end of the Kindau position around mid-day on 24 March 1966 after a preliminary artillery concentration. Then break contact, leave the battlefield to B Company, but be ready to close again on Kindau for further harassment from the east if called upon.

A Company. Carry out an artillery and infantry fire assault on Hill Top post and engage the Babang Garrison and the Risau 1 gun with observed artillery fire to divert attention from the HQ/C Company assault and subsequent action by B Company.

B Company. Establish the company in the area of 'Upper Macham' with an FOO[61] in an observation post (OP) on the pinnacle itself. Be prepared to harry Kindau from the north-west and ambush movement in and out of Kindau on the track towards Siluas, if this could be located.

D Company. Based on intelligence sources that indicated that Kindau was probably supplied on a weekly or bi-weekly basis by porter convoys from Siluas, D Company was tasked to: first, check whether Separan was occupied, because if it was it would pose a threat to any deep penetration to the south; and second, if

---

60 . Lines of Communication, that is to say its supply and reinforcement routes.
61 . Forward Observation Officer, to direct artillery fire.

Separan was unoccupied, it was to locate and ambush the Siluas–Kindau track south-west of Kindau.

All the companies deployed on their operational tasks between 16 and 20 March. By 19 March D Company had confirmed that Separan was not occupied and on 20 March it re-rationed itself by sending a platoon back to an LZ near the border to collect an additional five days rations. HQ Company was re-rationed on 20 March 1966 by the Pipes and Drums Platoon, which portered in the resupply. C Company joined HQ Company in their base near Kindau on 21 March 1966. A and B Companies and their respective FOOs were in position on 22 March. However, D Company had made slow progress crossing the flooded and swamp-flanked Separan River, which was 30 metres wide and running fast, and was unlikely to be in position in time for the assault on 24 March. Pike therefore decided to make a bold move on the night of 22 March along a track, visible on his air photograph, to get D Company more swiftly and directly south. At first light on 23 March, after an all-night move covering 4,000 yards, D Company established a hide in a patch of swamp and jungle. Unfortunately they had been spotted by a lone Indonesian farmer. Recce patrols sent out from the hide established that there were two enemy bases 1,000 yards to the south-west and south-east of the hide. Further recce was required and the same patrols went out again at first light on 24 March.

The date of the assault had been set for 24 March but this was delayed by 24 hours because the Brigade Commander, Brigadier Bill Cheyne, was not satisfied with the information Thomson had on the enemy dispositions at Kindau. The Brigadier had a reputation for keeping a tight grip on things and his decision makes clear that he knew what the operation entailed. Additional recce was undertaken and a clearer position emerged. Tensions were clearly running high. All five companies of 1/10GR were over the border and its only reserve was the Pipes and Drums Platoon under command of the Battalion Second-In-Command (2IC). Across the border the tension in D Company in particular must have been high. At 1400 hours on 24 March a group of 12 Indonesians arrived in the area of D Company's hide. They checked the main track on which D Company's footprints were clearly visible, sat down and cooked a meal within feet of a two-man OP 200 yards from the hide. The enemy clearly knew D Company was in the area even if they did not know its precise location: it is probable that the farmer had told the enemy of D Company's presence in the area. One of the two riflemen in the OP silently crawled back to the hide to warn the company, which quietly stood-to and manned its slit trenches. After three and a half agonising hours the enemy left without locating the hide. The patrols that had gone out at first light were safely back by last light and confirmed that two enemy camps, each for about 50 men, were under construction some 800 yards to the south-south-east and south-south-west of the hide. The patrols identified that the enemy were taller, paler and better built than normal. A new regular division had moved into the area.

That night Pike talked on the radio in whispered tones to Colonel Ronnie to discuss the options. Given that the enemy were alert to his presence, looking for the Kindau - Siluas track was probably too risky even for Pike; so a new plan was required. The first option was for him to move back north during the night and to try and break contact with the enemy, which was probably inevitable; or, he could lay an ambush on the complex of tracks which the enemy had used that day and would probably use again. An ambush had the advantage that it would act as a secure base astride Pike's route to the north, and inflicting casualties on the enemy might assist his get-away. Colonel Ronnie agreed that an ambush should be laid. That night D Company silently clipped a 500-yard tunnel through fern and secondary jungle and silently filed out of the hide; it crossed the track obscuring their tracks and took up three platoon ambush positions astride the main tracks in the area. At 1000 hours on 25 March, two civilians chose to rest in the shade in the rear platoon's ambush position. They were captured, tied up and blindfolded. At 1030 hours two enemy arrived; seven more joined them five minutes later and started eating, four yards from the muzzle of 10 Platoon's GPMG. A further five minutes later a third group of enemy joined the party. At that stage the GPMG group opened fire, the Light Mortar NCO threw two No.36 grenades into the midst of the enemy, and an LMG group engaged four enemy bunched in front of them. Ten yards further down the track Lance Corporal Hindupal Rai's section engaged three more enemy. At least eleven enemy were killed in this initial burst of fire, but not all had been silenced. Two or three extremely brave Indonesians lying still alive in the ambush area and within yards of our men started to fire back skilfully at any movement by 10 Platoon. Both machine gunners in the GPMG group were killed by a burst of enemy automatic fire and the Mortar NCO was seriously wounded in the arm. Hindupal's section was also heavily engaged by the enemy firing at any noise or movement in the thick jungle. The ambush had become a fire-fight. Knowing he had casualties to deal with Pike asked Captain Templar, the FOO, to call down the DF (SOS).[62] Six days from the last verified grid reference, and with only an air photograph to work off, the artillery fire from the 5.5 inch medium guns was brought down with unbelievable speed and accuracy to within a few yards of the track, with only one correction. This fire temporarily silenced and scattered the Indonesians. In the lull, 10 Platoon Commander, WO2 Jamanbahadur Rai, was able to extricate his two dead and one wounded without too much trouble, but Hindupal's section was still under severe pressure. On ordering his section to move back two riflemen were killed instantly and his LMG gunner badly wounded by two Indonesians at 10 yards range. Hindupal killed one and exchanged fire with the second; they both ran out of ammunition at the same time but with superb coolness and weapon handling skill Hindupal was the first to reload and he killed the second Indonesian at a range of five yards. Hindupal then rejoined 10 Platoon taking his wounded LMG gunner with him and immediately asked for assistance to recover the bodies of the two dead men he had had to leave behind. Long sporadic bursts of enemy fire continued from some way down the track, so to support the recovery Pike called for further artillery fire. This enabled a party under the Company 2IC, Captain (QGO) Bhimbahadur Sunwar, and guided by Hindupal, to return and recover the two dead bodies. As Colonel Ronnie wrote, 'Brave as Hindupal's conduct had been in the ambush itself, his recovery of the bodies at a time when every instinct urged immediate withdrawal, was beyond all praise.'

Pike regrouped D Company and by 1200 hours it was heading north towards the border and beginning the task of getting back, carrying their four dead, assisting the two wounded, and carrying the weapons, equipment and packs of the dead and wounded in addition to their own. News of D Company's action and casualties meant a rapid re-think was

---

62   . Emergency defensive artillery fire, arranged in advance.

required at Battalion Headquarters, especially as there were concerns about the possible need to evacuate the wounded and any further casualties by helicopter. The Brigadier visited Battalion Headquarters with the Assistant Director Medical Services (ADMS), and after talking to Pike to check on the state of the casualties, it was decided that a helicopter extraction could not be risked and to avoid the complication of further casualties the Kindau operation would be limited to fire assaults.

The Regimental History Vol.2 records:

> At 1525 hours 120 rounds of artillery fire were brought down on the enemy garrison at Kindau and HQ and C Companies conducted their fire assault on the enemy base from as close as 100 yards using GPMGs, LMGs and 2 inch mortars. The artillery fire was directed by the FOO, Lieutenant Hugh Welby-Everard, who was in an exposed OP up a tall tree 150 yards from Kindau, with Gunner Evans half-way down the tree and Captain Hughes, OC C Company, at the bottom of the tree on the Battalion radio net. This vertical arrangement allowed communications to be maintained throughout the action.[63]

Lieutenant Nick Worthington commanded the Recce Platoon during the Kindau operation has a different recollection. It was he and not Chris Hughes who was at the bottom of the tree relaying radio messages. Chris Hughes was commanding C Company during its part in the fire assault. Worthington recalls relaying Thomson's order 'Let fire commence' to Welby-Everard, then later, when the initial bombardment was complete and machine gun fire was hammering away in the background, and Welby-Everard sought further instructions, he recalls passing on Thomson's order to 'Swing it about a bit', and so the bombardment continued. The Kindau Garrison received a thorough stonking. Once it was over the attacking force set out on the return journey to Stass, but not before they had opened and emptied the contents of their unused ration tins to lighten the loads they were carrying.[64]

A Company carried out its fire assault on Hill Post and Babang with 81mm mortars and GPMGs as planned, and 2nd Lieutenant Bloxam, the FOO with A Company in an OP 800

63 . McAlister, Bugle & Kukri Vol.2, p.236
64 . NR Worthington, E-Mail dated 17 Dec 2017.

yards from Babang, brought down artillery fire on Babang and Hill Top. Bloxham came under fire from enemy mortars and machine guns and these were silenced by artillery and mortar fire. From an Air OP Captain Alcock, the Battery 2IC, neutralised an enemy field gun at Risau 1 and engaged opportunity targets at Babang, Risau I and Risau II for 90 minutes. Of the five companies involved in the operation only a frustrated Niven and B Company did not engage the enemy.

It was probably during his visit to Battalion Headquarters on 24 March[65] that the Brigadier gave Colonel Ronnie a severe dressing down. Andy Watt recalled:

> I do remember on our last Borneo tour when the Brigadier, Bill Cheyne DSO OBE, Commander of 99 Gurkha Infantry Brigade, came down to Battalion Headquarters in Bau, Captain Ian Corden Lloyd, who was Adjutant/Operations Officer, said to me 'Colonel Ronnie is being bollocked by Cheyne'. There was no doubt about it. You could hear the Brigadier through the thin atap – loud, clear and very angry! I think it was because Ronnie had allowed one of our company commanders too much leeway on a Claret operation – outside the parameters very, very strictly laid down on each and every occasion by HQ FARELF and MOD. Anyway, Ronnie was as cool as usual immediately after the tirade.

Such was the tone and the volume of the Brigadier's words, which were clearly audible through the thin atap walls of the Headquarters huts, that Corden Lloyd ordered everyone out of the Headquarters and thus out of earshot, including Watt, the Signals Officer, and Lieutenant Mark Cook, the Intelligence Officer. Cook also remembers the incident, but neither he nor Watt are certain what the admonishment was about. They do remember that Colonel Ronnie never mentioned the incident and his demeanour remained as calm, collected and focussed as always, on what continued to be a tense day.

Clearly something went wrong as far as the Brigadier was concerned, but exactly what brought about his harsh words to Colonel Ronnie may never be known.[66] It seems likely that he

---

65 . The 1/10GR operational log shows that the Brigadier also visited Battalion Headquarters on 31 March 1966.
66 . Brigadier WW Cheyne, DSO OBE died on 10 May 1970, Ronnie McAlister on 23 September 2015 and Lieutenant Colonel ID Corden Lloyd, OBE MC, on 17

felt Pike's ambush action, and the casualties, which was not the main focus of the Kindau operation, had compromised it, wasting considerable detailed planning and effort. It is possible that Colonel Ronnie did not clear his decision to let Pike set an ambush rather than withdraw. Ronnie knew the enemy were aware of D Company's presence in the area and the policy on cross border operations was that if your force was compromised inside Indonesia you made a quick withdrawal. Allowing D Company to set an ambush contravened that policy and it should have been referred to the Brigadier and authorised at a higher level. D Company's ambush battle undoubtedly did compromise the Kindau operation and reduced the impact that might have been achieved, and it was the Brigadier who then directed that the attack on Kindau be limited to a fire assault. Although Ronnie felt allowing Pike to lay an ambush was the less risky of two hazardous options under the circumstances, it nearly went badly wrong. Ronnie trusted the judgement of an experienced company commander and supported Pike's preferred option, but it is possible that this decision was not cleared with the Brigadier, and, given what happened, he probably thought Ronnie had made the wrong decision.

It is also possible that the Brigadier himself was under pressure from those higher up the chain of command. 1/10GR had five companies across the border when the rules laid down that only two were allowed to be over at any time. It is most unlikely that the Brigadier and the Director of Operations, Major General Lea, were not aware that the Kindau operation involved five companies on the other side at the same time. However, it is also possible that, in Ronnie's determination that 1/10GR should undertake a significant operation before it handed over the Bau sector to 3RAR there was, in a fast moving scenario, an element of mission creep that the Brigadier was not fully aware of. HQ FARELF and London may not have been aware what was going on and the Brigadier, who was coming to the end of a very successful tour in command of West Brigade, might have known that was the case. At a very sensitive time, when high level political talks about ending Confrontation were taking place between Kuala Lumpur, Jakarta and London, it is possible that the Brigadier may have been sticking his neck out and he was

---

February 1978, when he was killed in a helicopter accident on operations in Northern Ireland while commanding 1 RGJ.

only too aware that anything that broke the 'Golden Rules' or gave the Indonesians leverage would not be well received in London.

At 1615 hours on 25 March 1/10GR received orders that originated several thousand miles away in London, to pull back across the border.[67] Pike and D Company were already on their arduous journey back, and the remaining companies involved in the Kindau-associated fire assaults were also on their way back before about 1655 hours, when Captain Alcock, who was providing covering fire for the withdrawal, stopped engaging opportunity targets with the artillery and brought the operation to an end.

On the night of 25 March Pike established a strong defensive position but set off before first light covered by rear guard ambush parties leap-frogging their way back to the border. The lead party with the two wounded men reached the border at 1800 hours and the wounded were immediately evacuated by helicopter. The main party carrying the four dead reached the border in the dark at 1945 hours.

Colonel Ronnie's comments on the operation were as follows:

1. Major Pike showed tac[tical] skill in occupying, after a difficult march, a sound position covering a complex of tracks, thus regaining the initiative.

2. 10 Pl[atoon] had a fierce battle at p[oin]t blank range with an en[emy] who fought back bravely. LCpl Hindupal Rai, commanding a section at J[68], played an outstanding part in the action and in the recovery of two of the dead.

3. Major Pike kept his head admirably and conducted his withdrawal calmly and skilfully. The morale of the Co[mpan]y is very high, a direct reflection on their trust in their Co[mpan]y Com[man]d[er]'s leadership.

4. No S[ecurity]F[orces] had entered the area of this action before. We had not expected to find en[emy] camps so far West of KINDAU or so far north of SILUAS. There is scope for the harassment of the

---

67 . Nick van der Bijl, Confrontation: The War with Indonesia 1962-1966, p.231.

68 . The map associated with comments appears not to have survived.

L[ines] of C[ommunication] of those en[emy] positions. An endurance of 15 days might be needed for such ops indicating the requirement for a 'back-up' force on the SEPARAN to carry extra rat[ion]s and secure the withdrawal route. [69]

These points indicate Ronnie certainly thought his decision to let Pike carry out and area ambush on his withdrawal route was right. That the enemy did not interfere at any stage of D Company's difficult withdrawal suggests the ambush action did achieve a clean break as intended. There were however lessons to be learned after a sharp, close quarter battle during which 4 men were killed and 2 wounded. The debriefing of those involved was clearly thorough and in considering what happened, and similar incidents in Borneo, Ronnie's training experience came to the fore and he sent a thoughtful, questioning letter to the Company Commanders and copied it to the School of Infantry at Warminster and the Training Depot Brigade of Gurkhas with his ideas on how the teaching of minor tactics and shooting in the jungle might be improved. Titled MINOR TACTICS AND SHOOTING – DEALING WITH THE UNSEEN ENEMY he wrote:

1. In both D Co[mpan]y's contacts, in C Co[mpan]y's Tebedu battle and on a recent 42 C[oman]do op[eration], unseen, unlocated and therefore undealt with enemy intervened unexpectedly; on three occasions with devastating effect. In our case, two recruits were killed and one wounded at a stage when it seemed the battle had been won; two of these, when told to withdraw, stood up and attracted attention to themselves by moving the undergrowth.

2. It is clear to us all, I think, that the old dogma "one round one enemy" must go forever if it hasn't already; it is human nature to react to the enemy you can see and, of course, our soldiers must be able to shoot straight and fast at those enemy in sight. There is no point harping on the obvious.

---

69   .1/10GR Assessment of Operations 1st – 31st March 1966 dated 3 April 1966.

3. But "one round one enemy" is so far short of the methods needed to cope with the dangers of a close quarter battle in the jungle, that it is positively suicidal to teach soldiers that they must not fire at all unless they can see to fire an aimed shot.

4. In First Tenth we have all hoisted in the need to "win the fire fight". This means heavy fire must be directed at the enemy initially. Anyone who talks of fire control and conserving ammunition at this stage of a battle is naïve. But "winning the fire fight" too does not, it seems, go far enough either. To stop firing when the enemy stops firing makes some sense: but it must not be assumed that the enemy are all dead.

5. When this stage is reached men must be taught:

    a.   to listen as well as look

    b.   to fire in the direction of any suspicious sound

    c.   to search methodically with fire any bit of ground not yet dealt with. (This is the sort of "fire control" we want)

    d.   to move <u>along the ground</u> forwards (if it is in attack) or backwards (if it is a withdrawal or move back from an ambush). The days of charging in extended line died in 1959 with the last Malayan CT [Communist Terrorist]; this should be revived when next we come up against bandits instead of soldiers

    e.   NOT to get their heads up too soon, nor to stand up, or half stand up, unless they are clearly in dead ground.

    f.   NOT to give their positions away by shouted fire orders. This means <u>some</u> latitude to men to fire <u>without</u> orders

    g.   to cover each other at all times, even though it seems that the immediate danger is past.

6. <u>Moving along the ground</u> needs a little explanation. I believe you either crawl slowly forward or backwards on your tummy, or, rolled up like a ball and moving as

close to the ground as possible, you dash quickly to the next bit of cover, perhaps three to five yards away.

7. I wonder, too, whether DOWN – CRAWL – OBSERVE – SIGHTS – FIRE has much value in training the would be jungle fighter.

8. Other thoughts will occur to you and your QGOs [Queen's Gurkha Officers] / NCOs [Non-Commissioned Officers]. I want you to discuss this subject over the next ten days, sucking the brains of all who might contribute, however junior and let me have your ideas and suggestions in writing.

9. I would welcome your views, too, on what advice we might give on training the recruit. Dare we, for example, ask that the new recruit is told to kill all the enemy he can see and then "search" dangerous areas with prophylactic fire? By doing so will he get the wrong idea and will <u>we</u> then have to instil some fire discipline? Or do we teach him "one round one enemy" at TDBG [Training Depot Brigade of Gurkhas], and then, on arrival here, release some of his inhibitions and teach him to fire intelligently at what he cannot see?

10. This subject is a matter of life and death and therefore lies at the heart of professional infantry soldiering: dash and elan have their place but those who display such characteristics are often short lived. We have got to go on fighting <u>and</u> living.

11. As a matter of urgency we must all clear our minds on what we really hope to achieve and what we mean by "fire control", "fire discipline" and "winning the fire fight". Although the "war" is now being fought at Company level, it is at section/platoon level that a battle is won or lost in terms of casualties inflicted and suffered.[70]

---

70 .1/10GR PMO 409 G(Ops) dated 30 March 1966.

Sadly, none of any subsequent correspondence appears to have survived.[71] However, what is clear is that Ronnie felt better training and different tactics and rules on fire discipline in the jungle would have prevented some casualties.

On the whole operation, Ronnie certainly thought his decision to let Pike carry out an area ambush on his withdrawal route was right and that D Company's battle on 24 March was a victory as his Special Order of the Day published in Battalion Routine Orders on Saturday 9 April 1966 at Cambrai Camp, Bau makes clear:

SPECIAL ORDER THE DAY

BY

LIEUTENANT COLONEL RWL McALISTER MBE

COMMANDING OFFICER

1st BATTALION THE 10th PRINCESS MARY'S OWN
GURKHA RIFLES

(BRIGADE OF GURKHAS)

CAMBRAI CAMP, BAU

SATURDAY 9 APRIL, 1966

1. On 24th March 1966, in the BOKAH area of SARAWAK, an enemy incursion force, some 80 strong, moved into an area being patrolled by D Company.

2. The Company's patrol base, situated in close secondary jungle, although well concealed was not tactically sited to cut off the enemy's withdrawal.

3. On the morning of 24th March three recce patrols left D Company base to search for the enemy. While away from the base, thus making it impossible for the company to move, an enemy recce party, 12 strong, acting on information given by civilians, found D Company tracks and sat only ten feet away from a D Company OP manned by Rfn KALUSING LIMBU, who with great coolness and courage maintained his

---

71 . Shortly after the end of the Confrontation with Indonesia orders were given that any documentation that referred to Claret Operations was to be destroyed. Not all of it was but very little exists.

position for over six hours, ready to fire at once if the enemy should move towards the base yet equally ready not to give D Company's position away by movement.

4. On the return of the recce patrols, two of which, by skilful fieldcraft, had located the main enemy bases, Major Pike decided to move by night to occupy a better position on the enemy's withdrawal route. Starting at 0300 hours the company carried out a difficult and hazardous night move. At first light the company occupied a cleverly conceived position dominating a complex of tracks thus regaining the initiative and putting the enemy at a disadvantage.

5. At 1000 hours on 25th March a force of some 25 enemy approached the position occupied by 10 Platoon, commanded by WOII JAMANBAHADUR RAI. In a fierce firefight much of it at less than five yards range, 13 enemy were killed but not before four of our own men were killed and two wounded by a brave and aggressive enemy.

6. The following casualties were suffered by D Company:

Killed in action: 21149977 Rfn Bhalaman Rai
                    21154193 Rfn Krishnabahadur Rai
                    21156591 Rfn Prasadsing Limbu
                    21156684 Rfn Lachhuman Rai
Wounded in action: 21140991 L/Cpl Prembahadur Tamang
                    21148709 L/Cpl Birbahadur Rai

7. When all have done so well, it is often invidious to mention the names of individuals. However, I feel I must congratulate L/Cpl Hindupal Rai, who at the outset, killed 5 enemy personally at point blank range, and who, at the end of the battle, and still under enemy fire, guided the party, led by Capt (QGO) BHIMBAHADUR SUNWAR, to recover two of our dead from the most exposed position.

8. D Company would not wish me to forget the part played by the FOO, Capt Templar, who so accurately directed the fire of the medium guns of F Tp 132 Bty (Bengal Rocket Troop) RA; this fire undoubtedly broke the enemy resistance and forced their withdrawal at a crucial moment of the battle.

9. The Commanding Officer again wishes to congratulate Major CJ Pike and all ranks D Company for their tactical skill, coolness and courage in action. No one rifle company in the history of the Borneo emergency can equal the record of 50 enemy killed in the space of three weeks. The First Tenth is used to establishing records; this one is likely to take some beating.

Sgs XXXXXXXXXXX
(RWL McAlister, MBE)
Lieutenant-Colonel
Commanding Officer[72]

Pike was awarded the DSO for his very successful river ambush on 4 March and D Company's subsequent ambush battle, and also for his skilful handling of an exceptionally difficult withdrawal from the Kindau operation on 24–25 March. Hindupal was awarded a well-deserved DCM. However, in the Kindau ambush battle, D Company had suffered four men killed and two wounded, high casualties by Borneo standards, and some questioned whether it really was a victory. Against the losses, at least 13 enemy bodies were counted in the ambush area and the volume of small arms – and more specifically the 5.5 inch artillery fire at close quarters – probably caused further enemy casualties. The effects of the fire assaults by HQ, C and A Companies were more difficult to determine. Cross-border traders, whose information was notoriously unreliable, suggested that seven Indonesian military personnel were killed in the Kindau base. The Indonesian artillery gun at Risau 1 was knocked out by a direct hit from our artillery. It did not fire back that day and it is probable that some of those manning it were casualties. It is not known whether the enemy suffered further casualties from A Company's infantry fire and the artillery fire on Babang and Hill Top, but it would not be unreasonable to assume that they did. So, against the loss of four men killed and two wounded, at least 20 enemy were killed and a number wounded, in a deep penetration operation that would have would have unnerved the enemy and put them into an even more defensive mind-set.

---

72 . The rules on secrecy in relation to Claret Operations were such that the classified 1/10GR War Diary for 26 March records: '10 Pl when on patrol on G.RAYA ridge at GR 882057 walked into en APERS minefield trap. Casualties 4 killed 2 wounded.'

At a political level the situation was changing fast. In early April Indonesia established diplomatic and commercial relations with Singapore and then on 12 April, Suharto, who had replaced Sukarno as the President of Indonesia, indicated that Indonesia would recognise Malaysia. Major General Lea immediately suspended all Claret Operations but insisted that recce patrols should continue. 'Still reeling from the loss of 4 men killed', according to historian Nick van der Bijl,[73] 1/10GR handed over the Bau sector to 3RAR on 26 April and took over the Serian sector south of Bau from the Argylls.

The Argylls had had a difficult tour in the Serian area, with few successes. Among the challenges they described on handing over to 1/10GR were the difficulties they had encountered in crossing the broad, fast-flowing river that ran parallel to the border inside Indonesia, and also in approaching a strong Indonesian base on the north bank of the river, surrounded by open ground where they had suffered casualties. In his first three days in the Tebedu area Pike checked 1,000 yards of the river, identified four possible crossing points and, donning sub aqua flippers, crossed the river at his preferred crossing site in broad daylight with four NCOs and conducted a recce of the south bank area. Not to be outdone, Niven, based at Tebakang, found a covered route to the river near the enemy camp on the north bank and over five days checked the post from every angle and at close range, bringing back a detailed plan of the layout of the camp which gained the admiration of the hard to impress Brigadier Cheyne. In a matter of days the Battalion had achieved what the Argylls thought for four months was not possible. In May all cross-border activity was stopped, but Ronnie felt it might be appropriate to have a contingency plan for an operation on a back burner in case diplomatic talks broke down. This proved to be a sensible initiative when out of the blue at 1300 hours one Sunday afternoon in June an unannounced helicopter landed at Serian with an urgent message for the Commanding Officer from the Brigadier. Colonel Ronnie recalled that:

---

73 . Nick van der Bijl, Confrontation: The War with Indonesia 1962–1966, p.231. In 2016/17 the author offered the suggestion that 1/10GR was 'Reeling from the loss of 4 men killed' to Pike, Niven and Hughes, the surviving company commanders of 1/10GR, and to Watt and Cook, who were respectively the Regimental Signal Officer and Intelligence Officer in 1/10GR at the time, and they all refuted it.

Brigadier Cheyne wanted by four o'clock that afternoon, a plan to assault Niven's river post. I grabbed John Brake, my battery commander, and we flew down to Tebakang. With Niven's help, Brake and I drew up a plan, complete from warning, assembly and move out, to deception, artillery support, timings, H hour, medical, logistics, radio-rebroadcast, codewords, the lot. I wrote out an operation order and attached a diagram produced by Niven. The whole thing was in the Brigadier's hands by 1600 hours. The point to be stressed here is that on 99th Brigade's five-battalion front, the only really detailed knowledge of an enemy position at the time was that produced by Niven. To be asked to produce the contingency plan was a tacit recognition of Niven's outstanding courage and competence. I'm glad to say he was later Mentioned in Despatches for his work at Stass and in the Serian sector.[74]

Although the closing date for the award of the clasp 'Borneo' on the 1962 General Service Medal was 11 August 1966, agreement had been reached between Malaysia and Indonesia by 4 June that the Confrontation between the two countries should end. By 28 May the Director of Operations, Borneo, Major General Lea, had directed that British Forces Borneo should revert to internal security duties and guarding the border. The Battalion's final weeks, before it handed over to 1st Battalion The Buffs[75] in late July, were therefore quiet, and it was able to carry out useful watermanship training on the river near Tebakang, and to concentrate the Mortar Platoon to carry out refresher training and live firing.

On 6 July 1966 Ronnie initialled the first report he received as a Commanding Officer. It was written by Brigadier Cheyne who graded him 'B', that is 'Above the standard required of his rank and service'. It is an interesting report, describing Colonel Ronnie as having 'one of the clearest and best brains of any of the 25 Commanding Officers who have served in West Brigade in the past twenty months'. The Brigadier expands this by writing, 'I like the way he analyses a problem and the speed with which it is resolved and the guts got out of it. He gets the point even before one has finished speaking.' Yet the Brigadier wrote, 'To begin with I did not think he was commanding his Battalion

---

74   . McAlister, Bugle & Kukri, Vol.2, pp.238–239.
75   . The Royal East Kent Regiment.

effectively. I had the impression that he was frightened of his Company Commanders and was doing what they wanted him to do. I do not now believe this to be true. I was wrong, though at the time it had an element of truth in it.' Either, in the opinion of the Brigadier, Colonel Ronnie was frightened of his Company Commanders or he was not. The Brigadier records that Ronnie was not, but equivocates. I asked the surviving company commanders whom I was able to contact – Pike, Niven and Hughes – for their comments on this and they all said the suggestion that Colonel Ronnie was in anyway in awe or frightened of them was nonsense. Pike said that the 1/10GR officers at the time were a strong team, and a team that got on well together. Operations were discussed in a parliamentary way. Ronnie gave everyone the opportunity to put forward suggestions and state their opinion. He was an exceptional listener. However, once he had heard what others thought or proposed, he made his own decisions and gave instructions accordingly; and, once given, there was no doubt those instructions were orders. Pike made it clear there were occasions when he did not agree with his Commanding Officer's decisions, but there was no doubt about who the boss was, and what was to be done.[76] Pike was adamant that the Company Commanders had absolute confidence in Colonel Ronnie generally, and in particular with his written ability and verbal orders. In comparing his style to that of his predecessor, Pike said that when talking to 'Bunny' Burnett, as the Commanding Officer, it was like talking to a friend. He would say things that friends might discuss: with Ronnie discussions were professional, he rarely did small talk and almost never talked about himself.

In the report the Brigadier also wrote, 'He can give the impression of not wanting to make a mistake.' This is an odd comment, given the public rocket that the Brigadier gave Ronnie, and the rather obvious point that in warfare, when soldiers' lives are at stake, a sensible and caring commander will seek to avoid mistakes. Ronnie took calculated risks, which a commander not wishing to make mistakes would not have done. He had all five companies of 1/10GR over the border inside Indonesia on the Kindau operation. He agreed that Pike should establish an area ambush rather than follow policy by withdrawing fast when the enemy knew D Company was in the

76 . Telephone conversation Pike–Litherland 25 Aug 2016.

area and close to two of their bases. Both these decisions indicate that Ronnie was not afraid to take considered risks. The Brigadier's implied criticism that Ronnie was cautious is difficult to rationalise based on what we now know. Commenting on the Brigadier's remarks, Bruce Niven writes:

> It is utter nonsense to think that General Ronnie was in any way frightened of his company commanders or that he did not want to make a mistake ... I only met the Brigadier once and he came across as a very forward, forthright extrovert who liked to be seen and to be heard as he dominated proceedings ... the very opposite to General Ronnie, so there was room for a personality clash in that the Brigadier may have reckoned that anyone worth their salt had to be like him?[77]

In Ronnie's report the Brigadier went on to write, 'In fact he has had a successful first tour on operations commanding a high class Battalion,' However, for some reason he feels he cannot give Ronnie too much credit and then writes, 'in this respect, of course, he has had it easy; he has been the jockey on the back of Golden Miller.'[78] Ronnie himself wrote that his company commanders were exceptional,[79] as quoted earlier, and he probably discussed them with the Brigadier when considering their confidential reports and almost certainly on the citations for awards.[80] It is possible that Ronnie told the Brigadier that 1/10GR's company commanders were first class. They were, but to have this 'played back' – if that is what happened – to imply that Ronnie had an easy ride seems unnecessarily harsh when the command and control of a group of exceptionally talented and head-strong company commanders could be said to be a greater challenge than having to deal with less assertive ones. Ronnie himself wrote that the only issue he had with his company commanders was 'a problem only of reining them in'. He knew they all had more recent operational experience in Borneo than he did and at the level at which most operations were being

---

77 . BM Niven, E-Mail dated Saturday 27 Aug 2016 at 3.21am.

78 . Golden Miller (1927–57) was the thoroughbred racehorse that won the Cheltenham Gold Cup in five consecutive years and the 1934 Grand National.

79 . McAlister, Bugle & Kukri, Vol.2, pp.229–230.

80 . Pike was awarded the DSO, Hughes the MC and Niven was Mentioned in Despatches.

conducted. He was nevertheless highly regarded and respected by his company commanders, who recognised that he, too, was a competent operational commander. The Brigadier's caveats suggest something was not quite right and hint that there was a personality difference.

Rightly, the Brigadier goes on to highlight a part of Ronnie's character that was considered a weakness in some military circles, writing '…he is not impressive to meet and he makes no effort to sell himself, but as I have got to know him better, I realise why he has such a high reputation in the Brigade of Gurkhas; it is fully justified. He could have a big future ahead of him'. He goes on to recommend that 'he needs to come out of himself just a little more so that he can inspire as well as lead. This will happen as he has the brain, the ability, the outlook and ambition. He must take a leaf out of Lucifer ….. and sparkle, or to steal another advertisement … show a little 'scweffervescent'.[81] It is probable that the Brigadier and Ronnie had military backgrounds and outlooks that were sufficiently different for them not to be kindred spirits. Cheyne was the last commanding officer of the Seaforth Highlanders and had a 'special forces' background. He was probably used to projecting a forceful leadership style, as he demonstrated when giving Ronnie a rocket in the hearing of others, and he may have expected others to lead in the same way. That was just not Ronnie's style; he was by nature calm, collected and measured; and his sharp mind, unflappable character and the clarity of his orders were such that he did not feel he needed to impose himself or be overtly dominant. His military background commanding Gurkhas, who are by their nature highly self-disciplined and amenable to a calmer, more paternal form of authority, developed in him a leadership style based on a calm but steely determination, behind clear direction and example. His upbringing and manner were devoid of showmanship.

Ronnie was awarded a Mention in Despatches for his efforts in command of what was a fragmented operational tour. In the first three and a half months the Battalion took the fight to the enemy and was engaged in some serious fighting in the Bau sector, and he commanded a battalion-size operation when five companies were involved in the Kindau operation. A battalion-

---

81 . 'Schweppervescent' perhaps? A reference to the sparkle in a Schwepps tonic?

size operation was unusual at the time and although that operation did not achieve all that had been intended, it was a success. The insistence of the Australian Government that 3RAR move into the Bau sector disrupted the Battalion's activities part way through an operational tour, obliging it to take over and familiarise itself with a new area; then before the Battalion could undertake operations in the Serian sector, most offensive military operations were curtailed as the politicians brought Confrontation to an end. Some thought Ronnie was unlucky not to have been awarded the OBE for what the Battalion did under his command, and put that down to his differences with the Brigadier. Writing for the 'News from Members' section in the 3GR Journal Ronnie modestly wrote: 'My own news is that I was lucky to be 'Mentioned' for what my officers and men did for me during the closing stages of the Borneo Campaign.'

The Battalion was back at Cassino Barracks in Hong Kong by the end of July 1966, and after a brief spell of leave it settled down to the first protracted period of peacetime soldiering it had enjoyed since April 1963. Training cadres were run; the Battalion took part in Internal Security (IS) and Counter Revolutionary Warfare (CRW) demonstrations and exercises in the Colony, as enemy and friendly forces; and, for the first time since 1962, classified[82] its weapons on the rifle range and staged a ceremonial parade. In December 1966 it was announced that size of the Brigade of Gurkhas was to be reduced significantly. The 15,000 Gurkhas that had been required for the Confrontation against Indonesia were no longer needed and plans to reduce the Brigade to 6,000 men had been drawn up. Although some men, attracted by the opportunity to acquire immediate capital in the form of the £360 gratuity, volunteered to leave a hundred men who had borne the brunt of five operational tours in Borneo had to be told they would be made redundant in 1967. At the same time the Regiment was told that its 1st and 2nd Battalions would amalgamate in August 1968. The news was not entirely unexpected as similar plans had been drawn up after the end of the Malayan Emergency in 1961, and the Battalion took a positive view, looking forward rather than

---

82 . All ranks were classified as either a Marksman; 1st Class Shot or 2nd Class Shot according to their score in the Annual Personal Weapon Test on the range. On this occasion 73% of the Battalion classified as Marksmen on the Self-Loading Rifle (SLR) and 74.5% as Marksmen on the General Purpose Machine Gun (GPMG). McAlister, Bugle & Kukri, Vol.2, p.243.

back, in the knowledge that disbanding the Brigade of Gurkhas had been one of the options under consideration.

In the competitive field of inter-unit sport within the Colony the Battalion swept the board on the hockey field and more than held its own in other sports, while within the Battalion its inter-company competition was fought as fiercely as ever. The 200th anniversary of the raising of the Regiment in 1766 was celebrated and several initiatives that had been parked for operational reasons were now taken forward. Work began to assemble the material required for the second volume of the Regimental History; medals of former distinguished officers and men in the Regiment were acquired, including four awarded to the 10th Madras Native Infantry[83] in the First, Second and Third Burma Wars (1824–1887). Also, for display in the Messes and Guardroom, cases were commissioned that showed miniature medals for all the campaigns the Regiment had fought in, and others with miniatures and the gallantry awards, below which the names of the recipients of honours were recorded.

There was time for golf. The professional at the Fanling Golf Course, Joe Hardwick, presented a hickory-shafted putter to be a golf trophy. It came to be known as the 'Colonel's Putter' and the rules were quite simply that, as a Stableford competition, it was to be played for as frequently as possible.

The Battalion achieved a great deal in a relatively short period of time and Commander 48 Gurkha Infantry Brigade, Brigadier Peter Martin, was clearly impressed by Ronnie's performance and the way he was commanding and leading his battalion. In his annual confidential report for the period 1 June 1966 to 30 June 1967, the Brigadier wrote, 'I have been immensely impressed by this officer' ... 'Though not physically imposing he is head and shoulders above the other Commanding Officers in the Brigade in ability.' The report goes on: 'He has a strong and delightful personality compounded of charm and gaiety, integrity, imperturbability, imagination, determination and an incisive mind. He is above all a leader, who has the ability to give exceptionally clear and precise orders and who leaves his subordinates alone to get on with the job. He stands no nonsense within his unit, but has a happy knack of being able to unbend with his officers and men without ever losing their

---

83 . The 10th Madras Native Infantry (10MNI) was an earlier incarnation of the 10th Gurkhas.

respect. He has some very strong-willed and critical subordinates but he can do no wrong in their eyes.' The Brigadier praises his ability as a lecturer and leader of discussion; indicates that the quality of his reports on his officers are models of how confidential reports should be written, and writes 'I value his judgement and advice on all matters'. He then adds, '1/10GR has the deserved reputation of being a thoroughly tough, fit, aggressive, efficient and happy Battalion. In this it reflects its commander.' Graded 'OUTSTANDING', Ronnie was given an unequivocal recommendation for command of a British or Gurkha Brigade, and these recommendations and the report were strongly endorsed by both the GOC Hong Kong and the Commander Far East Land Forces. It should be noted that Brigadier Martin, the GOC Hong Kong and also the Commander Far East Land Forces were not from Gurkha regiments, so one can dismiss any suggestion that the report was written to correct whatever short-comings might have been perceived in his 1966 report; however, the contrast between the two reports is stark enough to raise a quizzical eyebrow.

Throughout this period storm clouds were gathering; in August 1966 Chairman Mao had launched his Cultural Revolution and widespread unrest erupted throughout China and threatened to spill over into Hong Kong.

Chapter 8

A Mixture of Deadly Earnest and Charades

In 1967 the Sino-British border followed the Shum Chun river from its mouth in Deep Bay in the west in an easterly direction along a wide valley and across to the village of Sha Tau Kok, a small fishing village on the east coast of the peninsula in Mirs Bay (See Map p.99). The border was about 22 miles long and where it ran along the Shum Chun river the boundary between China and Hong Kong was clear.[84] It was less well defined for three miles at the eastern end by 20 small boundary pillars, eight of which went through the centre of Sha Tau Kok village, along Chung Ying Street. In the west where the Shum Chun river was deep the surrounding area was marshy and formed a natural barrier, but from Ta Ku Ling to the east the river was easily fordable so the border was more or less open. There was an old chain-link fence in a poor state of repair and in many places it had been removed. A short distance away from the border on the British side, in 1962, a barrier of triple coil dannert wire had been erected to deter illegal immigrants, but this too was in a poor state and had been removed in places, because the Hong Kong Government had failed to meet the local farmers' demands for compensation for the land under the barrier that they could no longer cultivate.

Lo Wu was the first real contact point between the two countries on the border. It was where the Kowloon-Canton railway that carried produce and people between Hong Kong and China crossed the border. It was also a recognised crossing point for certain farmers who owned and worked land on the opposite side. They had an inalienable right, whether based in Hong Kong or China, to cross to the other side to work their land. The majority of the farmers with land in the border area lived in China so crossings to work were predominantly from China into

---

84 . The border was actually the high-water mark on the northern (Chinese) side of the river, although this technical nicety was not widely known or taken into account by either side.

Hong Kong. A mile to the east of Lo Wu was Man Kam To, where there was a 60-foot Bailey bridge across the Shum Chun river. Large numbers of livestock and vast quantities of vegetables were exported from China to Hong Kong across the bridge, and as at Lo Wu it was a recognised crossing point for local farmers on both sides of the border. Another mile to the east there was a foot-bridge at Ta Ku Ling opposite the village of Lo Fang on the Chinese side. It, too, was a recognised crossing point for farmers. At Ta Ku Ling the river becomes shallow and from Ling Ma Hang it could be crossed easily. From there to Sha Tau Kok the two countries were separated by the broken line of the two fences, or their remains, but on the ground the border was ill-defined. Here the area was dominated by hills: China Mountain to the north and the Robin's Nest range on the British side.

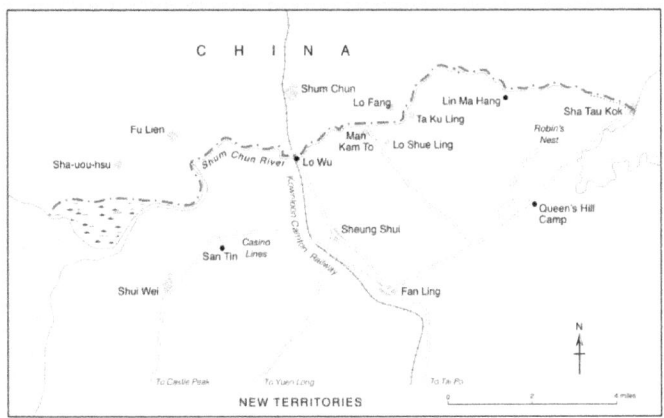

The Sino-British Border ca 1967

The Hong Kong Police (HKP) were responsible for the border. Police posts were established at strategic points along the border but they did not provide visual coverage of the whole of it. Effective control of the border did not exist. Occasional political purges in China brought floods of refugees that simply overwhelmed the Police and in 1956 and 1962 the Army was called in to help stem the tide. On occasions political escapees were pursued by uniformed Chinese soldiers[85] into British territory and the Chinese Communist Militia[86] pretty much came and went as they wished.

Between August 1966 and May 1967 the effects of the Cultural Revolution swept outwards from Beijing and the revolutionary fervour built up in Kwang Tung,[87] the province on the Chinese side of the border. People of the border, predominantly the farmers, with 'followers' (Chinese militia and 'Red Guards'[88]), began to cross over into Hong Kong to work the fields in significant numbers. They held meetings expounding the thoughts of Chairman Mao and it was not long before red flags and posters appeared and pamphlets began to be distributed. Political freedom was one of the essential rights in Hong Kong so no pressure was put on the farmers as they carried out their new activities. There were inflammatory speeches and posters damning the 'Imperialist running dogs' and derogatory messages were plastered on the walls of government and private buildings in Man Kam To and Sha Tau Kok. By May 1967 the Cultural Revolution was having a major impact in Kwang Tung and large rallies could be seen and heard by observers on the British side of the border. The mood of the farmers and their sympathisers on both sides of the border became more violent and their links to communist cadres and the 'Red Guards' strengthened.

The disturbances in Hong Kong started in an artificial flower factory in Kowloon when an industrial dispute over the unfair dismissal of some workers turned into a riot. The communist-dominated Federation of Trade Unions immediately intervened on behalf of the workers. On 15 May 1967 this in turn was backed by the intervention of the Chinese Ministry of Foreign Affairs in Beijing. A statement of protest was passed to Mr

---

85 . The People's Liberation Army (PLA) was the Chinese Army. Uniformed, professional, disciplined and well-armed. It was under the control of China's Premier, Zhou Enlai, whose agenda was to try and keep it aloof from the Cultural Revolution.
86 . The Militia were uniformed locally recruited, armed part-time soldiers under local control. They sympathised with the Cultural Revolution and tended to assist the Red Guard.
87 . Kwang Tung province is also referred to as Kwangtung or Guangzhou.
88 . Red Guards were locally-organised armed gangs of zealots, rabble-rousers, trouble-makers and murderers who had Mao's blessing to advance the Cultural Revolution and his directive to purge the population of its elites and the bourgeoisie (middle class).

David Hopson, the British Chargé d'Affaires in Beijing, which was followed by anti-British protests there and elsewhere, and sympathetic editorials in the *People's Daily* newspaper. This was interpreted by Hong Kong's left-wing radicals as a clear sign for action in Hong Kong. Demonstrations and strikes supported by media propaganda in the left-wing press followed. While events in downtown Kowloon and on Hong Kong island were hotting up, the border area and New Territories were relatively quiet. 1/10GR was the designated Frontier Battalion and remained on stand-by in case anything should happen on the border. It was on continuous notice for eight weeks, mostly at four hours' notice to move, but this was occasionally reduced to one hour's notice and more than once the Battalion was put on immediate notice and deployed to a forward assembly area. Loaded vehicles were kept ready in company lines and the men had their Internal Security (IS) scales of ammunition, grenades, detonators and loaded magazines with them all the time. The 'ready to move but not needed' status with the restrictions it placed on training and other activities was irritating. In mid-May Labour and industrial unrest stirred up by the communist-dominated trade unions turned into major rioting in Kowloon, and by late May also in the Victoria and Central districts on Hong Kong island. A major 'poster' campaign was mounted on Government House.

It was during this period that a Gurkha soldier was brought before Ronnie to be charged for some misdemeanour under Commanding Officer's Orders. Colonel Ronnie, as was the practice, was seated at his desk with his hat on. It being in the days before air-conditioning, he had his back to an open window. Standing hatless as advisers/witnesses on either side of the CO's desk were Captain Andy Watt, now the Adjutant and responsible to the CO for disciplinary matters, and the Gurkha Major, responsible for keeping an eagle eye on all matters Gurkha. The hatless Gurkha who faced the charge, followed by a Gurkha escort with drawn kukri, was marched in by the Regimental Sergeant Major (RSM) to a position in front of the CO's desk. The RSM retired from the room and the proceedings began. With everyone standing to attention, on what is always a solemn occasion, Colonel Ronnie began to read out the charges faced by the accused. As he did so, Watt and the Gurkha Major began to twitch and sniff and their eyes began to water; then the accused and the escort also began to twitch and sniff. This was too much for Colonel Ronnie who ordered everyone out and told them to get a grip of themselves. On standing up he too got a powerful dose of the CS gas that had been blown over the top of his head and reached the others first. The ever-diligent Pike and D Company were doing some realistic IS training up-wind from Battalion Headquarters![89]

At altogether higher levels in the political and diplomatic world there were different pressures and slightly different aims. The Governor Sir David Trench's primary concern was to maintain his effective governance of Hong Kong; with his strong colonial administration background and experience, he was inclined to take a tough line. So, too, was the Colonial Secretary, Michael Gass, his deputy.[90] At the British Embassy in Beijing, Chargé d'Affaires David Hopson was determined to maintain an effective operation, or at least the presence of the British Diplomatic Mission in Beijing. He and his staff were trying to keep operating in the face of considerable 'anti-imperialist' pressure, and he signalled London to say 'in the game of diplomatic warfare the Chinese can trump our every card. They control everything here, and probably do not much care about their staff abroad.'[91] The line that the Foreign and Commonwealth Office (FCO) and Her Majesty's Government (HMG) took was to adopt a firm but unprovocative policy. The Communists in Hong Kong, led by the 'Anti-Persecution Struggle Committee', thought the British would capitulate in the face of their action and hand over control of the Colony to them, as the Portuguese Colonial Government had done in Macau. They miscalculated. When it became clear that Trench would not accept their demands the communists had to escalate the disruption. This came in the form of a 'work stoppage' campaign and a 'poster war'. As fast as the protesters put up defamatory posters the Police took them down, and the protesters claimed this was an insult to Mao Tse-Tung. In spite of mass walk-outs and intimidation many essential services continued to function. A general strike was called for 24 June and a food stoppage for 28 June, and for three days no produce

---

89 . AJJ Watt, E-Mail dated Wed, Aug 17, 2016, 3.22 pm.
90 . Sir David Trench returned to England in June 1967 for health reasons and Michael Gass was the Acting Governor during Trench's absence.
91 . Cheung, Hong Kong's Watershed: The 1967 Riots, p.104-105. A reference to the restrictions HMG had imposed on the staff of the Chinese Embassy in London.

came into Hong Kong from China across the Man Kam To bridge. However, these actions did not receive widespread support. Many of Hong Kong's residents had fled communist regimes in China, many were apolitical and most were predominantly interested in making money. It became clear that the Communists were determined to raise the stakes but Trench decided firm action was required. He was convinced that the initial disturbance was not a pre-meditated one orchestrated by Beijing. He said, 'There is every indication that this (the original industrial dispute in Kowloon) was spontaneous', and the latest wave of militant unionism was 'a reflection of the increased freedom allowed to the 'masses' as a result of propaganda based on the Cultural Revolution in China.' He argued that the escalation of events was largely a result of the Hong Kong communist leaders' survival instinct. They needed a victory for the thoughts of Chairman Mao in Hong Kong to save their own necks.[92] Although Hopson in Beijing was not entirely happy, London agreed with Trench and he gave the Police the authority to go on the offensive. They raided known communist premises and seized arms, bomb-making equipment, assorted offensive weapons, documents and posters. Support for the communists waned, several of the Anti-Persecution Struggle Committee fled to China and some to the Chinese side of Sha Tau Kok village on the border, but their hard core resorted to an extensive bombing campaign, during which, between July and December 1967, 16 people were killed and 340 injured.

Sha Tau Kok

In May and June the border area was relatively quiet. However, the Police Special Branch learned that a demonstration and an attempt to take down and burn the Union Jack on the Police Post at Sha Tau Kok was to be made on 24 June. Two hundred coolies stormed the Police road block and a cordon that had been established to protect the Police Post and thwart the removal of the Union Jack. A major riot followed, which the Police dealt with by firing wooden baton rounds, smoke and tear gas. The coolies threw Molotov cocktails (petrol bombs) and burnt Police vehicles. Some coolies and Police were injured but the Police had the better of the confrontation, by using a reserve company

---

92   . Bickers and Yep, editors, May Days in Hong Kong Riot and Emergency in 1967, p.23.

specially trained to deal with riots. This had formed up in riot squad formation outside the Rural Committee building, which the Police occupied.[93]

Although the Police got the better of the militants on 24 June steps were taken to reinforce Sha Tau Kok when information from Special Branch indicated that the militants had plans to do something there on 8 July. An additional Pakistani platoon from the EUNT of the HKP was deployed in the Police Post (see Map p.113). The post was a substantial two-storey stone building topped by an observation tower and surrounded by a chain-link fence. It was to all intents and purposes a small Police Station with its own offices, cells, barrack rooms, armoury and cookhouse. The windows were protected by strong wire mesh and the first floor walls had firing loopholes. It was about 20 yards from the border and in the post on 8 July there were 86 Hong Kong policemen, predominantly Pakistani with some Chinese. A Police Tactical Unit (PTU) company of three platoons was based in the Rural Committee building 150 yards behind the Police Post, while Inspector Jim Main's Tau Ku Ling frontier platoon was at Sha Tau Kok Main, a mile behind the border, as a reserve. Main had reason to be wary about Sha Tau Kok; he and his platoon had been on duty there during the 24 June incident.[94] Main's landrover had been set alight by a Molotov cocktail when he was inside its central radio compartment reporting on crowd numbers. The crowd broke through the cordon his platoon was providing in front of the Police Post close to the border. Main was not aware that the vehicle was on fire and was saved by his driver, who abandoned his position in the cordon, leapt into the burning landrover and drove it out of harm's way, scattering the rioters as he went, and then, under a hail of stones and bottles, dragged Main clear of the landrover and into the Police Post.[95]

At 0900 hours on 8 July Main was directed to take his platoon forward to reinforce the PTU company. He reached the Rural Committee building shortly after 0915 hours, by which

93 . Main, JS, Assistant Commissioner (Retired) RHKP, 'The Sha Tau Kok Incident, 8 July 1967', unpublished account dated 24 June 2017 sent to R. Litherland.

94 . Main, 'The Sha Tau Kok Incident, 8 July 1967', unpublished account dated 24 June 2017 sent to R. Litherland.

95 . Inspector Main's driver PC 1421 TANG Wong-yau received the Colonial Police Medal for Gallantry.

time there had already been a build-up of people on the Chinese side of the border. Shortly before 1000 hours there was a sudden upsurge of noise and 300 to 400 people surged across the border and using stones, bottles and 'fish-bombs' attacked the Police Post and two unmanned Police 'armoured cars' that had been placed across the road as a barrier.[96] The Police Post was clearly under pressure so the PTU company formed up in riot formation eight-abreast outside the Rural Committee building; 10 Platoon was in front followed by 12 Platoon and then 11 Platoon. They formed up, as they had done on 24 June, on the main Sha Tau Kok road that went straight up to the small square on Chung Ying street (the border), where there was a pillbox building on the Chinese side. Main's platoon also formed up eight-abreast in riot formation behind the third platoon of the PTU company. 10 Platoon was ordered forward and advanced 100 yards until it was outside the Fire Station. Once there it fired tear gas at the rioters. It has been suggested that firecrackers were then set off by the militants probably as a signal to the crowd to disperse and, as it did so, a Chinese automatic weapon opened fire from an elevated position, probably on the flat roof behind the pillbox. It fired over the pillbox, the armoured car barrier and the heads of the remaining rioting militants. Much of the fire appears to have gone over 10 Platoon, because 12 and 11 Platoons to the rear suffered the initial casualties. Main heard the rattle of machine gun fire, saw spouts of dirt coming off the tarmac road and saw the PTC company and his own men scattering. One Policeman in 12 Platoon was killed instantly, another died of his wounds and several were wounded. Main took cover beside the PTU company commander's landrover, which was parked outside the Rural Committee building.

The precise time that the Hong Kong Government ordered that a battalion of Gurkhas be sent forward to Sha Tau Kok Main Police Station is not clear, but after a quick 'O' Group in Ronnie's office at Cassino Lines the leading elements of the Battalion deployed. Ronnie later wrote, 'By early July, we had grown so used to standing by, but never being used, that the events of Saturday, 8 July, found us initially off balance.'[97] In an effort to help others, Lieutenant Nick Worthington, the Motor Transport Officer (MTO), had loaned out some of the

96 . A 'fish-bomb' was an illegal bomb used by fishermen to stun fish.
97 . McAlister, Bugle & Kukri Vol.2, p.249.

Battalion's vehicles, so its operational deployment was hampered by a shortage of the correct types. B Company 'went to war' in the white buses that usually took the Battalion's children to school.

All Ronnie knew was that rioters from across the border had attacked the Police Post at Sha Tau Kok and when a Police reserve company formed up in IS box formation and prepared to march forward, it had been accurately fired upon by a machine gun from Chinese territory. Ronnie with Tac HQ and D Company, commanded by Pike, reached Sha Tau Kok Main Police Station, about a mile back from the border, at about 1030 hours just as the initial automatic firing died down. Other companies followed as transport that had been unwittingly dispersed was gathered up and a troop of armoured cars, manned by The Life Guards, arrived in support. Information was scarce and precisely what had happened was not clear; what was known was that the opposition, whoever they were, had fired at the Police reinforcements causing casualties and the Police in the Sha Tau Kok Police Post and the Rural Committee Building 150 yards behind it were under siege and pinned down by accurate sniper fire from China and positions inside British territory. The spasmodic and over-excited Police radio transmissions indicated that there had been further Police casualties. What was even less clear was what Colonel Ronnie and 1/10GR were permitted to do to assist the Police. The Hong Kong Government was loath to commit the military in the border area and certainly did not want to start a shooting war with China. They procrastinated and referred the matter to London, where, given the eight-hour time difference, only a skeleton night staff was on duty. The Policemen under fire and trapped in Sha Tau Kok had a desperate wait while the decision-makers in London were roused from their beds.

There were 86 Policemen trapped in the Police Post, the men of 10 Platoon were caught in the open beside or behind the locked Fire Station and most of the men in 12 and 11 Platoons and the Tau Ku Ling Platoon took cover in the area of the Rural Committee building. Those who scattered to the left, or west, of the Sha Tau Kok road had little cover in the paddy fields and scrub and ran the risk of being shot when running for the cover of the buildings. It was an uncomfortably hot day and anyone who emerged in the open was shot at. They were in a desperate situation and there was little they could do. They were under strict orders not to fire over the border and they were inadequately equipped: the majority were not armed or trained to deal with armed militia, let alone the Chinese Communist Army (CCA).[98] A few Policemen were armed with .30in M1 Carbines and the Police Post did have one .303in Bren Gun, or LMG, but the majority just had riot guns or revolvers, or were unarmed. Their weapons were no match for the number and type of those at the opposition's disposal. Sniper fire from well-concealed positions was immediate and so accurate that any movement near a window or opening was likely to result in a casualty. A Policeman[99] in 10 Platoon was killed by a sniper and two Pakistani policemen[100] in the upper lookout tower were killed by machine gun fire when they tried to set up the LMG to return fire through the lookout's fire slits, several were wounded and they needed better medical attention than any of the positions were equipped to provide. Dr CY Sam, from the Jockey Club Clinic, was in the Police Post and administered such first aid as he could, and said afterwards, 'It was pretty hectic up there. You couldn't stand or sit up because of the flying bullets. We had to crawl on our hands and knees to reach wounded men.'[101] Outside the Police Post they could hear hostile crowds moving still closer and attempting to blow up the protective fence around the post. They did not know whether an armed assault on the post was imminent or what the next moves of the opposition might be. Their position was dire and the completely unexpected killing of their comrades had an understandable effect on their morale; however, the fight had not gone out of all of them and they shot at close range one of two saboteurs placing a satchel bomb adjacent to the Police Post fence.

---

98 . In a typical Police Platoon there were four sections of eight men (A corporal and seven constables). No.1 Section was 'Minimum Force' equipped with an 18-inch rattan shield and an 18-inch wooded riot baton; No.2 Section was 'Second Stage Force' armed with four 1.5 inch pistols that fired tear gas cartridges and four 1.5 inch Federal guns that fired smoke shells; No.3 Section was 'Armed Force' with four Martini-action Greener shotguns that fired 12 .303in pellets about 30 yards and four .30in M1 Carbines, light rifle of WW2 vintage; No.4 Section was 'Lock-Up', equipped with short batons and handcuffs. The Platoon Commander had a .38in revolver, the Platoon Sergeant a Sterling sub-machine gun and the Platoon HQ Orderly a .30in M1 Carbine.

99 . PC 7266 Wong Loi-hing.

100 . PC 3015 Khurshid Ahmed and PC 3033 Mohamed Nawaz Malik both from EUNT, No 1 Platoon.

101 . South China Sunday Post-Herald, Hong Kong, Sunday, July 9 1967, Front Page continued on p.2. col. 3.

In the Rural Committee building the position was not dissimilar. It was not long before gunmen from the Chinese side had worked their way into firing positions on a series of knolls inside Hong Kong to the north-west of the Rural Committee building, and gunmen were firing from positions just across the border in China. At least one sniper was in the area of the flats near the public toilet block to the east of the Rural Committee building. The firing from the knolls made Main's cover by the PTU landrover untenable and he moved to the Rural Committee building where most of his platoon and the PTU company were holed up. Although they were pinned down by automatic fire from at least three positions inside Hong Kong, two police corporals, both the type who in normal times hovered on the edge of insubordination and disciplinary charges but who when the chips were down produced something extra, organised a determined resistance. They gathered all the M1 Carbines, about 20 in total, and the ammunition, and called for volunteers to man the firing loopholes on a roster basis. What followed was what seemed like a long afternoon of sporadic exchanges of fire. On his third stint at a loophole Main and others engaged two armed men seen moving between positions, both were hit and fell, and lay where they had fallen. The occupants of both the Police Post and the Rural Committee building fought back as best they could, but they were hopelessly outmatched. Five policemen, two of them Pakistanis and three of them Chinese, had been killed, and 13 had been wounded. Main, although not one of those recorded as wounded, was hit by a ricochet, the hot, almost spent round, lodging in his arm. The Police had no idea what might happen next and they knew the only reinforcements who might be able to help had to be the Army.

At around 1310 hours Colonel Ronnie was finally given orders to go to the assistance of the Police. He recalled:

I shall never forget the stark clarity and brevity of Brigadier Peter Martin's orders to me over the telephone. 'Can you hear me?' he said. 'Yes' – 'Quite clearly?' – 'Yes' – 'You are to clear British territory of armed infiltrators. Have you any questions?' I said, 'No' and rang off. I was, however, not quite so confident as I may have sounded, for the ground was quite new to us and our vantage point on the roof of the Sha Tau Kok Main had not permitted us, even with binoculars, to get a complete picture of the ground; nor had

Police radio information, trickling back spasmodically and always over-excitedly, and even at times hysterically, been of much help. I was launching the Battalion into the unknown. I consoled myself with the thought, which many Commanding Officers of Gurkha Battalions must have had before me, that any inadequacies in my plan or orders would surely be more than balanced by the resolute actions of the soldiers. So it turned out.

For some this recollection might suggest that the CO of 1/10GR and his Battalion had not done their homework. Why was he launching his Battalion into the unknown and why did he not have a complete picture of the ground? For at least three months 1/10GR had been the designated 'Frontier Battalion' and there had been ample time for them to carry out detailed reconnaissance of the border. The problem was that the entire border was a closed area, the prevailing view of the Hong Kong Government, and presumably of London, being that the risk of provoking the Chinese by sending the Army up to the border was not to be taken. So 1/10GR, despite being the Frontier Battalion, had not been permitted to enter the 'closed area' on the border. A political decision prevented it from carrying out the basic first step that is essential for any likely operation.

Planning and discussion took place between 1030 hours and 1310 hours, while London was consulted, and Ronnie knew his tasks were:

a. To secure Sha Tau Kok Village up to the line of the Border and clear British Territory of armed aggressors.

b. Having secured the village, to evacuate the Police from it.

He had also discussed with Brigadier Martin what rules of engagement should be applied. Nothing had officially been laid down. Policemen had been killed by fire from both sides of the border and there was no knowing what the reaction of the armed aggressors would be to the arrival of well-armed troops. It was clear that in achieving the tasks the aim was to avoid a shooting war if at all possible. The Brigadier had therefore told Ronnie to obey the principle of minimum force. British troops were only to shoot back in self-defence when the fire against them was effective; however, if there was a full blooded attack on them the situation could be treated as one of war.[102]

Colonel Ronnie held a quick 'O' Group to confirm the position and after the orders had been disseminated the Battalion advanced, with D Company moving off first to the left of the road, through the scrubby hills and over a series of tactical features towards Lone Tree Hill that dominated the village and Shan Tsui village from where an opposition machine gun was reported to be firing. A Company, supported by a troop of The Life Guards in armoured cars, was on the right, moving up the line of the road into Sha Tau Kok. They moved off at about 1410 hours.[103] Colonel Ronnie with his Tactical Headquarters was immediately behind 2 Troop, B Squadron, The Life Guards, commanded by Lieutenant Bickmore.[104] B Company of 1/10GR was in reserve, and its OC Bruce Niven, from the roof of Sha Tau Kok Main Police Station, acted as a radio rebroadcast link between Colonel Ronnie in dead ground and Brigade HQ now set up in Fanling Police-Military HQ.

As the 1/10GR force advanced a further firefight started between the snipers and the Police in the Rural Committee building. Then, as the leading Saladin of The Life Guards and A Company rounded the bend on the Sha Tau Kok road that brought the village into sight, one medium machine gun and some light machine guns started firing straight down the road, along which A Company, the Life Guards and Tactical HQ were advancing.[105] Colonel Ronnie recalled:

> Brigadier Martin landed on the road by helicopter right beside my Tac HQ and told me to press forward at best speed. We walked up the road together and had just come level with the troop leader's armoured car when the MMG opened up. The armoured cars 'closed down': the leading one was hit by a few rounds which ricochetted off into the distance. The Brigadier and I took cover behind the troop

---

102 . Martin, P.L.de C, Confrontation on the Hong Kong Border 1967, Appendix 5 to Bugle & Kukri Vol.2, pp.492–506.
103 . The Acorn, Regimental Magazine of The Life Guards, Autumn 1967, Vol. 1, No. 4, p.12.
104 . The Acorn, Autum 1967, p.66.
105 . There is some confusion about the fire that was opened. Brigadier Martin suggests 'all hell broke loose' with a heavy machine gun and light machine guns firing. IWM 12778, audio recording of PL de C Martin, Reel 17, dated '1992-11-12'.

leader's vehicle and we were joined by Captain (QGO) Bhaktabahadur Limbu DCM.[106] I found his presence comforting. As the MMG continued to fire short bursts, we periodically looked round our cover trying to pin-point the origin of the fire. None of us could tell and it improved morale no end to find that Bhakte's pin-pointing of the enemy was no better than mine.

A round from the MMG, possibly a ricochet, passed between Andy Watt's legs and hit the Tac HQ landrover beside which he was standing. Nick Worthington was also there, having brought the Commanding Officer's landrover forward. They both took cover in a ditch behind a small clump of bamboo, the MMG fire prompting Watt to say 'This is war'. After about five minutes the MMG stopped firing and the advance continued. As Colonel Ronnie marched forward he saw Watt and Worthington in the ditch and said 'What are you doing down there? Get up!'

Jonathan Edwardes' recollection of A Company's advance is that there were two different occasions when the opposition opened fire. He wrote:

Shortly after we had fanned out with two platoons leading, followed by Company HQ and the third platoon, there was a heavy burst of firing from the area of the village. We all hit the ground but it seemed that it was not aimed at us. It lasted for not more than a few minutes. After a period of time, during which there was no firing, we moved forward with some caution. It was not long before there was more firing and of course we hit the ground again, but on this occasion, it was abundantly clear that we were the target. For my part I ended up behind a bank with my wireless operator. The splashes caused by the bullets hitting the water of the paddy field immediately behind me was all the evidence I needed! The sound of the firing indicated it was small arms and LMG fire, although in my case whoever was firing was firing single shots. The firing was intense and lasted about 15 minutes. We were unable to pin-point exactly where the firing was coming from and there was no urgency to engage and return fire. On reflection, the proximity of the bullets splashing so close behind me, indicated that the firing was

---

106 . Captain (QGO) Bhaktabahadur Limbu DCM was the Second-in-Command of A Company.

from a height because of the trajectory. Shortly after the firing stopped, the CO called me on the radio. 'Are you alright?' he asked. 'Yes.' I replied to which he responded. 'Thank God for that.' It was the only radio contact we had. In fact it turned out that we had one minor injury – a Rifleman lost a finger from a bullet. There then followed a long period when nothing much happened – no firing and no movement. The impasse and situation changed with the almost simultaneous appearance of a Saladin, battened down, moving slowly along the road towards the village – a very reassuring sight – and the CO striding along at a pace passed my protective bank uttering the words 'It's all over, follow me.' At times like that, priorities change quite rapidly, and my primary thought was to give some form of protection to the CO. The nearest platoon had some difficulty keeping up with him, as their forward movement was somewhat more tactical than the CO's. As we passed the Rural Committee Building four or five Chinese ran out in their underpants. At least three headed towards the village and Fire Station, overtaking the CO in the process. I then set about deploying the company to occupy the village and it was not until much later that I had a look around. I saw no bodies or wounded but there was quite a lot of blood everywhere. As we prepared for the night within yards of the border I was in a state of some bemusement over what had gone on and what might follow. What I never anticipated was the sight and sound of the Pipes and Drums the following morning marching along the road that had been a killing field the day before. [107]

Edwardes is convinced it was the Police in the Rural Committee Building who, thinking the advancing Gurkhas were Chinese militia, fired at them from the Rural Committee Building. That some of them, having discarded their uniforms, fled from the Rural Committee Building away from the advancing Gurkhas and towards the Police Post would support this, and suggests the Police had not received the message that the Gurkhas had been ordered to secure Sha Tau Kok and rescue them from their ordeal.

---

107 . JAS Edwardes, Letter and Attachments relating to Hong Kong 1967, dated 8 Oct 2018.

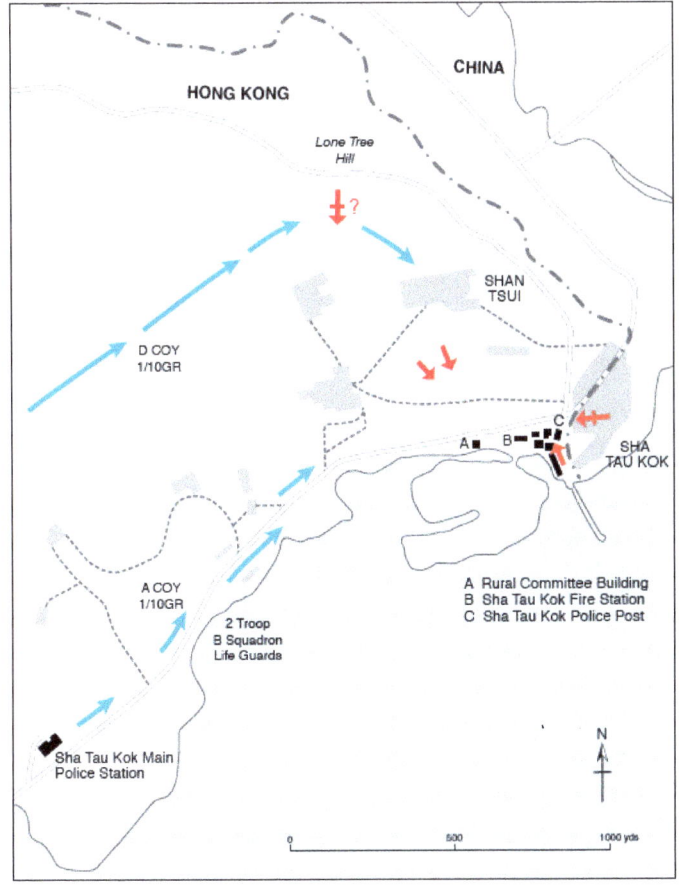

Sketch Map – 8 July 1967 Sha Tau Kok Incident

The diary entries made by Gilly Edwardes, Jonathan's wife, are interesting. She wrote:

> *08 July 1967. Had hair done. 1/10GR went to Sha Tau Kok. 300 Chinese came over the border, five policemen killed. 1/10GR are manning the police post. All rather nasty. Hope J will be OK. Dinner with Sally (McAlister).*
>
> *09 July 1967. J eventually came back at 7.30 pm, worn out but rather pleased about everything, 1/10GR did very well. Ronnie (McAlister) very brave.*

In its obituary on Major General RWL McAlister, *The Times* covered this advance and suggested:

> The voice of the British Gurkha battalion commander could be heard across the paddy fields: 'Kukris out!' Within an instant, the sun reflecting off the steel of the Gurkhas' curved, unsheathed knives sent a flash of brilliant light into the sky.
>
> It was the defining moment in an action that could have led to war between Britain and China over Hong Kong — and it instilled sheer terror into the minds of the hundreds of Chinese troops who had burst over the border into Hong Kong's frontier village of Sha Tau Kok. They retreated.[108]

Quite where this 'boys' own' version of what happened came from is not known, but it was an astonishing fabrication for such a renowned newspaper. Colonel Ronnie gave no such order. Kukris were not drawn, there were no brilliant flashes and glinting kukris did not instil sheer terror in the minds of hundreds of Chinese troops. What actually happened was rather more mundane. In the face of two companies of armed Gurkha soldiers, supported by armoured cars with 76mm guns, the other side did not oppose 1/10GR's deliberate tactical advance. The Chinese militia who had been in British territory, and there were not hundreds of them, melted away. Brigadier Martin later recorded that with the benefit of hindsight he thought the machine gun fire he and Ronnie took cover from behind the Life Guards' Saladins was in fact covering fire by the opposition to help their forces to withdraw back across the border.[109] *The Times* obituary on Major General Peter Martin records that:

> Martin was ordered to retake the police post, release the hostages and clear the village. He chose 1/10th Gurkha Rifles under Lieutenant Colonel Ronnie McAlister to lead, with a troop of Life Guard armoured cars in support followed by his own tactical HQ. The approach was over paddy fields devoid of cover but McAlister turned this to advantage by deploying his companies in extended order on

---

108 . The Times, Obituary for Major General RWL McAlister CB OBE, Sep 12, 2015. The same obituary suggested Ronnie quoted Shakespeare, despite being told by Sally McAlister that he did not. He did quote Burns and Kipling.
109 . Martin, PLdeC, audio recording by Conrad Wood, IWM catalogue no.12778, dated 1992-11-12.

114

each side of the central road. When the Gurkhas were 300 yards short of the village, the invaders fell over themselves in a race to the border, some, in the words of a hostage policeman, 'browning their trousers as they fled.'[110]

The last sentence may be as fanciful as the glinting kukris in McAlister's obituary, but on the arrival of 1/10GR and the Life Guards the shooting certainly stopped. The myth about the terror that Gurkhas instil in their opponents, which some writers feel it is necessary to perpetuate, is of course helpful. Getting your opponents to run away is one of the better ways of securing a victory.

Main remembers that late in the afternoon there was a sudden and to him alarming outbreak of furious, heavy and sustained firing, during which a number of rounds hit the Rural Committee building. When the firing stopped after several minutes, he looked out and noticed the two fallen bodies had gone. Pike was the first British Officer into the Police Post at about 1630 hours; neither it nor the Rural Committee building were pretty sights, with discarded uniforms and the blood of the casualties much in evidence. By 1700 hours the British section of Sha Tau Kok had been secured. The wounded and five dead were evacuated; the Police were relieved and C Company, still commanded by Captain Chris Hughes, came forward to help A and D Companies consolidate the position. D Company dug in on the little hills to the left of the village, A Company built defensive positions on the top of every commanding building within 100 yards of the border, while C Company did the same further back in the area of the Rural Committee building. Tac HQ occupied the Fire Station 50 yards from the border. Colonel Ronnie wrote:

> It was an unmilitary, uncanny, unreal feeling for commanders at all levels, standing in the open directing soldiers to the best fire positions while perhaps 200 Chinese soldiers and Militia trained their weapons at us at ranges of fifty yards or less, across an unwired, scarcely discernible border in a scruffy village of minimal value to either side.[111]

---

110. The Times, Obituary for Major General PL de C Martin CBE, Feb 15, 2006.
111. McAlister, Bugle & Kukri, Vol.2, p.252

Back at Sha Tau Kok Main that evening, Niven watched refugees coming up the road from the village. Men, women and children drove or pulled livestock and carried household belongings in bundles at the end of coolie poles or pushed hand carts. As they passed by, his thoughts ran along the lines of 'these are people of the frontier who have a feel for the place and country cousins on both sides: they must know there is more and bigger trouble ahead. What will the night bring and are the refugees a forewarning of things to come?' An uneasy but uneventful night followed and next day 1/10GR was relieved by 1/7GR. 1/10GR was tasked with preparing for similar incursions, demonstrations and incidents along the whole border, which, as the Frontier Battalion, it was responsible for. It was not long before they were back in action.

The Sha Tau Kok battle was regarded as a victory by both the Communist Chinese and their supporters in Hong Kong. In Beijing Hopson asked for an interview with Chinese Deputy Foreign Minister, Lo Kuei-po, to protest about what had happened. This was granted but before he made his protest he was handed a Note giving the Chinese version of what happened. The text of the Note was later published by the New China News Agency. It stated:

On July 8 people on our side of Sha Tau Kok and Chinese inhabitants of the 'New Territories' in Kowloon held a rally on our side to voice support for our patriotic countrymen in Hongkong and Kowloon in their just struggle against brutal persecution by the British authorities in Hongkong. After the rally, they demonstrated along different routes. When the Chinese inhabitants were returning to the 'New Territories' in Kowloon from the demonstrations, fully-armed policemen and 'riot-police' of the British Authorities in Hong Kong flagrantly carried out a premeditated sanguinary suppression at them, throwing tear-bombs and opening fire at them, and at the same time fired at our side.

The Chinese frontier guards at once fired warning shots against such atrocities and provocations by the British side. But, in total disregard of the warnings from our side, the policemen and 'riot police' of the British Authorities in Hongkong continued to fire at the demonstrators, killing one and wounding eight of them.

Our frontier guards also fired back at the policemen and 'riot-police' of the British Authorities in Hong Kong.[112]

The Chinese demanded a public apology and guarantees that nothing similar would happen. They also demanded that the culprits be punished and compensation be paid to the relatives of the dead and wounded, and those arrested in the previous 'sanguinary atrocity' in Sha Tau Kok. Hopson refused to accept the Note and lodged a strong counter-protest against the Chinese. It was brushed aside by Lo Kuei-po. Later the Foreign Office announced Britain's official protest to China, supporting Hopson's version of events.

On the Hong Kong side of the border the Government's avowed policy of being 'firm but unprovocative' was the instruction to all involved; in typical British Army fashion the soldiers re-phrased this into the more down-to-earth soldierly phrase 'be kind to coolies', which was to be applied whatever they did. This presented problems, as is often the case at the beginning of any confrontation, because it gave the opposition the initiative; and it was difficult to understand and work out what might happen next. The revolutionary masses had no instructions or rules of engagement and they were not being controlled; indeed, in the fever of the Cultural Revolution they were out of control and had little idea of how they were going to further their anti-imperial rhetoric. The Sha Tau Kok battle was a wake-up call, and as it transpired a turning point. A simple appreciation of the situation led the authorities to conclude that the Police were neither trained nor armed to deal with similar armed aggression and the Army should take over responsibility for the border. Permission was granted for the border security to become a Police-Military responsibility. The Police were the local experts with detailed knowledge of the ground and border people; they were, of course, predominantly Chinese and it was important that they should not be seen to have been relieved of their responsibilities or to have lost face.

On 12 July crowds gathered at Lo Wu and A Company 1/10GR was sent in to support the Police. Jonathan Edwards recalled being told there had been a standoff between a crowd of militants and the Police, but by the time A Company reached Lo Wu, in the middle of the night, the station was completely

---

112. Cooper, John, Colony in Conflict: The Hong Kong Disturbances May 1967–January1968, p.108.

empty. He had never seen the place before and without anyone to discuss the situation with he established a defensive position and the company spent an eerie night stood to. Asked in the morning whether he needed anything he asked for two railway carriages to provide some accommodation for his men. They were delivered within hours. At this stage Police morale was low so, on 13 July, the Army took over all the main border posts and Police stations. It was far from clear how the Army should act and what it was permitted to do. The Brigadier sought advice. The Political Advisor from the Hong Kong Government said he hoped that somehow the border should be maintained without getting involved in a war. The Psychological Warfare team were more helpful and said that the Army should carry out its duties in a ceremonial manner rather than an operational one because the construction of defensive positions and digging in would only provoke the Chinese into doing the same; the Chinese had far greater resources close by and the arrival of large bodies of Chinese soldiers on the border would have a disastrous effect on the morale of the population of Hong Kong. The rules of engagement were clarified and it was laid down that:

a.   If fired at from British territory, British troops could retaliate immediately.

b.   If fired at from Chinese territory, British troops could retaliate if the fire was effective, but only with the same type of weapon as was being used against them, and then only if they could identify where the fire was coming from. But there was a provisio that we could not answer mortar or artillery fire with mortars or artillery without the prior consent of the Government, except in the gravest emergency.

The last two weeks of July were relatively quiet. It was subsequently learned that this was probably because the beginning of August heralded the return to the border of some 800 Chinese Militia who had been away for a fortnight of intensive training. Increasingly bold demonstrations that crossed into British territory, and the use of children to thrown stones at British troops, put a severe strain on 'turning the other cheek' and 'being kind to coolies'.

General Sir Michael Carver, Commander-in-Chief Far East being briefed by Colonel Ronnie on the border July 1967[113]

On 3 August B Company, under Niven, dispersed a stone-throwing mob at Lo Wu three times, by using tear gas.

The Man Kam To 'Tea Party'

On 5 August an incident at Man Kam To, later described in the press as the 'The Man Kam To Tea Party', illustrates well how those involved had to think on their feet when dealing with unpredictable revolutionaries. That morning the coolies who crossed the bridge daily with vegetables on trollies for loading onto lorries on the British side came across as usual. There were about 50 of them. Noticing that their posters had been taken down, they had a quiet talk together and turned as if to march back across the bridge, but then 'jumped' the ceremonial style policeman and sentry on duty and disarmed them, taking the policeman's Sterling sub-machine gun and the Gurkha rifleman's rifle. Lieutenant (QGO) Dhanraj Rai, the local Platoon Commander went forward unarmed and began to talk to the coolies. He was joined by Pike who continued to parley with the coolies. The Brigadier, who happened to be nearby at Tau Ku Ling, was alerted. He ordered a troop of armoured cars

113 . 1/10GR Photograph Album, Gurkha Museum.

forward to Man Kam To and went to the scene, and, as he himself suggested later, he rather foolishly got involved. He was astonished that Pike was calmly talking to the coolies while they held the weapons that they had seized. The Brigadier spent the next three hours trying, through a Police Sergeant interpreter, to carry out a logical discussion with people to whom logic was entirely meaningless. He asked them what the trouble was. They responded by saying someone had taken their posters down and they demanded that whoever did it should be punished and must promise never to take their posters down again; that there should be no reprisals for the seizing of the weapons of the policeman and the soldier and that they must be allowed to sing and chant the thoughts of Chairman Mao and work in peace. The Brigadier said that he could not punish anyone for taking the posters down as inflammatory posters were against the law. He asked the coolies if they would expect him to obey the law if he went to China. They agreed he would have to obey the law. They then asked how they were expected to know the law in Hong Kong. The Brigadier said he would get someone to explain it to them. The coolies then said they did not wish to know the law in Hong Kong and again demanded that whoever took down the posters should be punished. The Brigadier then asked the coolies whether they studied the thoughts of Chairman Mao. They said of course they did. The Brigadier then asked them why they had disobeyed them. The coolies asked how they had disobeyed the thoughts of Chairman Mao, which allowed the Brigadier to point out that Chairman Mao had said you must never hurt anyone first. Why then had they attacked the policeman and soldier? For a moment this put the coolies on the back-foot, but one of them said the sentries had pointed their weapons at them. The Brigadier responded that that was nonsense and they knew it and drew their attention to another of Chairman Mao's thoughts which was that if you do damage, you must pay for it. The Brigadier pointed to the broken tiles on the roof of the Police Post which the stone throwing children had done. The coolies said they had no control over their children, which allowed the Brigadier to question how they could expect their children to follow the thoughts of Chairman Mao if they had no discipline. At this stage, when the coolies were looking rather sheepish, two coolies appeared from the Chinese side carrying buckets of tea. A tea break followed with both sides sharing the Chinese tea. After the break the Brigadier asked the coolies why their posters were so important to them; they responded by saying that they were an inspiration to them and helped them work harder. The Brigadier then suggested that if we permitted them to put up posters in our territory it would only be fair that they let the British put up posters in their territory. There was a general murmur of consent but one of their number went back across the bridge to get official guidance and came back later to say it would not be possible for the British to put up posters in Chinese territory because they did not work there. The Brigadier then asked why they put up inflammatory posters on our side and why they attacked the policeman and soldier. The coolies suggested they were supporting their compatriots in Hong Kong against the British oppressors. Pointing to the Gurkha soldiers quietly drinking their tea, the Brigadier asked whether they looked like oppressors, adding that if they were oppressors they would have shot you for attacking our people. The Brigadier then offered to take two of them in his staff car on a conducted tour of Hong Kong to see the situation for themselves. The coolies were clearly tempted but the offer was declined. The Brigadier then pointed to one of the posters which said 'Kill all the Hong Kong British' and asked the coolies whether they wished to kill him. They were quick to assure him that they did not wish to kill him which allowed him to ask them why then had they put up such inflammatory posters.

The discussion had become quite friendly so Brigadier said we would have no objection if they put up a reasonable number of posters provided they carried the thoughts of Chairman Mao as contained in the red book. The coolies suggested that Chairman Mao was always having new thoughts but the Brigadier insisted that only the thoughts in the red book could be used. One coolie suggested he had read somewhere in the book that the British were Revisionists. The Brigadier said that he had no idea what that meant but if it was in the red book that would be all right with him. He then asked the coolies whether they would respect posters on the thoughts of our great Chairman Harold Wilson if we put them up on the walls of the Police Post or whether they would paste their posters over the top of them. They said that they would respect the thoughts of Chairman Harold Wilson. At this stage Trevor Bedford, the New Territories District Officer, arrived and a statement outlining what could and could not be done when on Hong Kong territory was drawn up and handed to one of the coolie leaders. The

Brigadier then suggested they shake hands to settle the matter, however the coolies said they wanted him to punish whoever had taken their posters down. The whole discussion started all over again. Eventually the coolies accepted the statement, handed back the weapons and returned peacefully to work.

Thinking a potentially nasty situation had been resolved in a common sense manner the Brigadier returned to Brigade Headquarters feeling quite pleased, but the arrival of the Political Advisor by helicopter put a different complexion on things when he said: 'Brigadier, do you realise the appalling situation we are now in, you have signed a Treaty with Red China'. As it transpired this was not the case, because treaties have to be signed by both parties and the coolies had not done so. The Brigadier then told the Political Adviser that some posters bearing the thoughts of Harold Wilson were required and received the response: 'But he has not had any.'[114]

Opinion varied on the outcome of the Man Kam To Tea Party. Old China hands thought it had been well handled and that the Man Kam To coolies, who were of course Man Kam To militia, were likely to have been reprimanded for throwing away a tactical advantage without gaining any concessions. On the other hand the hawks felt it was appalling that a bunch of coolies had been allowed to get away with disarming a policeman and a soldier without being shot or imprisoned as a result. The hawks thought the Brigadier had been wet. Colonel Ronnie thought otherwise and summed up all that happened quite simply by writing:

> Brigadier Martin handled this situation superbly. When the coolies' spokesman said they always put up posters of Chairman Mao's 'thoughts' wherever they were working, and it was an insult to pull them down, the Brigadier agreed to respect them in future provided the coolies respected our posters on the 'thoughts' of Prime Minister Harold Wilson.[115]

The coolies tended their farms diligently for a few days. It was clear they were Militia as they marched to and from work in formed squads. What was not so clear was that they were

---

114 . Martin, PL de C, Confrontation on the Hong Kong Border 1967, reproduced as Appendix 5 in McAlister, Bugle & Kukri, Vol.2, pp. 499–501.
115 . McAlister, Bugle & Kukri, Vol.2, p.253.

smarting from a reprimand and were looking for an opportunity to stir things up again.

As this was happening on the border the Acting Governor Michael Gass took further firm action.[116] For some time there had been consideration of taking action against the nine pro-Beijing newspapers, which had a circulation of some 400,000 in Hong Kong, and published pro-communist propaganda, inaccurate communist versions of events, gave moral support to the trouble makers and provided cues for action and mobilisation, and also encouraged radicals to take action against the 'imperialists'. Gass obtained agreement to act from London and on 9 August five editors and publishers of three prominent pro-communist papers were arrested and charged.

That 'Damned' Photograph

On the border during the evening of the same day, 9 August, coolies put up posters all over the Man Kam To market square and on the walls of the Police Post in a defiant breach of what had been agreed at the Man Kam To 'Tea Party' on 5 August. The Brigadier decided the posters had to come down. They were taken down on 10 August and to prevent further posters being put on the Police Post and other Government buildings it was decided that some form of protection was required. Initially 1/10GR erected a dannert wire fence around the buildings and instructions were given to 69 Gurkha Independent Engineer Squadron to replace the dannert wire with a chain-link fence during the evening of 11 August. The coolies did not come to work as usual on 11 August; protesting instead from the Chinese end of the bridge by pointing at the Police Post and the obvious disappearance of their posters and at the dannert wire, which protruded a few feet into the road along which the coolies trundled their trolleys of vegetables. It did not prevent them from doing so. A representative from the Man Loon Transport Company, which collected produce from the British side, crossed the bridge to find out what was happening. He reported, although he had been told that on no account was he to inform the British, that the coolies were angry about the removal of their posters and had said that the wire projecting into the road was dangerous and someone might get badly hurt. The Man Loon representative said he thought the British Authorities,

---

116 . The Governor, Trench, was unwell and had returned to UK for treatment.

being reasonable people might agree to adjust the wire. The dannert wire was adjusted so that it could not be construed as an obstacle. By this stage Lt (QGO) Jitman Rai, the platoon commander and a very competent and experienced officer, reported what was happening. Alerted to the situation, which obviously had the potential to develop into a more serious incident, Colonel Ronnie went forward to assess matters and visit the 15-strong platoon based in the Police Post. On his arrival at 1415 hours the CCA stood-to along the border adjacent to the Man Kam To bridge and Police Post. They were in full battle order, with veils over their faces and foliage camouflaging their equipment; they occupied defensive positions and moved forward to the Shum Chun river bank. A 75mm recoilless gun was brought forward, its ammunition was unloaded from boxes and piled beside it and it was trained on the Police Post. Informed that there was a situation brewing, Trevor Bedford, the District Officer based at Tai Po, flew to the border by helicopter and made his way to the Police Post where he joined Colonel Ronnie. On the British side it was clear something was going to happen but nobody knew what or when. At 1430 hours a trolley full of vegetables was pushed across the bridge by half a dozen militants dressed as coolies. It was deliberately rammed into the dannert wire and overturned. One of the coolies threw himself to the ground screaming in agony and his comrades carried him back across the bridge. It was, to the observers, a splendid theatrical performance. In minutes 50 to 60 coolies were protesting at the dannert wire demanding that those who put the wire up should be punished, compensation should be paid for their injured colleague, the wire should immediately be removed and promises given for it never to be erected again. Inspector Jim Main arrived at the Police Post at between 1545 and 1550 hours. He had driven over from Tau Ku Ling, the Frontier Police HQ, where on return from a routine break he had changed into his uniform, before setting off to Man Kam To to relieve Inspector Jim Walker. No one at Tau Ku Ling was aware that anything was amiss at Man Kam To, and Main had no real inkling of what he was walking into as he passed through the chanting militant coolies, by then a familiar sight on the border. They let him through, the Gurkhas hurriedly opening a gap in the dannert wire, but the coolies did not let Walker out. Main came in for some light-hearted ribbing, his colleagues using the analogy that he had left the comparative safety of the lifeboats to return to the stricken *Titanic*.

The British forces of the Man Kam To Police Post garrison now included, from the Army, Colonel Ronnie, 15 Gurkhas, WO2 Pound and a number of Gurkha Engineers, who were building the chain-link fence; the District Officer, Trevor Bedford , and from the Police, Superintendent Paton, Inspectors Main and Walker, and about 12 Police rank and file. For the next six hours on a hot Hong Kong day, they were surrounded by militant coolies and kept confined within the dannert wire around the Police Post. It was an area about the size of a tennis court. Trevor Bedford talked to the coolies while the Gurkha engineers drilled holes and erected the chain-link fence and the small garrison remained alert while relays of militant coolies shouted and chanted and tried to remove the wire. Each time Bedford seemed to be making progress with the coolies a new bunch would arrive, stir up the crowd and he would have to start all over again.

Militant coolies protesting opposite Ronnie McAlister and Trevor Bedford[117]

As it began to get dark, when it was clear the talks between Bedford and the coolies were getting nowhere, there was increased activity on the Chinese side. One of the Police constables in the post drew Main's attention to a large-calibre weapon that was being set up by Chinese militia. Main in turn drew the matter to the attention of Paton who was standing next

117 .1/10GR Photograph Album, Gurkha Museum.

to Colonel Ronnie. They went into the post and from the strongpoint viewed the weapon. Colonel Ronnie said words to the effect of 'Yes, it looks like a Carl Gustav.[118] Don't worry Inspector, it may go off with a bang but it won't last long.'[119] At the time Main thought Colonel Ronnie's remark was rather condescending, and he remains uncertain what Ronnie actually meant. Colonel Ronnie had absolute confidence in the Battalion's war fighting skills and I suspect he may have been trying to indicate that if the weapon was fired it would quickly be taken out by the Gurkhas immediately behind the Post, but did not wish to expand on the damage it might cause to the Police Post. Shortly after this Paton said to Main 'I don't like the way things are going, Jim. I want you to withdraw all the Police into the Police Post and set up a strongpoint with arms and ammunition.' Pound, Walker and Main set up a strongpoint using sandbags on the forward edge of a table, on which they mounted an LMG pointing down the corridor to the main door 25 feet away. Others, armed with an assortment of Sterlings, M1 Carbines and revolvers, adopted defensive positions behind whatever cover they could make within the post.[120]

By 2030 hours when it was dark it seemed clear to Colonel Ronnie and Trevor Bedford on site, and to the Brigadier, who was in contact with Colonel Ronnie by telephone, that the coolies were intent on stopping the completion of the chain-link fence, which would effectively separate the Police Post from the coolies' working area. The Brigadier decided to seek permission from the Police/Military Operations Room in Hong Kong to disperse the coolies back to their side of the bridge using only such force as was necessary. Permission was refused. The Police/Military HQ thought the coolies would soon run out of steam and return home of their own accord. Asked what he thought might happen the Brigadier responded: 'I am not sure what will happen, but I am sure we will have a disaster of some sort.' He rang Colonel Ronnie and told him that he and the small Police-Military garrison would have to stick it out.

---

118   . The British Army issue Carl Gustav was a shoulder-held 84mm recoilless anti-tank weapon.
119   . Main, JS, 'The Man Kam To Incident, 11th–12th August 1967', unpublished account dated 25th May 2017 sent to R. Litherland, paragraph 30.
120   . Main, 'The Man Kam To Incident, 11th–12th August 1967', paragraph 31.

At about 2330 hours, just as the last sector of the chain-link fence was about to be secured, the coolies waved a paper and called Bedford to take it. As he did so the coolies leapt the dannert wire fence and seized him. In a co-ordinated attack other coolies had attached, in the dark, grappling hooks to the dannert wire nearest the bridge, and armed with axes, cargo hooks and pistols quickly surrounded the small garrison. Colonel Ronnie had seconds to react. The wind was in the wrong direction so the use of tear gas to rescue Bedford was not a viable option. Colonel Ronnie tried to draw his pistol but Bedford, who had a knife at his throat, shouted 'Ronnie do not shoot.'[121] Opening fire was not an option, given the presence of the heavily-armed and alert Chinese Army soldiers just across the border only yards away, and the general melee of people from both sides would certainly have resulted in the death of Bedford and others, and it would have escalated the situation to the level of the shooting war that the British were under orders to avoid. It is unlikely, as Pike observed, that Colonel Ronnie could or would have fired as within seconds he, too, had a knife at his throat, was taken hostage and relieved of his pistol. Paton made an attempt to rescue Colonel Ronnie and Bedford but could not get to them. He then attempted to close the main door into the Police Post which the coolies were trying to force. Then, just as the defenders were contemplating whether to open fire, Paton interposed himself between the militant coolies and the Police Post defenders, and ordered them not to fire by shouting 'Do not shoot, Jim, do not shoot. Put down your guns.' Reluctantly they obeyed and put down their weapons, Pound taking the magazine off the LMG and laying it on the table beside the LMG. For Jim Main, this was the single moment of greatest danger in the whole incident; had Paton not decisively ordered them not to fire they probably would have done so.[122] Captain (QGO) Nandabahadur Rai, OC C Company, and Lieutenant (QGO) Jitman Rai and Lieutenant Madankumar Subba had by this time gone forward from the company position behind the post to try and help. They, too, were disarmed and taken hostage along with the rest of the garrison. At Brigade HQ the Brigadier had been receiving a running commentary from Pike, who along with D

121 . Bedford, Trevor, interview by R. Litherland, 10 July 2017.
122 . Main, 'The Man Kam To Incident, 11th–12th August 1967', paragraphs 27–38.

Company, was dug in on the top of Man Kam To hill behind the Police Post. Pike sent two platoons forward to try to affect a recovery of the hostages, but a loudhailer was thrust into Colonel Ronnie's hands and he was told to tell the Gurkhas if they came any closer the hostages would be killed. Corporal Nandabahadur Rai MM, who was with the Recce Platoon in an OP also observing the situation, remembers Colonel Ronnie saying through the loudhailer: '*Khetaharu gholi bilkul na hannu. Gholi hanchhaubhane hamilai mardinchha.*'[123] Bedford also used the loudhailer to say he wanted to be given time to talk his way out of the situation.

The Brigadier told Major Phil Phillips, 1/10GR's Second in Command, to make a plan using two companies to prevent at any cost the abduction of the prisoners across the bridge into China. Pike and Niven, with Phillips, drew up a plan.

From his vantage point on the hill Pike witnessed everything that happened, which he later recorded in an article published in *The Kukri* under the title of 'Coolies of Man Kam To'.[124] He wrote:

> At this early stage of the confrontation we were allowed to do very little without first discussing it with the District Officer and senior police officers. By mid-day, the District Officer, three police officers and the Commanding Officer were in attendance. Negotiations proceeded slowly with continual to-ing and fro-ing across the bridge for instructions. Six o'clock was the deadline when by law all coolies had to be over the border, and the bridge was closed. By five o'clock it had been agreed that the wire fence would be moved a few feet.
>
> A small party of sappers was called in to drill holes in the road for a permanent fence to be constructed inside the one through which all negotiations were taking place. The coolies were allowed to remain on British territory in order to witness the construction. Bearing in mind the key to all internal security problems is 'minimum force', or so we are told, there was little we could do about it anyway.
>
> By ten o'clock, and under the glare of the police arc lights which lit up the whole market area, the drilling was completed and the picquets were ready to be wired up. The

123 . 'Soldiers, under no circumstances open fire. If you fire, they will kill us.'
124 . Pike, 'Coolies of Man Kam To', The Kukri, No.24, May 1972, pp.92–95.

negotiators were all present, none of them paying much attention to the non-stop chattering on the other side of the wire; they were tired and bored but had to stay to see the job completed satisfactorily. Two of the coolies attracted the District Officer's attention, intimating that they wished to hand him a sheet of paper through the wire. He strolled over, and as he reached to receive it he was grabbed and held to the wire. Simultaneously four coolies appeared from behind the police post, arms were snatched and with a carbine levelled at the District Officer's head and a pistol covering the CO and one of the police officers, the coolies of Man Kam To were once again in control. The whole action was so quick that watching every movement from some high ground overlooking the police post it was impossible to see how it could have happened. The CO and section of Gurkhas were powerless. I then witnessed one of the most humiliating sights ever to befall any soldier, particularly a Gurkha; their weapons were taken from them and there was nothing anybody could do about it. So much for 'minimum force'!

Using a loud hailer the CO ordered that no action was to be attempted, but that negotiations would continue. We then witnessed regional militia forces at work and began to realise just how well trained they were. In next to no time the wire was removed, the area cleared, four sandbagged machine gun positions constructed and three machine guns appeared out of the darkness. Now we knew what we were up against. The only light left on; the one above the police post, glared down on an eerie scene; five officers[125] from various services seated in a row surrounded by coolies and Red Guards all brandishing weapons.

Niven, with B Company down in dead ground in the area of the lairage for animals and produce, recalled the part played by B Company in the night's events:

As tension mounted, Pike (on the hill) relayed all Brigade's orders to me. I could not hear Brigade from my lowly position. I decided to try to prevent an abduction by deploying my men up to the bridge from both flanks. On ordering my two platoons forward, I heard a deafening

---

125 . There were in fact seven hostages, as the photograph on page 112 shows.

sound (or so it seemed in the still, electric atmosphere near the bridge that night!) of old fashioned ammunition boots

'Not that damned photograph again.'[126]

Seated left to right: Lt Col Ronnie McAlister, Trevor Bedford DO, Public Works Department Rep, Sup Bill Paton HKP, WO2 Dave Pound RE, Insp Jim Walker HKP and Insp Jim Main HKP seated on the ground.

coming clumping down the tarmac of the approach road to the bridge. These boots belonged to the 10GR new recruits – just arrived from the Training Depot that day – and now going straight to war. I had to stop the noise somehow as the Chinese militia were by now extremely jumpy as they stood threateningly over the CO, DO and Superintendent Paton – and so I ordered the recruits to remove their boots. They thus went to war in their stockinged feet – but it was a dry night and they got to the bridge without too much noise.

At about 0230 hours the Brigadier spoke to General Worsley and told him that he thought the situation had to be restored before first light. With the Chinese Army in full battle order on the other side of the bridge, the Brigadier reasoned that they were bound to intervene if a rescue was mounted in daylight. He

---

126 .1/10GR Photograph Album, Gurkha Museum.

asked for permission to move on the bridge before first light, fully recognising that some, if not all the hostages might be killed in the process. At 0415 hours permission for him to proceed was given. Pike recalled:

> The night wore on. Activity under the light increased, as did the moth activity around the light above them. Interesting psychological situation; could they really afford to maintain this position at daylight and would the Political Commissar of the area allow them to abduct five of Her Majesty's officers, plus a considerable haul of arms and ammunition? Speculation was cut short at this point as orders were received, relayed from Whitehall, that irrespective of casualties the situation would be resolved by dawn and Chinese militia cleared from British soil. Who said anything about 'minimum force'!
>
> Under cover of darkness, Gurkhas, eager for action, moved stealthily closer and around the flanks. This was more like it, something they understood. The coolies were getting jittery, and on four occasions forced the District Officer to discourage any attack. An hour to dawn; whose nerves were steadier? We were on home ground, playing our game now and creeping ever closer.

Following the arrival of his new recruits, Niven's coverage of the night's events continued:

> 'Then some five hours later, with dawn not far off, Pike told me that the Brigadier had ordered that 'the situation be resolved by dawn'. To me this meant gambling on the lives of the CO, Bedford and Paton, as, even with a rushed assault, there was no way I could prevent the meat hooks from entering the throats of the captives. I had a troop of Saladins with me on the road and called one right forward, its engine revved back for silence. I positioned Lieutenant Nima Lama's platoon behind this piece of armour and briefed it and Nima to make for the bridge at full speed on my order, driving over the Chinese militia manning *our* machine gun in the lairage area en route to the bridge, and blocking the bridge with the Saladin while the rest of us fought it out hand to hand for the captives with every Chinaman on this side of the MKT bridge. I recall the Saladin was on the point of accelerating forward when I heard from Pike that our weapons were being taken onto the bridge. My mind raced:

were the weapons actually going right across the bridge, followed by the CO, DO and Paton or were they (the Chinese Militia) only going to photograph the weapons and hand them back? (There had been photographers on the bridge for some time now). I decided to wait a minute longer or until they began to move the CO, DO and Paton towards the bridge, when I would have ordered the Saladin and Lieutenant Nima forward. Fortunately, only photographs – a propaganda victory – were required by the other side and our weapons were moved back from the centre of the bridge to our side again. They were then returned to the (by now) somewhat confused men of C Company, and shortly after Lieutenant Colonel McAlister, Trevor Bedford and Bill Paton made their way wearily towards us in the morning twilight.

It had been a damned close thing; if Lieutenant Nima and the Saladin had gone forward, there would have been a lot of blood split but we would have resolved the situation by dawn. I got all my men redeployed and then went forward and dumped every piece of wire I could find into the centre of the Man Kam To bridge, windlassing all the wire to the sides of the bridge as best I could … as a deterrent, as I was sure the Chinese would come forward to try and reopen the bridge.

Niven and Pike's plan, to rush the bridge and block it to prevent an abduction and then to fight it out with the militia and coolies to free the hostages, was not the only plan hatched that night. Captain (QGO) Nandabahadur, Lieutenant (QGO) Jitman and Lieutenant Madan, although disarmed of their personal weapons, had decided that should the coolies attempt to abduct their Commanding Officer and the District Officer, or if there should be a rescue attempt, they would assault the coolies' gun positions with their kukris, which they still had on them. Luckily it did not come to that.

Pike records that there was now

Sudden increased activity under the light and the District Officer announced that they were proceeding to the bridge where a document would be signed and photographs taken. More humiliation, bigger and better front page coverage, but once again a tricky situation had been resolved without bloodshed.

At about 0415 hours just as it was beginning to get light Trevor Bedford became aware that troops were moving forward. The Chinese knew something was happening and the militant coolies were becoming increasingly agitated. Jim Main recalls general shouting and signs of alarm among the coolies, and thinking how unfortunate it would be if at the point of resolution the entire incident went badly wrong. Bedford also realised the situation was in danger of going badly wrong and used the loudhailer to tell the advancing British troops (Niven's B Company) not to do anything, explaining that under duress a document had been signed making all the promises and apologies the militants required and that the hostages were about to be released. It was the hiatus in the area of the bridge as seen by Pike and reported to Niven that made Niven hesitate, and then Bedford's announcement stopped the rescue attempt and averted what would undoubtedly have been a disaster. The weapons that the coolies had captured were taken to the centre of the bridge and photographs of them and of the captives taken by the Chinese Communists. The photographs were published in many of Hong Kong's newspapers, and elsewhere across the world, the next morning.

The Hostages on the Man Kam To Bridge shortly before their release. [127]

---

127 . 1/10GR Photograph Album, Gurkha Museum.

As Colonel Ronnie later wrote:

> It was not an episode we recount with any pleasure or pride, but in retrospect the preservation of a modicum of peace without bloodshed on the border is now seen as infinitely more desirable than a military massacre of unarmed, if aggressive, Chinese citizens. Subsequent events at our Chancery in Peking[128] underlined the wisdom of the 'no escalation on the frontier' policy.

Pike concluded:

> The Man Kam To coolies had won round two, but we had their measure now and were learning fast. Before dawn the bridge was completely blocked and sandbagged positions constructed at strategic points. A bulldozer was called in, and the police post and all other buildings were demolished. Gurkhas dug furiously, wire was erected, and the beginnings of a sound defensive position underway. We would play it our way from now on and eagerly awaited round three.
>
> We won round three and all subsequent rounds. Few, however, will disagree that in those early days of humiliation and frustration we were up against something we had not experienced before; we certainly learnt the hard way.

During the hostage crisis other minor dramas were playing out. The Adjutant, Captain Andy Watt, was the Battalion duty officer at the New Territories Police-Military Operations Room at Fanling. He had earlier informed the Brigade duty officer, Major Peter Will RTR (who was the Brigade's DAA&QMG) that Colonel Ronnie had been taken hostage by the CCA. Will asked what the Battalion was doing about rescuing him. Watt responded by saying that the matter was in hand and was being dealt with by Pike and Niven, two very experienced and successful company commanders who were on site. Later Will rang Watt and asked him for another SITREP. He later ordered Watt to effect an assault to rescue Colonel Ronnie and the other hostages. Brigadier Martin and the Brigade Major, Major Ted Hibbert, were in Kowloon and not in the New Territories at Brigade Headquarters at the time, so the Brigadier's orders were

---

128. A reference to the sacking of the British Embassy in Beijing, which was burnt down by Red Guards, on 22 Aug 1967.

being relayed by Will to 10GR's Battalion HQ (Watt) at Fanling by telephone throughout the whole incident. Watt was in contact with Pike by radio on the 10GR Battalion frequency. Responding to the order relayed by Will, Watt pointed out that a CCA regiment, 30 Border Regiment, was stood-to fully-armed with supporting weapons opposite our forces and the Chinese probably had a division behind that! Watt told him that an assault by two companies over open ground dominated by the CCA would result in a disaster – to say the least. Will insisted that 10GR do something and again ordered Watt to tell the two company commanders to assault and affect a rescue. Watt then, rather stupidly, told the DQ to 'F.... off' and put the phone down. Not to be outdone by Watt, Will then got on to the 10GR Battalion radio frequency and spoke directly to Pike. In January 2018 Pike told me that when Will ordered him to effect the rescue mission he refused to do so, and was then challenged with 'Are you disobeying the order?' to which he responded 'Yes'. He was then asked 'How much do you value your career?' to which he responded with words along the lines of 'it is less important than the lives that are likely to be lost if the order is carried out'. Pike nevertheless relayed to Niven what they had been ordered to do. In the same conversation in January 2018 Pike told me that he had never before mentioned his exchange with Will to anyone.

About an hour after Watt had put down the telephone a landrover arrived at Police-Military HQ at Fanling with two young British Gurkha Signals captains on board. They told Watt they had come to arrest him; one would take him to Brigade HQ while the other would take over his responsibilities as duty officer! However, and fortuitously for Watt, Colonel Ronnie then walked into the Police-Military Operations Room in Fanling, having been released. That evening the Brigadier spoke on the phone to Colonel Ronnie about the incident and, *en passant*, said Watt had been extremely rude to Will. Colonel Ronnie quizzed Watt about it. He agreed that Watt had behaved correctly in disobeying the order but said there was absolutely no excuse at all for being rude and told him to go and apologise to Will. Watt did so, but will always remember that Colonel Ronnie backed him up. The incident was not mentioned again.

Colonel Ronnie rarely spoke about being taken hostage but a number of snippets give an insight into how painful it must have been to endure what some considered was a serious humiliation.

It was a sensitive matter. In December 1990, the then General Ronnie came out to Hong Kong on a Regimental Association visit to celebrate the 10GR's centenary as a Gurkha Regiment. At a function in the British Officers' Mess the regimental photograph albums were laid out on the billiard table, providing an opportunity for the 'old and bold' to reminisce over them and their time in the Regiment. Going through a 1/10GR 1967 album with General Ronnie and others, we came to a page with the Man Kam To 'hostages' photograph, with Ronnie looking thoroughly dejected on it. In his wonderfully understated way, he simply said: 'Not that damned photograph again'.

Released after a long and harrowing night as a 'hostage' and 13 hours at the sharp end in a tense situation, Colonel Ronnie was the same calm, assured man whom his subordinates knew well. He did not discuss with them what had happened, but he must have been struggling to come to terms with the indignity and humiliation of being 'captured' and the awfulness of knowing that his powerlessness to do anything to prevent it would be criticised by armchair warriors who were not there. At some stage he must have discussed it with Brigadier Peter Martin, who wrote:

> You can imagine the distress in the mind of Colonel McAlister, who was quite one of the best Commanding Officers in the British Army, but, in trying to console him, I pointed out that no territory or arms had been lost, only 'face'; there had been no bloodshed. I said I was sure that in six months' time, when we could look back on events more calmly, we would realise that indignity was preferable to a slaughter which could have resulted in great loss of life on the border and lasting bitterness. [129]

When he eventually got home to relax and rest Colonel Ronnie did not even mention what had happened. Sally, who was heavily pregnant, only learned about it from that well known source of information in most regiments – 'the wives' net'.

So, what of that event? On a sweltering Hong Kong summer day, Colonel Ronnie was confined to the Police Post area from 1430 hours to 2300 hours. The Police Post was three metres

---

129 . Martin, PL de C, Confrontation on the Hong Kong Border 1967, reproduced as Appendix 5 in McAlister, Bugle & Kukri, Vol.2, p.503.

from the end of the Man Kam To bridge on the British side. Immediately outside it were 50 to 60 protesting and aggressive coolies armed with an assortment of axes, meat hooks and pistols, and backing them up was an unknown number of fully-armed and alert CCA soldiers, from 30 Border Regiment, whose weapons, including a 75mm recoilless gun, were trained on the Police Post. Ronnie was joined by Trevor Bedford and Bill Paton, who were able to parley with the opposition. Each time the talking appeared to make progress the opposition changed the negotiators. The other side held the initiative and the 'no escalation on the frontier' directive meant that he, Trevor Bedford, Bill Paton and the small garrison could do little other than watch over the Gurkha Engineers from 69 Squadron as they erected a chain-link fence around the post, and wait, not knowing what the villagers, 'coolies' (alias Militia) and the CCA might do next. After eight hours the opposition played their hand and under the cover of darkness the small garrison was surrounded and taken hostage. The key personnel had meat hooks or knives held to their throats, they were covered by their own weapons which had been seized and were told to warn their back-up forces to take no action or they would be killed. It must have been a frightening ordeal. From that moment they were no longer in communication with our forces. They were then held for at least five humiliating hours seated in a row surrounded by coolies, who for the most part were not as aggressive as they had been; possibly because they too were tired and uncertain about what to do next. It is probable that they were waiting for instructions on what to do next. Trevor Bedford, whose Cantonese was considerably better than Bill Paton's, continued to parley with the militant coolies. Bedford recalled that the coolies' blood was up and any provocation might have occasioned the killing of the 'white imperialist pigs'. Bedford was certain the CCA were calling the shots, and if had they not been, the militant Red Guards would have willingly killed them all. Colonel Ronnie played no part in the proceedings, nor could he have done; he could not speak Cantonese and could only sit it out, powerless and humiliated. Bedford knew Ronnie well and judged that as a proud man he was severely dejected and deeply shocked by what had happened, and humiliated because he was unable to control events or do anything about it. Ronnie probably knew that our forces would mount an operation to prevent the Chinese from abducting them into China and knew any such operation would lead to bloodshed and the deaths of those he was responsible for protecting. That he and his fellow Europeans would probably be among the first to be killed must also have preyed on his mind. Bedford had said he wanted time to try to talk his way out of the situation and he recognised early on that the only way it was going to be resolved peacefully was to agree to the coolies' demands. The coolies were undoubtedly being told what to do. They were almost certainly getting their instructions from the CCA, but who was really pulling the strings?

In his report, 'Confrontation on the Hong Kong Border 1967', Brigadier Martin suggested that he had established an effective way of communicating with the Chinese Army. After the Sha Tau Kok incident the Chinese used loudspeakers to put across propaganda to the villagers on the British side of the border, and, in return, we made broadcasts back to them from our side. Our broadcasts suggested the Chinese Army did not approve of the actions of the militant coolies, and in an effort to get a message across to the Commander of the Chinese troops in Sha Tau Kok the thoughts of Chairman Mao were invoked, following the throwing of a bomb at 1/7GR patrol on 9 July in Sha Tau Kok. This specific broadcast pointed out that Chairman Mao had said that no one should ever harm anyone first, but if someone harms you, you should hurt them back. Referring to the bomb incident the broadcast suggested Chairman Mao would not have approved of it, and while the British would not harm anyone first, if anyone did harm us in future we would hurt them back. The broadcast asked for the Chinese Commander's co-operation in ensuring that there was no further incident. The broadcast went out twice and on the second occasion the Chinese Commander came to the border to hear it for himself. The Chinese Army were listening; it was apparent they, too, wanted to keep the peace, and it became clear it was not only the loudspeaker broadcasts they were listening to. Earlier during the trouble at Lo Wu it had seemed that the Chinese were reacting to what was being said on the Brigade radio net. After a trial run when the Chinese reacted to something he said on the Brigade net, the Brigadier realised that this was a method by which he could communicate with the Chinese Army, bypassing the militant coolies. He then started to use the radio rather than the more secure telephone when talking to his commanding officers, if he wanted to convey something to the Chinese Army. The

Chinese had made broadcasts in Gurkhali,[130] so it was probable that they were also listening in on the Battalion and Company radio frequencies on which Gurkhali was spoken. Did the Chinese know that a rescue attempt was to be made before dawn? Why did they take the weapons to the centre of the Man Kam To bridge and photograph them in the dark just before this was to happen? Why did they allow Bedford to announce that a document meeting the coolies' demands had been signed just as Niven, B Company and the Life Guards' Saladin were about to launch the rescue attempt? It is possible that the Chinese Army, from radio intercepts, knew what was happening and reacted accordingly.

Watching events as they unfolded during the night, Pike was certain the CCA would not allow the situation to continue into daylight. He thought it was most unlikely that they would allow photographers on the British side to photograph the militants and coolies holding hostages who were quite clearly in British territory, and see the photographs plastered across every front page in the world. For the same reason he also did not believe the Chinese would abduct the hostages, and he reasoned that if the Chinese authorities really wanted to destabilise Hong Kong they were unlikely to do so by simply taking a few hostages. Pike found himself in a difficult position when he was ordered to affect the rescue mission and clear the militants out of British territory before dawn. He thought the decision was a bad one, and the order, which would escalate the conflict – something they had been instructed to avoid – would result in unnecessary deaths, including that of his Commanding Officer. Fortunately, the situation was resolved shortly after his verbal exchange with Will, and it was not raised again at the time or mentioned at all until he told me about it more than 50 years later.

Whatever was going on behind the scenes and whoever was actually pulling the strings on the Chinese side during the Man Kam To 'hostage' crisis, it ended, thankfully, without bloodshed. The Hong Kong hawks, and some in the military, thought the whole incident was a disgrace; British, Gurkha, Senior Hong Kong officials and policemen had been captured, disarmed and humiliated apparently without resisting, and Trevor Bedford, Colonel Ronnie and Bill Paton had signed a

---

130 . Gurkhali was the term used for the British Army's version of the Nepali language.

document acceding to the wishes of the coolies. Calmer heads realised that what might have been a major disaster was averted; they recognised the self-control of those involved and dismissed the document acceding to the militants' wishes as irrelevant, because it had clearly been signed under duress. In this regard the opposition were unintentionally helpful, because the photograph released by them and widely published in the press clearly showed a coolie holding an axe aloft in a threatening manner over the seated hostages.

An appreciation of what had happened at Man Kam To quickly followed. It was recognised, some have suggested before the incident, that Europeans, the 'white imperialist pigs' who were the real targets of the militants rage, should not have put themselves in a position where they might be seized. Steps were taken, therefore, to make sure that control of the border was done at a distance from it, thereby reducing the risk of physical confrontation with the opposition and placing any possibility of it happening on ground of our choosing. Police Posts were pulled back and defended, and mines were laid around the more isolated ones. The Police Post at the end of the Man Kam To bridge was demolished, the animal lairage area cleared of all obstructions and buildings, and a defensive position was dug and wired on a small hill overlooking the working area, about 150 yards from the bridge. It was also recognised that our intelligence about what was happening on the border was poor. A border Special Branch was formed and efforts were made to improve communications between the Police and the Army. It was also considered what steps, short of opening fire, might be taken.

There was a relative lull from 12 to 23 August on the border, but there was an incident at the Ta Ku Ling gate which involved an action that fell short of opening fire and probably sent a strong message to the other side. A small party of policemen and Gurkhas from 2/6GR, led by the Company Commander, Major Bob Duncan, went down to open the Ta Ku Ling gate and were promptly set upon by a large group of militant coolie farmers. Rapid action by the Police and Gurkhas restored the situation but a policeman was severely injured and had his Sterling sub-machine gun taken. An attempt by a coolie to snatch the personal weapon of a Gurkha soldier was less successful, and the coolie lost part of the hand with which he grabbed the rifle, when the Gurkha cut it off with his kukri.

Elsewhere, the five editors and publishers arrested on 9 August had been charged and sentenced and their papers ceased publishing on 17 August. The reaction of the radicals in Beijing to the closure of the three pro-communist papers was one of fury. On 20 August a strongly-worded protest was given to Hopson in Beijing, demanding that the editors and publishers be reinstated. Back on the border, from 20 August there was a noticeable increase in activity over on the Chinese side. More coolies and armed Red Guards with prominent red armbands were seen giving lectures and instructions to assembled civilians, and well-camouflaged CCA with heavy weapons were seen moving from one camp to another. Special Branch informed 1/10GR that the intention of the 'Struggle Committee' leaders was to provoke the British into opening fire, and it was clear something was about to happen. On 22 August a large crowd of left-wing radicals in Beijing attacked and burnt down the office of the Chargé d'Affaires. Hopson and his staff were badly manhandled, abused and beaten. Ultimately they were saved by PLA/CCA soldiers, who initially had failed to prevent the sacking of the Chargé d'Affaires' office and home. Then on 24 August orchestrated rioting at Lo Wu and Man Kam To erupted simultaneously.

Lo Wu

At Lo Wu the railway crossing and station remained open. C Company, now commanded by Captain Madankumar Subba,[131] was based at Lo Wu, and its 7 Platoon manned the Immigration Office, which was barricaded and wired against assault. Unlike other posts it could not be pulled back from the border, so the occupants were 10 yards from the opposition at the other end of the bridge. 8 Platoon was covering the rear of the station and Police Post, while 9 Platoon was in the Company's defensive position on the Point 350 feature overlooking the bridge, providing information from good observation points and ready to give covering fire if required. In the morning 40 farmers tried to break into the Immigration Office but were repulsed using tear gas. Tension rose as the day progressed and at 1600 hours the rioters came suddenly and in large numbers: at the peak of

---

131 . Madankumar Subba was a Sandhurst commissioned officer, and therefore classed as a British Officer rather than a Queen's Gurkha Officer.

the riot there were approximately 500 civilians, Red Guards, Militia and CCA at the Lo Wu end of the bridge. They also came prepared, wearing wetted face masks to mitigate the effects of the tear gas and some carried buckets and blankets to cover the tear gas grenades while others picked the grenades up and tossed them into the river. The rioters repeatedly attacked the Immigration Post with iron poles, spears, hooks, axes and stones. Some rioters swam the river to assault the Immigration Post from the rear. They were met by 8 Platoon. Tear gas was largely ineffective because of the direction of the wind so Madankumar Subba gave the order to use the Army's No.80 WP smoke grenade. Its highly effective smoke was generated by white phosphorous (hence the WP) burning on contact with oxygen when the grenade burst open. In contact with flesh it could cause nasty burns. During the 'battle', which raged for three and half hours, CCA machine gunners fired bursts of LMG or MMG fire close over the heads of C Company from a hill feature known as 'Wireless Hill', 200 yards over the border in China, and loudspeakers blasted out propaganda and music, including some broadcasts in Gurkhali. By 1945 hours the last of the rioters had been driven back; some had suffered quite serious burns, and in addition to the 87 tear gas grenades C Company had used 12 WP grenades.

On 25 August the rioters returned to the charge. This time there were fewer rioters but the attack was more vicious. About 10 Molotov cocktails (petrol bombs) were thrown at the Immigration Office and at one stage the roof was on fire; and, more seriously, six fragmentation stick grenades were thrown by the opposition; three landed on the roof of the Immigration Post blowing minor holes in it. So that Madankumar Subba could concentrate on the dealing with the rioters, Lieutenant Peter Reid, who commanded the Reconnaissance Platoon had been sent forward to observe from the Police Post tower and to report back to Colonel Ronnie. The CCA machine gunners lowered their sights and Reid reported that the bursts of fire were now barely clearing their heads. Water cannon were used to extinguish the fire at the Immigration Post, which rapidly spread to the sandbag defences. 7 and 8 Platoon used 28 WP grenades and 117 tear gas grenades during this confrontation. It was thought the rioters suffered no less than six or seven casualties from WP grenades and some had to be carried away on stretchers. As it was getting dark a platoon from D Company was sent forward to reinforce C Company but the rioters had withdrawn. C Company checked their positions and re-grouped, both sides switched off all their lights and C Company spent a long night 'stood-to', not knowing what might happen in the eerie silence that had descended over Lo Wu.

1/10GR had what was known as the 'Bahaduri Book'. *Bahaduri* means a brave person or a bravery award, and written citations, whether submitted for official recognition or not, were pasted into the Bahaduri Book and kept in Battalion HQ. A mention in the Bahaduri Book was a treasured and recognised honour within the Battalion. The entry covering the exploits of Rifleman Lakhdan Rai of 7 Platoon, C Company, give a flavour of what it was like in the front line at Lo Wu:

21154128 RIFLEMAN LAKHDAN RAI – C COMPANY

On 24 August 1967, Rifleman Lakhdhan Rai was a member of the platoon sited in the sandbagged Immigration Office Post at the border railway bridge at Lo Wu. During the morning, forty Communist Chinese farmers crossed into British territory and tried to break into the post. Rifleman Lakhdhan at once went forward to an open 'bay', and under his Company Commander's orders dispersed the mob using seven tear gas grenades. Tension rose throughout the afternoon and at about 4 pm the post was again rushed and subjected for over three hours to a sporadic hail of stones, bottles and Molotov cocktails from ten yards range, to the accompaniment of bursts of fire overhead from a military post on Chinese territory. Without relief throughout the action, Rifleman Lakhdhan, with great determination and initiative, stood in the bomb bay and repulsed every attack, personally throwing over fifty grenades, with the remainder of the platoon keeping him supplied.

On 25th August 1967, the post was again assaulted for three hours. This was a more vicious attack by fewer rioters, but many more Molotov cocktails and three fragmentation grenades were thrown into the post.

The LMG from Chinese territory again fired throughout the action, this time much closer overhead. Rifleman Lakhdhan, by now an acknowledged expert,

dominated the entire 'battle', throwing grenades non-stop from the open bay, refusing to take cover from the missiles or bombs, and completely ignoring the possibility that the Chinese LMG gunner might at any time lower his aim and fire straight at the post.

The courage and endurance of this young Rifleman in his self-imposed task during two days of severe strain and tension, were a fine example to all around him, in circumstances calling for an unusual mixture of defiance and restraint in the face of provocation.

Man Kam To

The border crossing point at Man Kam To was closed and the bridge at the British end was blocked by a wired barrier. The rioting coolies' objective was to clear away the barrier so that produce could flow across the border again and the farmers regain access to their land on the British side. Two platoons of B Company, under Niven, fought a four-hour tear gas and WP grenade 'battle' with the rioters. As at Lo Wu the rioters were now better organised; some had 1914-18 style gas masks, and they used barrows of straw as cover and to ram the barrier. Chinese machine gunners fired over the top of the Company's dug-in position and a number of rounds hit the position. The rules of engagement were that if fire was effective British troops could return fire. After the event, when Niven was quizzed about why he had not returned fire when rounds had hit his company position: he responded; 'Who said it was effective? ... none of us got hit.'[132] Niven's typically down-to-earth Scottish brevity hid a steely determination not to open fire in return as the opposition wanted. His determined style of leadership percolated down to his subordinates as another 'Bahaduri Book' entry records:

LIEUTENANT (QGO) DHANRAJ RAI – B COMPANY

On 24th August 1967, Lieutenant (QGO) Dhanraj Rai was commanding a platoon tasked to maintain intact a substantial barbed wire obstacle erected on the British

---

132 . '1st Battalion Notes', Bugle & Kukri journal, Vol.3, No.8, May 1968, p.384.

end of the Man Kam To road bridge on the Hong Kong border.

Some forty to fifty Chinese Communist workers attempted to remove this obstacle under cover of a barrage of stones and encouraged by a number of automatic weapons firing low over the heads of our troops from positions within 200 yards of the frontier.

Lieutenant (QGO) Dhanraj positioned himself some fifteen yards from the end of the bridge and, supplied with WP and tear gas grenades by his men, personally defied all initial efforts by the rioters to dismantle the obstacle. Finding they could not, in the open, stand up to the accurate barrage of grenades, the rioters brought up trolleys of straw to provide cover and act as battering rams. Lieutenant (QGO) Dhanraj attacked these with WP grenades and set them alight, forcing their withdrawal. At each sally, the rioters succeeded in cutting or removing a portion of the obstacle and eventually resorted to attempts to apply a grappling hook and drag the wire away. On three separate occasions Lieutenant (QGO) Dhanraj went forward to the obstacle and, at point blank range with the rioters, grenade in one hand, kukri in the other, succeeded in cutting the grappling ropes.

Finally, despite all our efforts, the last strands of wire were removed but with Lieutenant (QGO) Dhanraj and his men standing guard at the end of the bridge, no one dared advance onto British territory.

The personal courage, leadership and determination of this Queen's Gurkha Officer were prime factors in the repulse of a violent and aggressive mob in an action lasting nearly four hours.

After the confrontation at Man Kam To on 24 August, the Hong Kong Government agreed to open the bridge again; this took the opposition completely by surprise and the situation reverted to one of careful vigilance, with alert troops standing-by and ready for the unexpected.

Congratulations came from the Commander British Forces and Brigadier Martin for the way 1/10GR had stood firm and not been provoked into firing, as the Chinese radicals and the Hong Kong Struggle Committee would have wished and were

Coolies, alias Militia, gathering on the Man Kam To bridge August 1967[133]

trying to engineer. Colonel Ronnie took the view, suggesting it was rather ironic, that it was only when the situation escalated from stones and catapults to Molotov cocktails, grenades, white phosphorous and bursts of fire that he began to feel that the Battalion had got the measure of a uniquely sensitive and volatile situation.

With the benefit of hindsight and fresh research it is clear that the British and Chinese were communicating at several levels. However, it is probable that both sides were not communicating particularly efficiently and all that was going on was not being passed up and down their respective chains of command. In part this could be attributed to the different communication systems at the various levels, and especially between the Police and Army; to the lack of sophistication in the communications equipment, the cumbersome encoding and

---

133 . 1/10GR Photograph Album, Gurkha Museum.

146

decoding procedures of the time, the levels of secrecy, and a tendency to withhold information rather than share it. In addition, the time differences between Beijing, London and Hong Kong did not help. A major factor, however, was that when Mao Tse-Tung launched the Cultural Revolution he plunged China into chaos, and in 1967 there was no effective central control or clearly-recognised chain of command in China. Following the Sha Tau Kok shooting on 8 July, Jack Cater, [134] who had been given responsibility for security by the Governor, Sir David Trench, contacted the central leadership in China. It was clear that Zhou Enlai, China's Premier, had not approved of the incident at Sha Tau Kok, and according to Cater the response he got from China when lodging a formal complaint about the killing of the five policemen at Sha Tau Kok was:

> Beijing told us to 'hold on' and that they would help. But they were in chaos. There were riots and most provinces in China had serious problems. They could not do anything for us at the time. [135]

On the border those facing the chaos were unaware that the Chinese central authorities had said they would help, nor did they know it was simply a question of hanging on until China did help. If anything, events on the border suggested the Chinese authorities were encouraging and helping the Red Guards and militant coolies in their aggressive and provocative activities. Initially this was the case. Radical and uncontrollable militants and Red Guards purged China of its elites, academics and anyone considered privileged, and they were inclined to take the view that if you were not assisting them in radicalising the masses you were against them. The CCA had to tread a careful line between whole-hearted support for Mao's Cultural Revolution and the more moderate views of China's Premier – and their boss – Zhou Enlai. China was on the verge of Civil War in mid-1967. Zhou Enlai made it clear he was not happy with the militants' actions at Sha Tau Kok on 8 July; he expressed his displeasure when the Red Guards sacked and burnt down the British Embassy on 22 August and he ruled out the

---

134 . Later Sir Jack Cater, KBE, Hong Kong's Colonial Secretary 1973–76.
135 . Bickers and Yep, editors, May Days in Hong Kong Riot and Emergency in 1967, p.40.

possibility of a military invasion of Hong Kong when it was suggested.[136] By August 1967 the tide had turned in China and the excesses of the Red Guards and the chaos that the country had been thrown into caused Mao to change course. In addition the Communist leaders in China had lost faith in the Hong Kong communists, who they thought were unsuitable and inept. They had hopelessly distorted the truth of what was happening in Hong Kong in their reports to China and they had spent what were considered scandalous sums of money to further the disturbances. It did not help that the acknowledged communist leader in Hong Kong, Fei Yi-ming, who was exceedingly rich, arrived to lead the left-wing demonstration at Government House in a huge Mercedes-Benz. It also became known that many of his fellow Hong Kong communist leaders had transferred large sums of personal money to neutral countries when the trouble began. Then they did not help themselves by announcing that the 'Anti-Persecution Struggle Committee' would celebrate October the First by holding a ten-day feast, and they further upset the mainland communists by paying striking workers 480 dollars a month, hoax bomb planters 40 dollars and real bomb planters 200 dollars per plant. These sums were considered excessive and a waste of the funds earned by the blood and sweat of the workers. It was also apparent that far from winning over the majority of Hong Kong's inhabitants to their cause, their campaign, in particular their bombing campaign, had in fact alienated them, and even turned away a high proportion of communist sympathisers. It was also clear that China considered that Hong Kong was still economically important. So a combination of economic reality, a change of mind by the architect of the Cultural Revolution, and the ineptitude of the Hong Kong communists helped to bring the confrontation to an end. Small wonder the events on the Hong Kong border were described by the then Head of the Far East Desk at the Foreign Office as a 'Mixture of deadly earnest and charades'. In 1987, when reflecting on the matter Sir David Trench, remarked: 'How fatuous the whole thing was, there was no issue between us and the people who were rioting except they wanted to riot and we did not want them to.'[137] Those involved with the intrigue, grand-standing and self-interest of the various

136 . Cheung, Hong Kong's Watershed: The 1967 Riots, p.118.
137 . Bickers and Yep, May Days in Hong Kong, p.2

parties involved in the tragic events in Hong Kong in 1967 at a political level may well have thought the shenanigans were charades. On the border for the officers and men of 1/10GR, other units that manned the border during this time and the Hong Kong Police, who faced hostile provocation from militants that risked escalating the situation to one of war between China and the United Kingdom, it was a matter of deadly earnest. That officers and men of 1/10GR, who had so recently been involved in the undeclared war during the Indonesian Confrontation, were able to show such restraint is a remarkable tribute to their steadfastness, obedience and loyalty; and it also says much about the man at the helm.

The situation Ronnie faced on the Hong Kong border required remarkable resilience. It is never easy for anyone trained to command a force capable of delivering significant lethal force in high intensity conflict to turn the other cheek and show a level of restraint that makes one look weak. Ronnie's intelligence and ability to think quickly was underpinned by his absolute integrity and loyalty. He followed orders that the CCA were not to be provoked: hotter heads might not have been so resolutely calm nor conveyed to their subordinates an unflappable assuredness. The arm-chair pundits who were not there did not see that. He probably knew that his being taken hostage would be seen as a sign of failure and poor judgement. He may have felt that he unfortunately got himself into an unwinnable situation: he was 'damned' because he went too far forward and was taken hostage and he would have been 'damned' if he had not gone forward to assess the situation and reassure his men. The question of where a commander, particularly a Commanding Officer, should be in a confrontation is a subject that continues to divide opinion. Some would consider that he should never have put himself into a situation where he could have been taken hostage. It was not his job to be on the front line; a point made by Brigadier Peter Martin when, in relation to the Man Kam To Tea Party incident, he wrote, albeit with the benefit of hindsight, that he himself had 'rather foolishly allowed himself to get involved' talking to the coolies when he visited Man Kam To on 5 August, to find out for himself what was happening. He realised that, once involved, he could not stand back, nor could he from such a position command and control the situation or bring to bear the considerable resources at his disposal. That was his proper job, not engaging in conversation with hostile and irrational militants. In 1992 the then retired Major General Peter Martin made an audio recording of his military career, which covers his recollections of what happened in Hong Kong during the 1967 border confrontations. In it he says, 'After the Man Kam To Tea Party strict instructions had been given from above that no officer above the rank of major was to risk involvement with Chinese farmers or coolies; it was unlucky chance that Colonel McAlister happened to be in the Police Post when events began to move very fast.'[138]

Although there were several incidents on the border that caused the militant coolies to protest, the situation calmed down as the Cultural Revolution ran out of steam following Mao's change of mind. The CCA took back control, and they, like us, were determined that the situation should not get out of hand. The task of manning the border remained a Police-Military operation, but the border was quiet and became a dull routine of watchful vigilance.

On 14 September 1967, shortly before 1/10GR took over from 1/7GR in the Sha Tau Kok sector, Sally and Ronnie's second daughter, Caroline was born in the British Military Hospital in Kowloon. 1/10GR were at Sha Tau Kok from 19 September to 6 November 1967 and then the manning of the border was put on a roster system. Battalions did 14-day tours on the border with six to eight weeks between tours. Colonel Ronnie was not alone in his disapproval of this arrangement, which was extremely disruptive and allowed little time for meaningful training, and it was not long before tours on the border were increased to six weeks with a corresponding longer gap between border tours that allowed time for worthwhile training.

On 6 February 1968 Ronnie signed his third and final report as a commanding officer. The major incidents on the Hong Kong border in 1967 all happened in the period 1 July 1967 to 31 January 1968, which the report covered. Brigadier Martin initiated the report and he praises Ronnie for his admirable awareness of the political implications of events on the border and the need for restraint in difficult situations, and he

---

138 . Martin, PLdeC, audio recording by Conrad Wood, IWM catalogue no.12778, dated 1992-11-12.

commends him for his leadership qualities in never allowing the morale of the Battalion to suffer. The report highlights Ronnie's skilful handling of the relief of the Sha Tau Kok Police Station on 8 July, when the Battalion came under fire and were not provoked into a shooting match with the Chinese Army, also for his coolness and calmness, and ability to make rapid and sound decisions, when the Battalion routed the militant Chinese rioters at Lo Wu and Man Kam To on 24 and 25 August, using minimum of force even though they again came under fire. Brigadier Martin sums up the report by writing, 'Throughout the whole period of his command he has shown splendid qualities of leadership and has earned the admiration of his officers and men and the respect of all with whom he has come in contact.' He is strongly recommended for command of a Brigade – British or Gurkha. Graded A, that is 'Well above the standard required of his rank and service'. There is no mention in the report of the 11 August Man Kam To incident when he and others were taken hostage. The GOC Hong Kong, Lieutenant General Sir John Worsley, upgraded the report to 'Outstanding' and wrote, in response to the narrow range of staff appointments recommended by the initiating officer, that Ronnie 'he would be a success in any appointment', and adds, 'I believe that his outstanding qualities can be more effectively used elsewhere'. The 'Outstanding' grading is supported by the Commander Far East Land Forces, Lieutenant General Sir Thomas Pearson, who writes: 'He has done extremely well and deserves this good report.'

Lieutenant Colonel DR Green MC arrived in Hong Kong on 5 March 1968 to take over 1/10GR from Ronnie, who relinquished command on 13 March 1968. On his predecessor Duncan Green later wrote:

McAlister had commanded with distinction in Borneo and through the complex and testing internal security operations on the Hong Kong border. His brand of leadership combined an unerring instinct for the important issues and a willingness to give his officers full rein to exercise their responsibilities and initiative. This brought out the best in the Battalion which had already, so often in Malaya and Borneo, shown its mettle. Under his direction it established a reputation as a tough, alert and fast moving fighting machine. McAlister's departure was marked by a farewell befitting one of the Regiment's most successful commanders.[139]

Captain Andy Watt, who was able to observe Colonel Ronnie at close quarters, provided the following insights into his Commanding Officer:

> I was very lucky to have served as Regimental Signals Officer (RSO) under Ronnie during 1/10GR's last and most successful operational tour in Borneo in 1966 and as his Adjutant during the Hong Kong border troubles during the Chinese Cultural Revolution in 1967.
>
> When I was his Adjutant he had a habit, when bored and before setting off for golf promptly at 1500 hrs daily, of picking up my entire 'In Tray', dealing with it all immaculately, dumping it on top of my 'Out Tray' and then departing with his clubs in his staff car. When I recently told General Garry[140] about this he told me of the time when on operations in Borneo, Peter Myers, then CO 2/10GR, asked him and Kit Maunsell to draft an operational order for a Claret Op. Neither Garry nor Kit were in any way staff trained at the time, and both wondered how on earth they were going to complete even a basic draft satisfactorily. However, Ronnie, who was the Battalion Second in Command at the time, then entered the room, saw their predicament, picked up the paper work and in a very short time returned with an immaculately completed operational order ready for typing.
>
> I remember on one occasion when as his Adjutant being told by phone by Colin Maddison, Bn 2IC, that a four star staff car was 'stalled' outside our guard room at Cassino Lines and did I know who the general was inside it. I quickly informed Col Ronnie who told me to let the VIP car through and to direct it to Bn HQ. Meanwhile he and Colin went downstairs and met the general and came up with him and his ADC to the CO's office for a rather nasty cup of cold tea and a chat before departing in good humour. To this day I cannot remember who the VIP was and how I completely forgot the pending visit which must have been programmed by HQBF and Brigade HQ well in advance.

139 . McAlister, Bugle & Kukri, Vol.2, p.439.
140 . General Sir Garry Johnson KCB OBE MC.

But what really staggered me was that absolutely nothing was said to me by Ronnie in the form of an admonition afterwards. Was this a continuation of the previous Burnett policy: that any BO could do anything wrong once, no matter how awful, and be forgiven if at all possible, but a further and similar mistake would bring down the career curtains upon the hapless officer? Or was it because I had a CO who was not only a very kind man, but who was also blessed with a generous sense of humour. Probably a bit of both.

As CO Ronnie had one very distinct trait when in his office or whilst waiting on developments in the ops room. Over time, we would all notice that he would be very quiet for a short while, then he would roll up his sleeves, reach for his fountain pen or pencil, never a biro, take out a pad of paper and start writing without pause. There then followed anything from an operational citation, a Special Order of the Day covering a battalion battle honour, an officer's confidential report or a detailed response to a paper from on high. Whatever it was, it never required more than one draft, and this was invariably as a result of typing errors, and there was very minimal correction of the original. A rubber, lying pristine on his desk, was never used. He was a natural staff officer par excellence. When he corrected my drafts, or anybody else's, he always made a point of politely stating: 'The most difficult task when writing a paper or letter of any kind is the production of the first draft. Thank you for this; I will now just do a very quick check through it for you.' The final document, invariably returned to the author within the hour, often bore little or no resemblance to the original draft and was half the original length. Furthermore, it quickly became glaringly obvious that what you were trying to say was actually so utterly simple, clear and so easy to express. Ronnie really enjoyed paperwork which he regarded as a challenge to be met with both skill and enthusiasm, no matter how minor the issue.

What particularly impressed me about him was his absolute calmness when under pressure. He always appeared to be relaxed and good humoured and never once did I hear him raise his voice in anger, nor did I ever see him lose his cool. Combined with these rare attributes was his ability to think both clearly and quickly when confronted with tense moments, whether during Claret Operations in Borneo or whilst being held captive by the Communist Chinese Army at Man Kam To on the Sino-Hong Kong border.

One of his great tenets was that as an officer you should never work to your one hundred per cent capacity, but should always keep a reserve of twenty five per cent of your energy to meet and deal with dire occasions. This came out clearly when we were on Hong Kong border duty in 1967, during the really tense period, when he frequently played golf on the Fan Ling Golf Course in full uniform accompanied by his orderly and radio operator. Recognition panels were carried by his orderly for quick display so that he could be picked up by Sioux helicopter and taken to Fan Ling Polmil HQ in an emergency. This happened on several occasions.'[141]

In 1967 the military telephone network was based on a series of exchanges manned by operators. By modern standards it was infuriatingly slow and prone to break down, but not always because of its or its operators' failings. One hot afternoon when he was feeling rather bored and thought he was alone in the office Andy decided he would test the Hong Kong telephone network and try to see how easy it was to bring the entire military telephone system to a standstill. He picked up the telephone and made a sequence of requests through the Cassino Barracks operator, asking to be put through to Brigade at Sekkong, then the Garrison at Kowloon, then Force HQ at Victoria Barracks and then back through the same operators to Cassino, with a request to speak to the Adjutant – who the operator said was engaged. The whole system was thereby grid-locked. Thinking this act of mischief proved how vulnerable the telephone network was, and that radio was the best way to communicate, Andy was feeling slightly smug when he heard the quiet voice of the Commanding Officer through the hatch between their offices say: 'Adjutant, it's well time you took up golf.'

In a contribution to the 'News from Members' section of the 3GR Association journal, Ronnie wrote a more modest reflection on his time in command:

---

141 . AJJ Watt, e-mail dated Wed, Aug 17, 2016, 3.22pm.

My own news is that I was lucky to be 'Mentioned' for what my officers and men did for me during the closing stages of the Borneo Campaign. I hand over the 1st 10th in March 1968 and go to JSSC as a DS. This suits me fine, as I know the greens on the Harewood Down GC quite well, having been a student there and I much enjoy mid-week golf. My wife is also a keen and improving golfer, with a handicap nearing single figures.

Command has been great fun, but if I never see Hong Kong again I won't mind. I don't like Red Guards.[142]

Ronnie was appointed an Officer of the Order of the British Empire (OBE) in the Birthday Honours 1968 for his work in command of 1st 10th Gurkha Rifles. The citation for the award reads as follows:

Lieutenant Colonel McAlister relinquishes command of 1/10 Gurkha Rifles in February 1968 on completion of a highly successful tour.

The first part of his command was served in Borneo where his Battalion was responsible for some of the major successes achieved during the whole period of the confrontation, earning a DSO and many other awards. At the end of the confrontation Lieutenant Colonel McAlister brought his Battalion back to Hong Kong where it quickly achieved the reputation of a thoroughly fit, well-trained and aggressive Battalion with particularly high morale. These qualities have been well tested during the last six months of his command when the Battalion has been fully engaged in operations on the Hong Kong border.

On 8 July 1967 he conducted the relief of the Police in Sha Tau Kok Village that had been under heavy fire from Chinese militia and soldiers for several hours. Realising the dangers to Hong Kong inherent in a full scale clash with the Chinese Army, he conducted this operation with the greatest skill, and although his Battalion came under heavy fire at one stage, succeeded in relieving the Police without firing a shot.

In subsequent operations on the border he has shown the same admirable awareness of political implications

---

142 . 3GR Association Journal, No 24, Mar 68.

and has continued to follow the necessary policy of restraint without ever allowing the morale of his Battalion to suffer, as could so easily have happened.

For weeks on end his soldiers were subjected to stone-throwing and other provocations on the border without ever losing their discipline and morale, and when force has been necessary against militant Chinese from across the border Lieutenant Colonel McAlister has conducted operations calmly, imperturbably and firmly but always using the minimum force to achieve the immediate object. There is no doubt that by his sensible and cool-headed handling of his Battalion he has contributed enormously to the maintenance of some degree of peace on the border, a peace that might well have been impossible had bloodshed taken place.

Throughout the whole period of his command he has shown splendid qualities of leadership and has earned the admiration of his officers and men and the respect of all with whom he has come in contact.

He hands over a Battalion which is second to none in the Brigade of Gurkhas and he richly merits an award.[143]

It was a well-deserved and fitting reward for his command and leadership on operations that had required his officers and men to show military skills which could hardly have been more varied.

---

143 . TNA, WO 373/173/31.

Chapter 9

Command of the Berlin Infantry Brigade

Ronnie had not received a recommendation to be an instructor at the Army Staff College at Camberley or the Joint Services Staff College (JSSC, at Latimer) when he was a student at those colleges, yet he was posted to the latter as an instructor. It was a holding appointment, as he was selected for promotion to Brigadier and to command the Berlin Infantry Brigade. In the time he spent at Latimer he not only relished the opportunity for mid-week golf on a course that he knew from his time there as a student, he also showed that he was a high-grade instructor. It was not all plain sailing as there was an occasion when he was reminded of painful memories. During his time as an instructor one of the students at JSSC was Trevor Bedford, the Hong Kong New Territories District Officer, who had been taken hostage with him by the Red Guards on the Hong Kong border. Trevor Bedford suggested to Ronnie that the events leading up to and the hostage incident on the night of 11/12 August 1967 might provide an interesting Internal Security scenario for an exercise for the students to study. Bedford later said his suggestion was not well received nor was it taken forward. He felt Ronnie was still sensitive about the matter. Bedford added that if he had had the opportunity to comment as a student he would have said they should never have allowed themselves to be drawn into a place so close to the border and a situation which handed the initiative to the Red Guards.[144] Hindsight and the subsequent decision to control the border from positions further back make this appear obvious, but at the time no-one knew how the militant coolies and Red Guards would behave, and controlling the border was a question of reacting to events as they unfolded.

He was graded 'Outstanding' in the annual confidential report that covered the seven months he instructed at JSSC, and the report states: 'He is an extremely good teacher, one of the best I have seen, and he has a happy knack of bringing out the best in his syndicate particularly in discussion'; also 'He is very

---

144 .Bedford, interview, 10 July 2017.

good at expressing himself both orally and on paper and his critiques on students' work have been models of clarity and helpfulness.' He received a strong recommendation to attend the Imperial Defence Course, but he had already been selected for promotion to Brigadier and to command the Berlin Infantry Brigade.

Ronnie assumed command of the Berlin Infantry Brigade on 15 November 1968. He was 45 years old and he was the first Berlin Infantry Brigade commander since 1945 not drawn from the Household Division. His arrival created considerable interest among the staff and units in the Brigade. In the late 1960's Berlin was occupied by American, French, British and Russian forces which controlled the city and jointly oversaw the East and West Berlin local governments. The 'Berlin Wall' separated the Eastern (Russian) sector from the Western (American, French and British) sectors. West Berlin was an isolated city, separated from West Germany some 150 miles away along limited road, rail and air 'corridors'. Relations between the East and West were strained and there were signs of unrest in Eastern Europe, particularly in Hungary and Czechoslovakia. The Baader-Meinhof Group and the Red Army Faction (RAF) were a cause for concern both in West Germany and Berlin. Berlin was a city on edge and a possible flashpoint for conflict – civil or military. Diplomatic skills and a constant alertness for any eventuality were required of those in charge.

Although the Berlin Infantry Brigade was part of the British Army of the Rhine (BAOR), Berlin was in practice autonomous. In the British sector, the Berlin Brigade formed the major part of the British Forces. The American, French and Russian sectors were of more or less the same size as the British, with a military presence of similar strengths. The British Force was commanded at that time by Major General James Bowes-Lyon, and its role was mainly the co-ordination of British military strategy for Berlin with the UK Government, together with the other three occupying powers in Berlin and their joint handling of the German civil authorities. In addition to the military ground force the British presence included elements of the RAF, the Civil Service (including the Foreign Office), the Diplomatic Corps, the Intelligence Service and the Prison Service.

At that time the Berlin Infantry Brigade had a Headquarters and three infantry battalions: The Argyll and Sutherland Highlanders (in Montgomery Barracks); The Gloucester

Regiment (Brooke Barracks); and the Staffordshire Regiment (Wavell Barracks); all of which were on two-year tours. There was also an armoured squadron detached from an armoured regiment in BAOR, namely A Squadron, 1st Royal Tank Regiment (at Smutts Barracks) on a one-year tour. The remaining army units of the Brigade were permanently stationed in Berlin. These included 38 Berlin Field Squadron, Royal Engineers; 2 Regiment, Royal Military Police; 62 Transport and Movement Squadron, Royal Corps of Transport (RCT); 14 (Berlin) Field Workshop, Royal Electrical and Mechanical Engineers (REME); the Berlin Ordnance and Ammunition Depot, Royal Army Ordnance Corps (RAOC); the British Military Hospital, a number of specialist Security, Signal and Intelligence units and BRIXMIS (British Commander-in-Chief's Mission to Soviet Forces in Germany), which was not under command, but was administered by the Berlin Brigade Headquarters. In all it was a command of some 3,100 men.

On 5 July 1969 Ronnie played the opening hole of the Gatow airfield golf course in his capacity as Vice President of the British Berlin Golf Club. The course had been laid out by the Royal Engineers as an amenity for the British Forces in Berlin; it was a project that took the best part of a year to complete as the work had to be carried out when men and equipment could be spared from other duties. One feature of the course, which the Royal Engineers were proud of, was a water sprinkler system on every green. The course was officially opened by Air Marshal Sir Christopher Foxley-Norris, (the C-in-C, RAF, Germany) who then played the opening hole with Brigadier Ronnie. History does not record who won, nor whether it is true that someone was only stopped at the last moment from performing a ceremonial turning-on of the sprinklers as they stepped onto the first green.[145]

One of the duties that had to be performed in Berlin was the guarding of Rudolf Hess[146] in Spandau Prison. Guards were provided by each of the nations for a month on a rotating basis. At the end of 1969/beginning of 1970, Hess was in the British Military Hospital in West Berlin suffering from a perforated

---

145 . Lieutenant Colonel John Yerburgh, Royal Engineers, e-mail attachment dated October 2017.

146 . Rudolf Hess was given a life sentence for Nazi war crimes and had been in Spandau prison since 18 July 1947.

ulcer. The British guard on duty at Spandau Prison at the time had to continue to guard the empty 600-cell prison because the Russians insisted that they should do so. This apparently ridiculous waste of soldiers' time and the Russian insistence that it should happen was because Spandau Prison was situated in West Berlin and the guard duty allowed the Russians a legitimate access to the Western half.

At about this time Ronnie wrote a short piece for the 'News of Members' section in the 3rd Gurkha Association journal that was printed in the 1970 edition. He wrote:

'We have had a wonderful year in Berlin, socially hectic and militarily undemanding. We both played a lot of golf and tennis, quite successfully too, and had two good holidays to Kiel and later to Bavaria.

We have had a few minor crises: the holding of the Federal German Bundestag elections in March 1969, during which the Soviets and East Germans held Army-scale manoeuvres on the access 'Corridor' frequently interrupting traffic: there was a lot of student unrest, demonstrations, interference with lectures, etc., throughout the summer: and now we have Hess in the BMH and my soldiers guarding an empty prison this month (January 1970) so as not to rock the boat with the Russians, who, for the time being, are behaving most cordially over forthcoming talks on Berlin access. The present cosy relations probably spring from Russia's efforts to efface the horrid image of the Czechoslovak invasion; and a desire to keep the West quiet in view of the sharpening confrontation with China. Berlin is always affected by every such change of mood: this is what makes it so interesting.

Lieutenant Colonel Derek Boorman[147] was the commanding officer of the 1st Battalion of the Staffordshire Regiment in Berlin at the time. In remembering Ronnie he wrote:

Above all I am reminded of my good fortune in working under the command of Ronnie as a CO and then a brigade commander.[148] I will come to his personal characteristics below, but as a commander his ability to delegate, to be

---

147 . Later Lieutenant-General Sir Derek Boorman.
148 . Derek Boorman subsequently commanded 51 Brigade in Hong Kong when Ronnie McAlister was the Deputy Commander Land Forces, Hong Kong.

there when needed and to give indirect advice or encouragement, to remain in the background and not to score points from a position of authority (an approach not always displayed by senior commanders) was almost unique in my experience. Interestingly his style was so similar to Dwin Bramall and I wonder if this was a factor in his selection for the HK appointment. In Berlin the Battalion was put through a testing exercise in spite of the limitations of ground and space, and my memory is of creative settings placing challenges at every level and, of all-importance, imbued with a sense of fun and enjoyment but serious intent.

The person. Blessed with a natural eye, his ability and choice to engage in all manner of sporting activities (not only golf!) endeared him to all ranks. I suffered the joy of being soundly thrashed on both tennis and squash courts. A friendly, unassuming and always polite demeanour fits the old-fashioned description of a perfect gentleman. With the lovely and constant support from Sally, as a pair they attracted regard throughout Berlin and HK.[149]

Major John Yerburgh, who commanded 38 Field Squadron, Royal Engineers in Berlin wrote:

On first meeting, one realised that one was in the company of an exceptional man. He was at once youthful, highly intelligent, charming and one got the feeling he was really interested to hear what one had to say. Equally, one instinctively knew that he could be relied on to come up with exactly the right solution to any given problem. I was very prepared and happy to accept any decision made by him, knowing that all the parameters had been taken into account and that every decision had been based on a thorough analysis. I became particularly impressed with his determination to update the plans for coping with emergency situations both civil and military in Berlin, and the thoroughness with which he ensured that new drills were tested and introduced. Being, at the time, the commander of the engineer squadron and the senior Royal Engineer officer in the Brigade headquarters, I found out how much reliance the Brigade placed on the Royal Engineers carrying out their allocated tasks in time to enable the Brigade to fulfil its role.

---

149 . Sir Derek Boorman, e-mail dated 26 September 2017.

Brigadier Ronnie, I felt, fully understood our capabilities – and our limitations – and made the maximum use of his Sapper resources.

The British Forces in Berlin were extremely fortunate to have both General James Bowes-Lyon and Brigadier Ronnie McAlister as they were experienced soldiers and both excelled as diplomats capable of charming all and sundry into, more often than not, accepting their points of view. One manifestation of this was their unfailing courtesy in writing to thank their staff for tasks carried out which they considered had been well done, and asking that their thanks be passed on to all concerned. I still have and treasure a number of letters from both.

This tribute would not be complete without mentioning the tremendous support given to Ronnie, throughout their lives together, by Sally, who was always the most supportive wife, the most splendid hostess and one who was always most friendly, ready to give assistance and sound advice to all who asked. In particular, she never asserted her position or made one feel aware of her status. As a result, they acquired a wide circle of friends wherever they went. It was a privilege to be counted among them and to be able to continue this friendship for the rest of our lives.[150]

Brigadier Ronnie took over command of the Berlin Infantry Brigade from Brigadier David Tabor, a Blues and Royals officer, who in turn had taken over from an unbroken succession of officers from the Household Division since 1945. One of the reasons that the command of the Berlin Infantry Brigade became something of the Household Division tied appointment may well have been because one of the important annual public events there was the Queen's Birthday parade, when the eyes of other nations in Berlin, particularly the Russians, were on the British Army. The Brigade of Gurkhas, in comparison to the Brigade of Guards, was not well versed in the demands of ceremonial parades, and Guardsmen, and most British Army units, marched at 116 paces per minute, whereas Gurkhas, as rifle regiments, marched at 140 paces per minute. Ronnie's only ceremonial parade experience had been when he commanded a British

---

150 . Lieutenant Colonel John Yerburgh RE, e-mail attachment dated October 2017.

contingent on the Sultan of Jahore's Diamond Jubilee parade on 17 September 1955 and the marching pace for that was set at 110 paces per minute and he had not had to ride a horse.

Brigadier RWL McAlister OBE - Queen's Birthday Parade Rehearsal, Berlin 1970 or 1971[151]

Ronnie relinquished command of the Berlin Infantry Brigade on 3 August 1971. He and Sally then had a brief spell of leave from 4 to 27 August before they flew to Canada. Ronnie was one of four people from Great Britain who had been selected to attend Course XXV at the Canadian National Defence College, from September 1971 to July 1972. The course was designed to prepare senior military officers and government officials to positions of higher responsibility by enabling them to study together, in an atmosphere of an advanced graduate school, matters of national and international concern. The syllabus included studies of the major countries and regions of the world, to gain a better understanding of their strengths and weaknesses, how they were likely to develop and how they were likely to behave internationally. Twelve weeks of the course were spent on Field Studies to many of these countries and regions of the world. His, and Sally's, course report recorded:

---

151 . The McAlister Family Collection.

His experience, judgement and sound common sense were invaluable to both syndicate and central course discussions. He was an outstanding speaker and his presentations, both verbal and written, were outstanding. He was very active during our field studies around the world and again his experience and leadership proved invaluable to other members of the course. His wife also contributed to the activities of the course throughout the year and they were excellent representatives of their country.

The report concludes, 'with his experience and background combined with his personality, dedication and integrity, he should be well suited for higher command and responsibility.'

Sally and Ronnie returned to England on 29 July 1972. He was taken on strength on the United Kingdom's Commander-in-Chief's Committee (UKCICC) on 30 July 1972 and on 6 October 1972 he was appointed Exercise Controller UKCICC an appointment he held until March 1975. His confidential report for the period 6 October 1972 to 21 March 1974 states:

It has been a particularly difficult period in that while there has been no diminution of planning exercises, there have been great problems of actually executing them caused by restricted transport aircraft and by troops not being available. These conditions have made an especial demand for patience, perseverance, nice judgement of priorities, tactful handling of the many agencies and enthusiastic management. Brigadier McAlister has not merely taken these requirements in his stride, but has instituted a system of planning and preparation which has given new impetus to the more complex and ambitious mobilization exercises that are still to come. His planning has been meticulous and those exercises for which he has been responsible have been notably successful. He is a man of sound, likeable and tenacious character, who expresses himself, whether talking or writing, with enviable force and lucidity. He runs his team with a sure and light touch, and serves UKCICC with imagination, dedication and success – in short a first class performance.

The initiating officer, a major general, goes on to write: 'I have not graded him outstanding as I cannot be sure he will reach the rank of Lieut-General. But he has already been selected for promotion to major general in a command appointment, and he is equally and wholly fitted for a major general's appointment on the staff.' The acting Commander-in-Chief, in his remarks as the superior reporting officer writes:

> This is a perceptive report which admirably sums up this excellent officer. On two particular occasions, running an exercise in Cyprus and a Study Period in UK, I have been strongly impressed by his enthusiasm, his grasp, and his ability to express himself lucidly and forcefully, gaining the confidence of his audience. He is a most likeable man, easy to get on with, who only turns on the power when it is needed so that one doesn't get the impression of an intense tightly wound-up man, but rather one of many parts who knows how and when to relax.

Two aspects of the report are interesting: first, it is extraordinary that the initiating officer, a major general, should speculate on whether a brigadier might reach a rank higher than he himself had achieved, and, second that the superior reporting officer did not pick up on the remark and point out that it was not one for the initiating officer to make.

Although Ronnie remained in the appointment of Exercise Controller UKCICC for another year there is no report in his Confidential Report book which covers that period. It may be that he did not get a report because he had already been selected for promotion to major general and it was therefore deemed unnecessary. Reports on generals are not placed in their Confidential Report books, so thereafter that valuable information trail runs cold.

Chapter 10

Major General Brigade of Gurkhas

In March 1975 Ronnie was appointed Major General Brigade of Gurkhas and Deputy Commander Land Forces Hong Kong. He took over from Major General Bunny Burnett for the second time. General Ronnie was the last person to hold the appointment of MGBG as a tied Gurkha appointment.

The Hong Kong he returned to after an absence of seven years was quite different to the place he left on relinquishing command of 1/10GR in March 1968. The Hong Kong–Sino border had become an operation that required a watchful vigilance of the activities of the CCA and an alert readiness, but the situation was peaceful to the point of being boring for the soldiers who manned the border on six-week spells of duty. The Commander British Forces (CBF), Lieutenant General Sir Edwin Bramall, had concluded that one of the factors or limitations for those in the Hong Kong government and the Armed Services working on the new Defence Costs Agreement was that, 'At least for the foreseeable future, it was realistic to discard any idea of China taking over Hong Kong by force of arms.'[152] However, there was another side to being on border duty, and the main preoccupation of the troops in the Police-Military controlled area was the prevention of illegal immigration across the border into Hong Kong. This was a time-consuming, tiring and occasionally dangerous task, as thousands of illegal immigrants (IIs) tried to make a 'home run' and get to Kowloon or Hong Kong Island, where they were not pursued. Illegal immigration had always been part of the Hong Kong scene but it became a pressing issue in the mid-1970s when the numbers increased dramatically. The Chinese did not like their people fleeing China for the 'paved with gold' streets of Hong Kong and the Hong Kong government could not cope with unrestricted immigration, because it placed an unreasonable burden on the colony's finances and infrastructure planning.

---

152 . Tillotson, Dwin Bramall, The Authorised Biography of Field Marshal The Lord Bramall, KG,GCB,OBE,MC, p.151.

Therefore there was an agreement between China and Hong Kong that IIs would be apprehended on both sides of the border and those caught in Hong Kong would be sent back to China, where, in their 're-education centres', they would be made aware of the advantages of the communist way of life. In 1975 the Police and Armed Services, but predominantly the Army, were apprehending between 20 and 50 IIs every 24 hours. This influx had to be curtailed. The whole 22 miles of the land border was fenced and the 20-foot high chain-link fence was festooned with razor wire, but the IIs climbed it, cut holes in it, crawled through the drainage culverts under it or tunnelled under it. Soldiers manning observation posts scanned the border fence and monitored detection devices while mobile teams stood-by to go rapidly along the border road that ran parallel to the border fence, to reach suspected breaches. IIs built makeshift boats and floatation devices from inner tyre tubes and plastic containers, or swam across the shark-infested waters of Deep Bay in the West and Mirs Bay in the East, so all the islands and miles of the colony's northern shoreline in the New Territories had to be watched and patrolled, predominantly at night. Patrols had to deal with the swimmers who did not make it or failed to evade the sharks. There was the cat-and-mouse battle, dealt with predominantly by the Police, against the people-smuggling syndicates, or 'snakeheads' as they were called. The syndicates involved in exploiting the aspirations of desperate people made use of those who lived on the border and had a right to cross between China and Hong Kong to work their land, and paid them handsomely. The assistance ranged from hiding IIs in the livestock carriages on trains, to the use of exceptionally fast speed boats which the Army's rigid raiders, small landing craft and the Royal Navy's and Marine Police's patrol boats could not hope to match for speed. Most of the troops involved felt, and understandably, that had they been in the IIs shoes they would be trying to do exactly the same thing, so it was an unenviable and thankless task, especially when soldiers admired the tenacity of IIs who were caught for a second or third time. It was a task that had to be done and Gurkhas dutifully carried it out well, at a time when significant numbers of them were being made redundant.

The Vietnam War came to an end soon after General Ronnie's return to Hong Kong, but it was a stark regional reminder that hard training for limited war was a high priority and much needed to prevent the Hong Kong garrison becoming a mere colonial gendarmerie. Imaginative training exercises using the hills and islands provided some all-arms and tri-service training, while company-level overseas exercises in Australia, Brunei, Fiji and New Zealand provided welcome relief from the restrictions of Hong Kong. The spectrum of training also had to include Internal Security (IS) exercises for the more likely deployment of troops to assist the Police or help the Hong Kong Government under the catch-all role of 'Aid to the Civil Powers'. In Hong Kong the latter usually involved helping in the aftermath of the typhoons or severe tropical storms that occasionally hit the colony, causing widespread flooding and some damage.

In May 1975 this role was invoked in an unexpected way. The United States flag at their embassy in Saigon was hauled down on 30 April 1975 and many South Vietnam citizens fearing for their lives fled the country by whatever means they could. On 3 May, the day before the Queen was due to arrive on an official visit to Hong Kong, Headquarters British Forces was informed that the Dutch container ship *Clara Maersk* had sighted a sinking vessel in the South China Sea and taken on board an estimated 2,800 men, women and children, all refugees from Vietnam. The *Clara Maersk* was heading for Hong Kong and would dock there to put the refugees ashore, at about the same time as the Queen was due to land at Kai Tak airport.[153] The Police suggested they could only provide eight men as the rest were all committed to the royal visit, so dealing with the refugees fell on the shoulders of the armed forces. The garrison swung into action quickly. RAF helicopters winched doctors and medical staff onto the *Clara Maersk* to deal with the sick and injured and a refugee in need of immediate hospital attention was winched off. With 12 hours' notice 7GR established at tented camp on Sek Kong airstrip in the New Territories and 10GR reactivated the old training camp at Dodwells Ridge, also in the New Territories, and, until the Police and local authorities were able to take over some weeks later, both battalions found themselves in the unusual role of running refugee camps to accommodate the 3,400 Vietnamese refugees that the *Clara Maersk* brought to Hong Kong. Thousands more Vietnamese

---

153 . The Kai Tak runway on the eastern side of Kowloon jutted out into Hong Kong's harbour.

refugees followed them to Hong Kong and it was not until 1997 that the last were forcibly repatriated to Vietnam.

For the first year of Ronnie's tour Lieutenant General Sir Edwin Bramall KCB OBE MC was the CBF and hence his boss. Bramall, known as 'General Dwin', had a very high opinion of Ronnie, and recalls that he valued his common sense, absolute integrity and loyalty. He said, 'He was a terrific Number 2', and at a time when he was concentrating on the Defence Costs Agreement negotiations with the Hong Kong Government he had the greatest confidence in allowing Ronnie to handle Land Force and Gurkha matters.[154] In fulfilling this role General Ronnie visited all aspects of the garrison and, as MGBG, the scattered units in the Brigade of Gurkhas. Captain Philip Chaganis, who was General Ronnie's first ADC, recalls memorable trips to Nepal and India, to inspect what was quaintly still known as the Gurkha Lines of Communication (L of C), where the Gurkha recruiting depots, resettlement training farms and leave and welfare headquarters were located, at Paklihawa in West Nepal and Dharan in East Nepal; to Brunei to visit the British Brunei garrison with its resident Gurkha battalion and the Training Team Brunei, which ran British Army jungle training, and to South Korea, where a strong platoon, on rotation, from the Hong Kong garrison was part of the United Nations Korean Honour Guard. There was also a Gurkha battalion stationed at Church Crookham, near Fleet in England. General Ronnie's visit to South Korea coincided with an International Commemoration of the Korean War. Philip remembers standing next to General Ronnie in the line-up of international generals and dignitaries accompanied by their aides, waiting for their five-minute slot with General Lee Sae Ho, the Chief of Staff of the Republic of Korea's Army. The Defence Attaché had emphasised the importance of the gift to be given without indicating what might be appropriate. Philip felt nervous as most of the aides were carrying large, well wrapped gifts while the one General Ronnie had told Philip to get was small and inside Philip's briefcase. When their turn came General Ronnie said to General Lee that although he was representing the British Army he was actually based in Hong Kong as the Major General Brigade of Gurkhas, and it was in

---

154. Field Marshall Bramall, Telephone interview by R. Litherland, 24 May 2017.

that capacity that his gift to the General was being given. Wrapped in a yellow duster, Philip took out a standard issue Gurkha kukri in a highly polished black scabbard. General Ronnie got it absolutely right; General Lee was thrilled to receive a gift that marked him as a warrior. The meeting lasted 15 rather than the allotted five minutes, and that Christmas and for the next few years General Ronnie and Philip both received Christmas cards from General and Mrs Lee.

The intensity of the social scene at the higher levels of society in Hong Kong had to be experienced to be understood. On their arrival Sally and Ronnie accepted most of the invitations that were sent to them and took on the challenge of Hong Kong's frenetic socialising: there were cocktail parties, social dinners, official dinners, Officers' Mess dinners, curry lunches, barbeques, junk trips and picnics, and afternoons and evenings at the races. Philip Chaganis recalls that after three months Sally and General Ronnie were exhausted and he was instructed to cut back on their social engagements, particularly those emanating from Hong Kong government circles, and allocate time for relaxation in their programmes. Among other things that meant time for golf, which once programmed became sacrosanct.

Nonetheless, official entertainment continued and Sally and Ronnie were generous and welcoming hosts at their residence at 10 Shek O. The house staff were a mix of Chinese and Gurkhas and Sally recalls the occasion when a guest, who was a senior member of the Hong Kong community, asked, on arrival, for a 'Whisky on the rocks'. The Gurkha member of staff dutifully went off to meet the request only to return and report to the guest 'We have whisky but no rocks.'

In his annual report to the King of Nepal as Major General Brigade of Gurkhas, General Ronnie informed King Birendra Bir Bikram Shah Deva that his subjects continued to display 'the characteristics which have made them so famous'. He reported that 10GR had 'completed an outstanding peace keeping role in Cyprus where they earned the respect and good will of both the Greek and Turkish communities'. Gurkha shooting teams had won both the Major and Minor Unit Championships at Bisley and Corporal Surjasher Rai of 10GR had become the first Gurkha to win the coveted Queen's Medal as the individual champion shot. On the down side, he had also to report, with regret, that the Brigade of Gurkhas was to be reduced by about

1,000 men. The closing sentence in his report expressed his feelings, 'While I remain in charge of The Brigade of Gurkhas Your Majesty has my solemn affirmation that the interests and welfare of Your Majesty's subjects will remain foremost in my mind.'

In May 1976 Lieutenant General Sir John Archer KCB, OBE took over from General Bramall. One of the cost reductions agreed in the Defence Costs Agreement, concluded before Bramall left, and which transferred more of the costs of a reduced British Garrison to the Hong Kong Government, was that the second general's appointment in Hong Kong, the Deputy Commander Land Forces, would be axed. Thus, for what was to be his last year of service General Ronnie knew he would be the last Deputy Commander Land Forces Hong Kong. It was essential, however, not least for the morale of the Brigade of Gurkhas, that there should be a Major General Brigade of Gurkhas, and it was decided that the Commander British Forces Hong Kong would also have that title and role.

A substantial part of the Defence Costs agreement was in effect a 'land deal'. Land in key areas of the colony, including Victoria Barracks in central Hong Kong and the RAF facilities at Kai Tak, which both had significant development potential, were passed back to the Hong Kong government. These facilities had to be replaced and in 1976 the changes and rebuilding began. At a lower level Gurkhas took over all the tasks and roles that had been carried out by British soldiers in the Royal Engineers and Royal Signals, and this required more extensive training for soldiers in the Gurkha Engineers and the Gurkha Signals. [155]

In his 1976 annual report as MGBG to the King of Nepal, General Ronnie was able to report that Gurkha shooting teams took six out of the top ten places out of an entry of 63 teams at the Annual Bisley Rifle Meeting. He was undoubtedly proud that Gurkha shooting skills were so high, but he was not a great fan of Bisley shooting, believing that it was not particularly relevant to the battlefield. He may not have appreciated that the promotion of competitive shooting at Bisley in the early and mid-1970s was part of the drive to improve battlefield shooting in Northern Ireland, a campaign that Gurkhas were not involved

---

155   . Soon to become the Queen's Gurkha Engineers and Queen's Gurkha Signals, at the Silver Jubilee in 1977.

in. His views were probably tempered by the effects of the overwhelmingly better firepower that the British enjoyed over the Japanese, which he had witnessed as a young officer towards the end of the war in Burma; also by the short-range, close-quarter engagements that were the norm in the Malayan Emergency and the Indonesian Confrontation. He was a strong believer in the use of firepower rather than manpower in battle. In 1982 shortly after the end of the Falklands War he came to see me in my office in HQBG in the HMS *Tamar* building. I was the Brigade Major Brigade of Gurkhas at the time and General Ronnie dropped in while on a visit to 10GR as Colonel of the Regiment. The King of Nepal had asked, when consulted about the use of Gurkhas in the South Atlantic, that he be informed of any Gurkha casualties before the news reached any elements in Nepali society and the press who were hostile to the use of Nepalese citizens in the British Army. HQBG was tasked to do this, and to achieve it the Headquarters was included on the distribution of SITREPs and casualty reports during the Falklands war. This allowed me, with the help of Cpl Mangalnarayan Pradhan, to plot the course of the war. General Ronnie and I discussed aspects of what I had learned and I mentioned some of the casualty figures. During our discussion General Ronnie observed that a Parachute battalion and a Marine battalion appeared to have carried out battalion attacks on similar objectives, but in comparison to the Marine battalion, the Parachute battalion had suffered heavy casualties. This prompted him to say with some feeling that the Parachute battalion appeared not to have learnt that battles are best won using firepower and not manpower.

In the same report he informed the King of Nepal that responsibility for all communications to and from Hong Kong and for all field engineering work there had been taken over by the Gurkha Signals and the Gurkha Engineers. He mentioned that the depot at Paklihawa in West Nepal was to be closed, and he reported on the success of the pupils at the Gurkha High School in Hong Kong in the Nepalese School Leaving Certificate exam. In concluding his report he explained that he would shortly be handing over his responsibilities as MGBG to Lieutenant General Sir John Archer KCB OBE, and retiring from the Army. He said, 'I am sad to leave the Army and thus end my service with Gurkhas. But I do so without regrets, for it has been my good fortune, and my greatest reward, to serve with these splendid soldiers for more than 34 years.'

Philip Chaganis recalled that General Ronnie rarely talked about his career, but on one occasion he let slip that he had been convinced that the rank of brigadier would be his ceiling. He said he was surprised to have been promoted to major general. This, I believe, was a typical example of his modesty, but it also reveals that unlike many who reached two-starred rank he was not driven by ambition. Both Bramall and Archer had a high opinion of General Ronnie. Field Marshal Bramall said he was surprised Ronnie did not get a second two-star appointment,[156] as he was well qualified for a 'thinking' staff job, but he went on to mention that the Army was contracting, competition was fierce at the time and like many who knew Ronnie well he observed that he was a quiet, extremely modest and unassuming person.[157] It is possible that the image and manner he portrayed was not one that the Army wished its most senior officers to project at a time of reductions and uncertainty.

On 1 March 1977, shortly before his retirement, General Ronnie took over as Colonel of the 10th Gurkhas Rifles from General Bunny Burnett. In his letter on appointment he wrote with typical modesty:

Proud as I am to be Colonel of the Tenth Gurkhas, it is with a sense of humility that I assume the appointment. General Bunny Burnett's challenging job in Teheran made it hard for him to keep contact either with the Regiment or the Association. By default then, and after only two years 'in the chair' he has been succeeded by a lesser man. This is the third time I have taken over from Bunny: in command of First Tenth, as Major General Brigade of Gurkhas and now as Colonel 10GR. Familiarity with the process makes the task no easier! The Regiment will miss his uniquely galvanising personality. Who knows, in a few years from now, he may be asked to take over again.[158]

10GR provided a Guard of Honour to mark his retirement and departure from Hong Kong. It was commanded by Major

156 . As a major-general.
157 . Field Marshal Bramall, telephone interview by R. Litherland, 24 May 2017.
158 . Pearson, Bugle &Kukri: The Story of the 10th Princess Mary's Own Gurkha Rifles. Vol.3, pp.25–26.

Madankumar Subba and Ronnie was accompanied by his ADC Captain Nima Wangdi Lama. This was a fitting tribute in the company of two officers who had been with him at the sharp end when he commanded 1/10GR during the 1967 border troubles.

Chapter 11

Life After the Army

Ronnie, Sally and the girls left Hong Kong in late March 1977. They returned home to The Chalet. Ronnie attended an accountancy course as part of his resettlement training and his Regular Army service ended on 28 June 1977, when he was put on retired pay with a reserve liability as a major general until 26 May 1983. He chose as his second career to be the Bursar at Wellesley House Preparatory School in Broadstairs. The school was 10 minutes from The Chalet and in fine weather Ronnie cycled to work. He held the appointment from September 1977 until December 1988, retiring from the School at the age of 65 – which was five years beyond the normal retirement age for teachers and bursars at the time. As with everything he did he carried out his responsibilities with an assured thoroughness and care, and with understanding when dealing with the staff, pupils and parents. One of the early improvements he made was to computerise the school's accounts. Intended as a measure to improve the accounting procedures and to save time, things did not quite turn out as he would have wished. His workload actually increased as the school only had one computer and that was his. When a parent said 'I understand you were a Sergeant Major in the Army', rather than be drawn into what might have been seen as an aggrandizing explanation, Ronnie simply replied 'Yes …. something like that.' The proximity of Wellesley House Prep to The Chalet suited him well, and the long hours which he might have spent commuting to a more high-powered appointment elsewhere allowed him to devote time to his two principal interests – Gurkhas and Golf.

His career as a professional soldier had lasted for just over 35 years, but there was no let-up and he packed a great deal into the next 38 years. In addition to his second career as a bursar, he was Colonel 10GR (1977–85), President of the 3GR Officers' Association (1978–2008), Chairman Buckmaster Memorial Home in Broadstairs (1981–2009), Chairman of the Gurkha Brigade Association (1975–85), a Committee member, Captain and then President of the Royal St George's Golf Club,

Chairman of the Open Championship Committee in 2003. He was also a trustee of the Clan Donald Lands Trust. He wrote Volume 2 of the Regimental History of the 10th Princess Mary's Own Gurkha Rifles, completing it in 1985, and he was Editor of *The Bugle & Kukri*, the journal of the 10th Gurkhas, from 1997 to 2002. At home he was the Chancellor, Butler and Head Gardener.

On 23 February 1985 General Ronnie handed over his appointment as Colonel of the Regiment to General Sir Garry Johnson KCB, OBE, MC. In his tribute to General Ronnie, General Garry wrote:

> Ronnie has served the Regiment with devotion for many years, but his achievements as our Colonel will be specially remembered. Successive Commanding Officers have benefitted greatly from his wise advice; under his guidance the Association has flourished and the Regimental trust prospered; and from his hand has come the splendid [second] volume of the Regimental History. He and Sally have given an enormous amount of time and energy to the life of the Regiment in the last years, and we owe them both a debt of gratitude. Ronnie will, of course, continue to be active in Gurkha affairs as President of the Gurkha Brigade Association and I am delighted that he has agreed to remain a member of the Regimental Council.[159]

Volume 2 of the Regimental History covering the period 1948–75 was a significant undertaking and a major contribution to the history of the Tenth Gurkhas. It was published in 1984. It is interesting, informative and written in a style that allows the reader to understand the many facets of life in a Gurkha Regiment on operations and during periods of peace. It covers the important contributions made by both 1/10GR and 2/10GR in the Malayan Emergency and the Indonesian Confrontation and does so in a way that brings the challenges of those campaigns to life. Work on Volume 2 started when Ronnie was commanding 1/10GR in 1966–67. He tasked officers to start looking for, collecting and collating material on the regiment's activities since 1948, where Volume 1 ended. It helped that he had served in both Battalions, that he was interested in Regimental, Gurkha and military history and was keen to

---

159 . Pearson, Bugle & Kukri, Vol.3, p.150.

Sally and Ronnie McAlister[160]

promote and foster that interest within the Regiment. When he commanded 1/10GR he initiated the collecting of medals earned by distinguished former members of the Regiment and had them mounted and displayed in the Battalion messes and the Guardroom. Framed cases containing miniatures of campaign and gallantry medals won, with the names of the recipients under the gallantry awards, were made to commemorate campaigns the Regiment had fought in. This initiative raised the Battalion's knowledge and understanding of its own history. In 1966 the Annual Inspection parade theme in 1/10GR was the 200th anniversary of the raising of the Regiment as the 14th Battalion of Coast Sepoys, later the 10th Madras Native Infantry (10MNI). Colonel Ronnie revived the links to 10MNI knowing that the connection between the old Madras Army and the Gurkha Brigade (pre-1947) and Brigade of Gurkhas (post-1947) through the 10th Gurkhas was a sensitive matter within the Brigade. The 2nd Gurkhas in particular took understandable pride in being the oldest Gurkha Regiment, having been raised as a Gurkha unit, along with the 1st Gurkhas, in 1815. In 1890 a series of changes began whereby the 10th Madras Infantry ceased to enlist Madrassis and instead was authorised to enlist

160 . The McAlister Family Collection.

three companies of Gurkhas and five of Assamese hillmen. The Colours, Battle Honours, Honorary Badges, Mess and Band Funds and the chattels of 10th Madras Infantry were retained, and an important religious icon, the Mahabir Swami, was voluntarily handed on by the Hindu Madrassis to their Hindu Gurkha successors. Whether or not the old Regiment had been disbanded was a question that was debated and passed all the way up to Parliament, which decided it had merely been reorganised. In reality there were never more than 12.5% Assamese and by 1895 enough Gurkha recruits were available to complete the Regiment, and its title now became 10th Regiment (1st Burma Gurkha Rifles) Madras Infantry.

Despite this, when in 1903 the Indian Army was restructured and the Gurkha Brigade was formed, there was confusion over the Regiment's right to retain the pre-1890 honours and distinctions; the highest authorities again ruled that the entitlement was valid, yet the commanding officers of 1/10GR and 2/10GR (of 1902–07, later 7 GR) could not agree on what to do, and the Regiment did not have a Colonel who might have advised them or made a decision. Hence in 1903 the Regiment (now finally called 10th Gurkha Rifles) ceased displaying the pre-1890 honours and distinctions. This was soon regretted and in the 1930s the Regiment applied to re-adopt the pre-1890 Honours. Without access to all the papers, the application failed, yet hope lingered.

In the 1980s David Harding, as Regimental Archivist, conducted fresh research, uncovered the full story, and was able to show that there were strong grounds for making a new application. General Ronnie was currently Chairman of the Gurkha Brigade Association (GBA); he took David aside at a dinner and expressed strong doubts about applying for the Honours to be restored. In 1967, as commanding officer and with his 10GR hat on he had strongly supported the connection, but in 1987 he evidently felt he had to tread carefully while wearing his Chairman GBA hat. Many officers in the other Gurkha Regiments felt a connection with the 10th Madras Native Infantry (10MNI) was inappropriate to an organisation that strongly identified and prided itself as Gurkha, whereas Tenth Gurkhas were conscious that they had inherited their number from Tenth Madras, and took pride in it.

The Colonel of the Regiment, Lieutenant General Sir Garry Johnson, reviewed the historical evidence and precedents and had the Army Historical Branch do the same; they agreed that the case was very strong, especially as David had found that of the two other regiments which had undergone similar changes of personnel in 1890, one had retained their honours and the other had relinquished then successfully reclaimed them, and King George V had expressed interest in the latter case and approved it. General Garry took wide soundings within the Regiment and its retired members, and found the reaction was in favour of applying. On 3 March 1987 he submitted a formal application to Her Majesty the Queen, and on 3 March 1988 the old Honours and Distinctions were restored in Defence Council Instruction Army 26/88.[161] In the event the subject did not become an issue, and the pre-1890 Battle Honours and Badges are displayed on the drums of today's Gurkha infantry regiment, The Royal Gurkha Rifles, alongside the many others earned over the years by the 2nd, 6th, 7th and 10th Gurkha Rifles.

In 1997 General Ronnie was invited to edit the regimental magazine – *The Bugle & Kukri*. In his first editorial he opened with the following words:

> Most readers of this journal are retired, a majority probably over 60, and it is a privilege of the elderly to discuss what should be done to solve the great problems of the day, rejoicing in the knowledge that we are not actually responsible for finding solutions or implementing them. This is the rationale under which an editorial in an otherwise parochial journal can include some of the major themes and events of the year. These may also serve to give perspective to the year, particularly for overseas readers, and remind anyone who picks up the Journal some years hence of the wider issues which marked 1997.

In all five of the editorials that he wrote his reviews of 1997 to 2001 are as enjoyable to read today as they were when they were published. Well written and informative, they reflect his deep understanding of what was going on in the world and how well and widely he read and kept abreast of current affairs. His commentary on events is astute and not without sound predictions and a nice touch of humour. He also took the opportunity to gather in and involve members of the

161 . DF Harding, 'The Restoration of the Old Pre-1890 Battle Honours', Bugle & Kukri journal, Vol.2, No 7, 1988, pp.35–42.

Association, getting them to contribute so that the journal covered a rich mix of interesting stories. The section 'News of the Old & Bold' expanded significantly, bringing old comrades closer together and more importantly he persuaded many to write down their recollections of actions and battles they took part in. Excellent articles from former officers who served with 1/10GR, 3/10GR or 4/10GR in Burma, or with 2/10GR in Italy and with 3/10GR in Java and 4/10GR in Indo-China produced remarkable insights into aspects of regimental history that might otherwise have not been recorded. General Ronnie also wrote several articles that cast a different light on aspects of regimental history and in the process added immeasurably to the regimental archive and the Regiment's understanding of its past. He captured many tales before it was too late. In short, he edited five outstanding journals. It might seem to some that he was simply gifted when it came to putting things down on paper; I do not believe that was so; he undoubtedly had a natural literary ability but there was more to it than that; his writing was a matter of application and a pride in doing things well: the adage that 'hard writing makes easy reading' is appropriate.

Shortly after he retired from the Army he also became a trustee of the Clan Donald Lands Trust involved in the preservation and restoration of Armadale Castle, Gardens and Museum on the Isle of Skye. He served as a Clan Donald trustee for 21 years and during that time he and Sally formed a close friendship with Ellice and Rosa MacDonald, the American philanthropists, who also gave significant financial support to the Gurkha Welfare Trust. On relinquishing his appointment as a trustee he was awarded the Somerled Medal and Boat, caste in silver, in recognition of his exceptional service.

Golf played an important part in Ronnie's life throughout it: it was his principal form of relaxation. Wherever he was stationed he joined a local golf club and played regularly. He did not shy away from playing even when the situation was tense on the Hong Kong border. He had a very good eye, excelled at squash and racquets and was a good tennis player but it was golf he enjoyed most. It may well be that he inherited his interest from his father, who was a keen golfer and proposed Ronnie's membership of The Honourable Society of Edinburgh Golfers at Muirfield in East Lothian, believing Ronnie would choose to serve in the Argylls after the War and Partition. Ronnie had to tell his father he had chosen to remain a Gurkha officer. He had little opportunity to enjoy Muirfield as he was seldom in Scotland. He remembered being told by his mother that in her marriage to his father 'the Regiment came first, golf came second and I came third' and he almost certainly made a mental note of this and the implications of his mother's assertions about his father's priorities. It was not, however, a matter he had to pay any attention to while he was a bachelor, nor was it when he married, for in Sally Marshall Ronnie found the perfect partner. Sally had been introduced to golf as a 12-year-old and became, like Ronnie, an excellent single figure handicap golfer. They both excelled at the game and enjoyed playing together.

As mentioned earlier, in 1966 Jim Hardwick, the professional at the Fanling Golf Club in the New Territories, presented a hickory-shafted 'Clamity Jane' putter to the Regiment as a golf trophy. Inevitably, it came to be known as 'The Colonel's Putter' with an unwritten understanding that it was actually 'The Colonel Ronnie McAlister Putter.' It was a much sought-after trophy, contested for keenly. The rules were simple – it was a Stableford competition; it was to be played as often as possible; it could not be played for by fewer than four players and it was open to all officers of, or attached to, the Regiment. The winner had the privilege of paying for a silver band with his name and the date inscribed on it to be put on the hickory shaft. Once the shaft had filled up with silver bands the winners' names were put on small silver plaques hung on the putter, and it was displayed in the Officers' Mess mounted in a horizontal positon. Ronnie won the Colonel's Putter two and a half times. He was the outright winner in February 1967, before the confrontations on the Hong Kong border became serious, and in October 1967 after the tensions on the border had eased. Then in 1977, when he was MGBG, he and Major Nick Cooke GM shared a victory. That his name does not appear more often on the Colonel's Putter merely reflects that he relinquished command in March 1968 and rarely served near the Battalion between then and 1975. That he did not win it more often probably says much about his scrupulous adherence to the rules and his handicap as a regular golfer, as opposed to the dubious handicaps that some bandits among the infrequent players claimed.

It was, however, in retirement that his involvement and contribution to golf really took hold. The Chalet is very close to the North Foreland Golf Club and not far from the famous Royal

St George's Golf Club at Sandwich, which Ronnie joined in 1968. Ronnie's association with the famous old club was to be long and distinguished. At Sandwich he served on the General Committee for some years until his retirement from Wellesley House Prep School in December 1988, when he was appointed Captain Royal St George's Golf Club for the 1989-90 season. He was the Honorary Treasurer from 1991 to 1996 and in 1993 he was invited to be chairman of the ad hoc committee formed to manage the Open Championship, which was played at Royal St George's that year. Michael Attenborough, a fellow committee member at the Club, wrote of Ronnie's ad hoc committee chairmanship:

> It was a responsibility that required tactful but firm liaison skills both with The Royal & Ancient Golf Club of St Andrews and with the members at large, whose interests in the Championship were many and various. Ronnie carried out these duties with military efficiency coupled with charm and understanding. The 1993 Open, won by the Australian Greg Norman, was a thrilling affair and a huge success for the Club, the R&A and the thousands of spectators who made their way to east Kent to watch the world's finest golfers and to savour the joys of links golf at Royal St George's.

Ronnie was President Royal St George's Golf Club from 2004 to 2008. On Ronnie, Michael Attenborough went on to write: 'He swung the club smoothly, was always competitive and difficult to beat. He loved the game and all that came with it, and most especially the opportunity it gave him to encourage others making their way professionally in golf. To this end he proposed to Royal St George's that the Club should host annually a 36-hole golf invitation tournament for assistant professionals attached to clubs in South East Kent. This tournament, first held in 1991, has now enjoyed its 25th anniversary and remains an important event in the Royal St George's calendar – a splendid legacy from a great servant of the club.' In that very English way Michael Attenborough expressed his admiration for Ronnie when he said he felt Ronnie had one failing, which was that his contribution to the Club's bar profits fell short of what the other members of the committee managed. Throughout the Club Ronnie was admired for his contribution to golf as a golfer, an administrator and for being his own man.

Although golf was important throughout his life, and he put something back into the game in retirement, his real love, after Sally and the girls, was for the Gurkhas. He devoted much of his energy and time to their interests. His regimental career with 3GR and 10GR spanned 34 years, and he continued to serve in Regimental and Gurkha Association appointments for another 30 years after his full-time service ended. It was not until 2008 that he stopped his direct involvement in Gurkha matters, when he stood down as Chairman of the 3GR Association, when that Association was wound up 66 years after he joined it, and 61 years after 3GR was transferred to the Indian Army at Indian Independence in 1947. Even after that he remained a wonderful source of knowledge on Gurkha issues and regimental history, and was always happy to be consulted. His advice was unerringly sound and willingly given. There comes a time in most peoples' lives when they contemplate 'the road not taken'. I wonder if Ronnie ever looked back and considered whether he might have made different decisions and taken a different road. I doubt it. He was a career soldier and dedicated to the Gurkhas he served, and it is clear that he enjoyed both his career and serving his Gurkhas. He came from an Army family and although he was caught in the circumstances of his time and called up during the war he would probably have followed in his father's footsteps. That he did not choose to serve in the Argylls was almost certainly because his mother left his father, and meeting Bunjy Collins sowed the seeds of serving with Gurkhas for both Ronnie and Brian. It is clear from his article 'First Impressions' that in that decision he had found the career, people and lifestyle he wanted and that he enjoyed it all.

Ronnie died on 8 September 2015 surrounded by his family, not long after he had been diagnosed with pancreatic cancer and two days after his illness forced him to bed. He did not want anyone apart from his immediate family to know about his illness, but the word got out through friends at the Royal St George's Golf Club and in a reply to an e-mail from Bill Dawson, a regimental colleague, he replied: 'I am fully at peace with my future and having lots of laughs with the family (down for the bank holiday) ... So don't feel sorry for me ... I have had a great life. No church or memorial service for me – a quiet family affair. Tell everyone.' It was typical of the man to want no fuss, no memorial service, no celebration of his life and no sadness. His decision and wishes, however, left a void. Many of his numerous colleagues and friends would have wished to mark his passing with a celebration of his life and achievements. Ronnie was cremated after a family-only funeral and his ashes scattered in a place they loved and known only to Sally.

At a regimental lunch a month later, General Sir Garry Johnson, as President of the 10th Gurkha Regimental Association, took the opportunity to say a few words about 'Ronnie Mac', reminding those who knew him, and informing those who did not, what a tremendous contribution he had made to the Regiment and what an exceptional person he had been. General Ronnie had every right to be content. He was one of life's contributors: a man who gave more than he took; a man, who, in the process of giving, was modest to a fault. He never blew his own trumpet, never sought the limelight, never wanted a fuss and never failed to carry out his responsibilities and to do his duty, and whatever he did, he did it well.

Acknowledgements

I am grateful to the many people who helped me produce this biography on Ronnie McAlister, but especially to Sally, his widow, for having me to stay at The Chalet to talk about Ronnie and for allowing me to see his papers and files. I thank also Ronnie's daughter Angela McAlister for her thoughts about her father.

I am indebted to General Sir Garry Johnson, KCB OBE MC for his comments on my first draft and for writing the Foreword, also to David Harding, 10GR's unofficial archivist, who sub-edited this biography and in the process made numerous helpful comments and suggestions. I am in particular thankful to him for clarifying the detail on the restoration of the honours and distinctions of 10MNI. Without their sage advice, comments and encouragement my efforts would be the poorer.

I could not have tackled my subject without the contributions made by several officers of the 10th Princess Mary's Own Gurkha Rifles, in particular the late Brigadier Chris Pike DSO OBE; Colonel Bruce Niven MBE MA; Colonel Mark Cook OBE; Lieutenant Colonel Andy Watt MBE; Lieutenant Colonel Nick Worthington; Major Chris Hughes MC; Major Kit Maunsell MC and Captain Nandabahadur Rai MM.

Without the contributions of members of other British and Gurkha Regiments and the Hong Kong Police my insights into Ronnie's life and activities would have lacked balance, and I am indebted to: the late Field Marshal Lord Bramall KG GCB OBE MC; Field Marshal Sir John Chapple GCB CBE, (Late 2GR); Lieutenant General Sir Derek Boorman KCB; Major General Michael Tillotson CB CBE; Colonel Phillip Chaganis OBE (Late Queen's Gurkha Transport Regiment); the late Lieutenant Colonel Mike Barrett OBE (Queens Gurkha Signals); Lieutenant Colonel Yerburgh RE, Assistant Commissioner Jim Main CPM RHKP. I am most grateful to Trevor Bedford MBE, for sparing the time to talk through in detail the events when he and Ronnie were taken hostage in 1967.

My thanks go to all the staff at the Gurkha Museum and in particular the Director Gavin Edgerley-Harris. I am indebited to

Michael Attenborough for commenting on Ronnie's contribution to the Royal St George's Golf Club, and to Mrs Claire Hardings, the Headmaster's Secretary at Wellesley House Prep School.

Finally, to Jane, my wife, my eternal thanks for her patience in putting up with all I left undone that I should have done following my decision to attempt another contribution to 10th Gurkha regimental history, by writing a biography on Ronnie McAlister.

Bibliography

Interviews

Bedford, Trevor, District Officer New Territories, Hong Kong 1967; interview by R. Litherland Sunday 10 July 2017.

Bramall, Field Marshal Lord, CBF Hong Kong 1975–76; telephone interview by R. Litherland 24 May 2017.

McAlister, Sally (widow of Maj Gen McAlister); interviews by R. Litherland at Broadstairs, Kent, Thu 12 and Fri 13 July 2018.

Martin, PLdeC, audio recording by Conrad Wood, IWM catalogue no.12778, dated 1992-11-12.

Pike, CJ, OC D Company 1/10GR 1966–67, subsequently Brigadier OBE DSO; telephone interviews by R. Litherland 26 Aug 2016 and 12 Feb 2018.

Journals and newspapers

3rd Gurkha Rifles Association Journals and Newsletter, 1950–2008.

The Acorn, Regimental Magazine of The Life Guards, Autumn 1967, Vol.1. No.4.

The Bugle & Kukri, The Journal of the 10th Princess Mary's Own Gurkha Rifles, 1949–2002.

The Kukri, The Journal of the Brigade of Gurkhas, 1950–2002.

South China Sunday Post-Herald, Hong Kong, Sunday, July 9 1967, Front Page continued on p.2. col. 3.

The Times, London, 12 Sep 2015, Obituary for Major General RWL McAlister CB OBE.

The Times, London, 15 Feb 2006, Obituary for Major General PL de C Martin CBE.

Printed books

Barclay, Brig CN, CBE DSO, Editor, *Regimental History of the 3rd Queen Alexandra's Own Gurkha Rifles, Volume II (1927–1947),* (William Clowes and Sons Ltd, London 1953).

Bickers, Robert, and Yep, Ray, editors, *May Days in Hong Kong: Riot and Emergency in Hongkong 1967*, (Hong Kong University Press 2009).

Cheung, Gary Ka-wai, *Hong Kong's Watershed: The 1967 Riots*, (Hong Kong University Press 2009)

Cooper, John, *Colony in Conflict: The Hong Kong Disturbances May 1967–January 1968*, (Winsome Printing Press, Hong Kong 1970).

Gould, Tony, *Imperial Warriors* (London, Granta Books 1999).

Lyman, Robert, *Slim, Master of War, Burma and the Birth of Modern Warfare,* (Constable & Robinson, London 2004).

McAlister, RWL, *Bugle & Kukri: The Story of the 10th Princess Mary's Own Gurkha Rifles,* Vol.2 (10GR Regimental Trust, 1984; repr. 1985).

Pearson, Brigadier PTC, *Bugle & Kukri: The Story of the 10th Princess Mary's Own Gurkha Rifles*, Vol.3 (10GR Regimental Trust, 2000).

Pocock, Tom, *Fighting General: The Public and Private Campaigns of General Sir Walter Walker*, (Collins, London 1973).

Tillotson, Michael, *Dwin Bramall, The Authorised Biography of Field Marshal The Lord Bramall, KG, GCB, OBE, MC*, (Sutton Publishing Limited, London 2005).

Van der Bijl, Nick, *Confrontation: The War with Indonesia 1962–1966*, (Pen and Sword Books, Barnsley 2007).

Other sources

Edwardes, JAS, letter and attachments relating to Hong Kong 1967, dated 8 Oct 2018.

McAlister, RWL, 'R.W.L McAlister – CV', undated.

Main, JS, 'The Man Kam To Incident, 11th–12th August 1967', unpublished account sent to R. Litherland, 25th May 2017.

Main, JS, 'The Sha Tau Kok Incident, 8th July 1967', unpublished account sent to R. Litherland, 24th June 2017.

List of Abbreviations

10GR:	10th Gurkha Rifles
1/10GR:	1st Battalion of the 10th Gurkha Rifles
2/10GR:	2nd Battalion of the 10th Gurkha Rifles
2GR:	2nd Gurkha Rifles
3GR:	3rd Gurkha Rifles
6GR:	6th Gurkha Rifles
7GR:	7th Gurkha Rifles
2IC:	Second in Command
AA:	Anti-Aircraft
ADC:	Aide-de-Camp
AOP:	Air Observation Post
Argylls:	1st Battalion of the Argyll and Sutherland Highlanders
ASP:	Assistant Superintendent of Police
A/Tk:	Anti-Tank
BAOR:	British Army of the Rhine
BGGS:	Brigade of Gurkhas Golf Society
BMBG:	Brigade Major Brigade of Gurkhas
BMH:	British Military Hospital
BO:	British Officer
CB:	Companion of the Order of the Bath
CBF:	Commander British Forces
CCA:	Chinese Communist Army
CCO:	Clandestine Communist Organisation
CIA:	Central Intelligence Agency (US)
CO:	Commanding Officer
CT:	Communist Terrorist
DA:	Defence Attaché

DAA & QMG:	Deputy Assistant Adjutant & Quartermaster General (Abbreviated to DQ)
DCM:	Distinguished Conduct Medal
DF:	Defensive Fire
DF (SOS):	Defensive Fire (Save Our Souls)
DOBOPS:	Director of Borneo Operations
DS:	Directing Staff
DSO:	Distinguished Service Order
ECO:	Emergency Commissioned Officer
EUNT:	Emergency Unit New Territories
EWC:	Eastern Warfare Centre
FOO:	Forward Observation Officer
GBA:	Gurkha Brigade Association
GCB:	Knight Grand Cross of the Order of the Bath
GM:	Gurkha Major
GO:	Gurkha Officer
GOR:	Gurkha Other Rank
GPMG:	General Purpose Machine Gun
GR:	Gurkha Rifles
Hav:	Havildar (Indian Army Sergeant)
HKP:	Hong Kong Police
HQ:	Head Quarter
IBT:	Indonesian Border Terrorist
IS:	Internal Security
Jem:	Jemadar (Indian Army Lieutenant)
JNCO:	Junior Non-Commissioned Officer
KCB:	Knight Commander of the Order of the Bath
KGO:	King's Gurkha Officer
LCpl:	Lance Corporal
LG:	London Gazette
LMG:	Light Machine Gun
L/Nk:	Lance Naik (Indian Army Lance Corporal)
MBE:	Member of the Order of the British Empire
MC:	Military Cross

MCP:	Malaysian Communist Party
MGBG:	Major General Brigade of Gurkhas
MID:	Mention in Despatches
MIO:	Military Intelligence Officer
MM:	Military Medal
MMG:	Medium Machine Gun
MOD:	Ministry of Defence
MRLA:	Malayan Races Liberation Army
MTO:	Motor Transport Officer
NCO:	Non-Commissioned Officer
OBE:	Officer of the Order of the British Empire
OCTU:	Officer Cadet Training Unit
PKI:	*Parti Komunis Indonesian*
PLA:	People's Liberation Army
PTU:	Police Tactical Unit
QGO:	Queen's Gurkha Officer
RAEC:	Royal Army Education Corps
RAMC:	Royal Army Medical Corps
RHKP:	Royal Hong Kong Police
RMO:	Regimental Medical Officer
RTR:	Royal Tank Regiment
SLR:	Self-Loading Rifle
SOE:	Special Operations Executive
Sub:	Subadar (Indian Army Captain)
Sub-Maj:	Subadar Major (Indian Army Major)
TA:	Territorial Army
TNA:	The National Archives
TNKU:	*Tentera Nasional Kalimantan Utara*
USAAF:	United States of America Air Force
WO:	Warrant Officer

Glossary of Military Terms relating to a Gurkha Infantry Battalion in the mid-late 1960s.

Ranks, Groupings and Responsibilities:

At Platoon Level

Rifleman, abbreviated to Rfn, was the Gurkha soldier.

Lance Corporal, abbreviated to LCpl, usually a Section Second-in-Command, who commanded a half section of four men, more often than not this group included the section machine gun.

Corporal, abbreviated to Cpl, usually commanded a Section of eight men (a LCpl, six Rfn and himself). The Section usually had a two-man machine gun group (a Light Machine Gun (LMG) or a General Purpose Machine Gun (GMPG)) and the other six men were armed with a personal weapon (a 7.62mm Self-Loading Rifle (SLR), a 5.56mm Armalite (AR16) or a 9mm Sub-Machine Gun (SMG)).

Sergeant, abbreviated to Sgt, usually a Platoon Second-in-Command. He had specific responsibilities for the field administration of the platoon – ammunition, casualties and rations.

2nd Lieutenant/Lieutenant (British Officer (BO)) or Lieutenant (Queen's Gurkha Officer (QGO)), abbreviated to 2Lt/Lt or Lt (QGO), usually commanded a platoon which had a small Platoon HQ (the Lt, Sgt, a radio operator, a medic, a Rfn, who in addition to his personal weapon carried a 2-inch mortar, and a Rfn, who was the platoon runner (message carrier) and provided protection for the Pl HQ) and three sections of eight men each. Thus, ideally and on paper a platoon was 30 strong, but this was seldom the case, as there was no reserve to cover illness or any other absence.

At Company Level

Colour Sergeant, abbreviated to CSgt, was the Company Quartermaster Sergeant, abbreviated to CQMS, with specific responsibilities for ration and equipment resupply.

Warrant Officer Class 2, abbreviated to WO2, was the Company Sergeant Major, abbreviated to CSM, with specific responsibilities for discipline and ammunition resupply.

Captain or Captain (QGO), abbreviated to Capt or Capt (QGO), was usually the Second-in-Command of the Company. He had specific responsibilities for the field administration of the Company – ammunition, casualties and rations.

Major, abbreviated to Maj, usually commanded a Company comprising the Company HQ and three platoons each of 30 men. The size of the Company HQ varied depending on the number of attachments required for the type of operation; however it would usually include the Major (BO), a Captain (QGO), the Company Sergeant Major (CSM), the Company Quartermaster Sergeant (CQMS) who was more often than not back at the company base, two radio operators (one on the Company radio net and one on the Battalion radio net), a medic and two Rfn for protection.

Attachments from within the battalion might come from: the Mortar Platoon (Mor Pl) equipped with 81mm mortars with a Cpl Mortar Fire Controller (MFC); the Anti-Tank Platoon (ATk Pl); the GPMG(Sustained Fire) Platoon (GPMG(SF) Pl or the Assault Pioneer Platoon (Aslt Pnr Pl).

Attachments from outside the battalion might include: a Troop (usually three vehicles) from an armoured unit (tanks or armoured cars); a Forward Observation Officer (FOO) and his FOO group from the Royal Artillery (the FOO controlled the fire of any artillery guns in support) or a troop (platoon equivalent) from the Royal Engineers (for demolition or construction work).

At Battalion level

<u>Lieutenant Colonel</u>, abbreviated to Lt Col, was the battalion commander, known as the Commanding Officer, abbreviated to CO. The CO was supported by Battalion Headquarters, abbreviated to Bn HQ, which included the following:

<u>Second-in-Command</u>, abbreviated to 2IC, a Major.

<u>Gurkha Major</u>, abbreviated to GM. The GM was the senior Queen's Gurkha Officer (QGO). He was responsible for advising the CO on all Gurkha matters, covering Gurkha customs and traditions, family, tribal and religious issues, in particular matters that related to Gurkha welfare, discipline and morale.

The rank of QGO was unique to the Brigade of Gurkhas. It was a rank between British Officer (BO) and NCO (Non-Commissioned Officer). QGOs in a Gurkha battalion held most of the platoon commander and second-in-command appointments. This meant the number of British Officers in a Gurkha battalion was limited to about 12 officers, as opposed to about 45 in a British battalion (The 12 excludes the Royal Army Medical Corps (RAMC) doctor, the Royal Army Education Corps (RAEC) Education Officer and the Royal Army Pay Corps (RAPC) Paymaster).

In British battalions a number of appointments have traditionally been held by officers commissioned from the ranks. The same applied in Gurkha battalions and those officers commissioned to hold British appointments were known as Gurkha Commissioned Officers (GCO).

<u>Adjutant</u>, abbreviated to Adjt, a Captain, responsible as the principal staff officer to the CO, for the receipt and issuing of orders, instructions and correspondence up and down the 'chain of command'. In a Gurkha battalion he usually commanded the Pipes & Drums Platoon which on operations was the Bn HQ defence platoon and provided the Battalion's stretcher bearers. The Adjt was supported by a Head Clerk and several clerks.

<u>Regimental Signals Officer</u>, abbreviated to RSO, a Captain or Lieutenant, commanded the Signals Platoon that was responsible for radio and telephone communications up and down the 'chain of command'.

Intelligence Officer, abbreviated to IO, a Captain or Lieutenant, commanded the Intelligence Section and was responsible for the collation of intelligence, mapping and air photographs.

In a Gurkha battalion there were four Rifle Companies (A, B, C and D Coys), a Support Company (Sp Coy) and a Headquarter Company (HQ Coy). The composition of the Rifle Companies is described above.

Support Company, commanded by a Major, with a Captain (QGO) as the Second-in-Command, usually comprised the Mortar Platoon (8 x 81mm mortars each manned by a crew of three, usually grouped in sections of 2 x 81mm mortars); the Anti-Tank Platoon (8 x Wombats – a 120mm recoiless rifle manned by a crew of three); the Reconnaissance Platoon (7 x 4 men groups who were close reconnaissance experts and also trained as snipers) and the Pioneer Platoon (3 x sections with responsibility for minor engineering tasks like demolitions, helicopter landing pad construction, mine laying, wiring and the clearing of wire obstacles and minefields).

Headquarter Company, commanded by a Major, with a Captain Second-in-Command, included the Signal Platoon (which provided signallers on the Battalion net; on the Brigade net and at re-broadcast/relay stations), the Pipes & Drums (who on operations were the Battalion HQ defence platoon and stretcher bearers; the Quartermaster Department (storemen and cooks), the Motor Transport Platoon (which provided all the drivers for the Battalion's vehicles (landrovers, 4-ton trucks and staff cars), the Clerks, the Regimental Medical Officer (RMO), a Major or Captain from the Royal Army Medical Corps (RAMC) and his medical section; the Paymaster, a Major or Captain from the Royal Army Pay Corps (RAPC), and his Unit Administration Team and the Education Officer, a Major or Captain from the Royal Army Education Corps (RAEC) and the education team who, on operations, became the Battalion Intelligence Section.

The Brigade of Gurkhas

The Brigade of Gurkhas is the generic term for all the Gurkha units in the British Army. In the 1960s the Brigade of Gurkhas comprised four infantry regiments, the 2nd, 6th, 7th and 10th Gurkha Rifles (GR) each with two battalions, the Gurkha Engineers (GE), the Gurkha Signals (GS) and the Gurkha Transport Regiment (GTR). There was also the Gurkha Independent Parachute Company, a Gurkha Dog Company, the Training Centre Brigade of Gurkhas (TCBG) and British Gurkhas Nepal (BGN). A small headquarters (HQBG) was responsible for overseeing recruiting, manning, Gurkha terms and conditions of service, Gurkha matters and the interface with Nepal.

Gurkhas

Gurkhas are the soldiers of the Brigade of Gurkhas. They were recruited from the Tibeto-Burman tribes from the 'hills' of Nepal.

Gallantry Awards

Broadly speaking Army gallantry awards during the 1960s were awarded along the following lines:

Highest Gallantry: The Victoria Cross (VC). Open to all ranks.

Level 2 Gallantry: The Distinguished Service Order (DSO). Open to officers.

The Distinguished Conduct Medal (DCM). Open to other ranks.

Level 3 Gallantry: The Military Cross (MC). Open to officers.

The Military Medal (MM). Open to other ranks.

Level 4 Gallantry: Mention in Despatches (MID). Open to all ranks.

© Rupert Litherland 2020

Lightning Source UK Ltd.
Milton Keynes UK
UKHW022020051120
372857UK00004B/154/J

9 781800 318397